# The Complete LINDA LOVELACE

## A Deeper-Than-Deep Look at **America's First Porn Queen**

Eric Danville

POWER PROCESS PUBLISHING • NEWYORK

The Complete Linda Lovelace



Printed in the United States



Library of congress info

ISBN 978-0-9859733-0-8

Second edition

Art Direction by John Faraci, www.johnfaraci.com

**Certificate of Exemption**

POWER PROCESS PUBLISHING LLC hereby certifies upon penalty of perjury that all visual depictions of actual or simulated sexually explicit activity displayed in this book are exempt from the provision of 18 U.S.C. §§2257, 2257A and/or 28 C.F.R. §75, because the visual depictions were created prior to July 3, 1995.

This book is dedicated with love to Noodle,
the world's coolest poodle!

**DISCLAIMER:** It is the belief of the author and publisher that the use of book, magazine, newspaper and interview quotes; book, magazine, album and CD covers; and ad mats and promotional stills in *The Complete Linda Lovelace* falls within the doctrine of fair use as set forth by the U.S. Copyright Office.

**On Fair Use, from the U.S. Copyright Office website copyright.gov, in part:**

One of the rights accorded to the owner of copyright is the right to reproduce or to authorize others to reproduce the work in copies or phonorecords. This right is subject to certain limitations found in sections 107 through 118 of the copyright law (title 17, U.S. Code). One of the more important limitations is the doctrine of "fair use." The doctrine of fair use has developed through a substantial number of court decisions over the years and has been codified in section 107 of the copyright law.

Section 107 contains a list of the various purposes for which the reproduction of a particular work may be considered fair, such as criticism, comment, news reporting, teaching, scholarship, and research. Section 107 also sets out four factors to be considered in determining whether or not a particular use is fair.

- The purpose and character of the use, including whether such use is of commercial nature or is for nonprofit educational purposes
- The nature of the copyrighted work
- The amount and substantiality of the portion used in relation to the copyrighted work as a whole
- The effect of the use upon the potential market for, or value of, the copyrighted work

The distinction between what is fair use and what is infringement in a particular case will not always be clear or easily defined. There is no specific number of words, lines, or notes that may safely be taken without permission. Acknowledging the source of the copyrighted material does not substitute for obtaining permission.

The 1961 Report of the Register of Copyrights on the General Revision of the U.S. Copyright Law cites examples of activities that courts have regarded as fair use: "quotation of excerpts in a review or criticism for purposes of illustration or comment; quotation of short passages in a scholarly or technical work, for illustration or clarification of the author's observations; use in a parody of some of the content of the work parodied; summary of an address or article, with brief quotations, in a news report; reproduction by a library of a portion of a work to replace part of a damaged copy; reproduction by a teacher or student of a small part of a work to illustrate a lesson; reproduction of a work in legislative or judicial proceedings or reports; incidental and fortuitous reproduction, in a newsreel or broadcast, of a work located in the scene of an event being reported."

## Thanks to

Victoria Luther, for being my favorite person

My mother and sister for always putting up with me; David Orbach and Debra Cohn-Orbach for their constant support; Howard Thompson for being one of my best mates; my designer John Faraci, for taking all his hard work and skill and making this look like a real book; Sally Walker, for making sure this all makes sense; Alexis Ford, Joshua Thompson and Corrine Butler-Thompson, Lainie Speiser and Cheyenne Picardo for all their help with my book trailer; every bartender in the East Village who listened to me babble about this project for three years; Robert Rosen; Jeffrey Emerson, Tessa Davis, Tom Clark and everyone at 2A for all their help; Ashley West and Gerard Damiano Jr. for a great show; James D. Sasser; Irv O'Neil, David Flint and Jade Lindley for all the kind words about my *Linda Lovelace* script; Marc Medoff, without whom. . . ; Alan Smithee; the fine folks at Dijifi; Lenny Aaron for making everything look so good; everyone at Lightning Source; Annie Sprinkle; Jennifer Peters; Leslie Day; 42nd Street Pete; Mike Linn and SMP Digital Graphics; Crystal and Enviro-Tote; Mark Snyder and everyone at the Museum of Sex; Ray Pistol and David Bertolino for the honor of being mentioned in their lawsuit deposition (bwahahahaha!); Zoe Hansen; Lenny Bruce, George Carlin and Alice Cooper for the inspiration and making life just a little more bearable; Al Goldstein, for being the toughest boss a pornographer could want; Mike Vraney and Lisa Petrucci for loaning me some Linda; Legs McNeil; anyone I've forgotten to mention here; and last but not least Linda Boreman, for trusting me and being my friend.

# CONTENTS

# INTRODUCTION

I began the first edition of this book by pointing out what *The Complete Linda Lovelace* isn't. This book isn't a "biography," at least not in the traditional sense of the word. *The Complete Linda Lovelace* is a "bio-bibliography," or an analysis of a person through critical reviews of media reports surrounding that person. By approaching a subject that way, it's possible to take a step back and see as much as possible of what's already been presented and place it into a context that would be impossble in a more conventional biography. I hope I've succeeded in doing that here.

There's one more thing *The Complete Linda Lovelace* isn't: "complete." This book will *never* be complete, because in the 40 years since Linda Lovelace sucked her way into the American consciousness—and in the more than a decade since Linda Boreman's death—the public still can't get enough of her; the past decade alone has seen the release of several documentaries in theaters and on television, one feature film and more books and music featuring America's First Porn Queen.

That being the case, it was impossible to include every bit of information and every reference I've found since *The Complete Linda Lovelace* was first released. And because this book is again being self-published, it would have simply been too big (yes, size does matter sometimes); the extra number of pages would have raised the overall production cost which in turn means I would have had to charge more for it. For that reason, all the research and information gathered over the years that isn't included here will be offered in a series of updates, issued periodically as downloadable PDFs.

So what *is* this book? *The Complete Linda Lovelace* is the most thorough reading and analysis of The Linda Lovelace Story that's ever been assembled. Anywhere.

**Bonus Content**

To that end, I've placed a series of QR codes throughout the book that link to different media I hope will increase your enjoyment of *The Complete Linda Lovelace.* You can hear clips from interviews through Soundcloud; download PDFs of early-'70s vintage advertisements for Linda Lovelace magazines and films through MediaFire; watch video on YouTube; and more. If you're unfamiliar with QR codes or don't have a smart phone, most of it is available by logging onto the URL next to the codes.

If you'd like to see more about *The Complete Linda Lovelace*, you're invited to use any of the codes or URLs below.

To follow us on Twitter, scan this QR code or go to twitter.com/ThCmpltLndlvlc

**TUMBLR**

To follow us on Tumblr, scan this QR code or go to thecompletelindalovelace.com

**SOUNDCLOUD**

To follow us on Soundcloud, scan this QR code or go to soundcloud.com/EricDanville

**YOUTUBE**

To follow us on YouTube, scan this QR code or go to YouTube.com/ThCmpltLndlvlc

So get ready for a story unlike any other in pop culture. Whether you're a fan of pornography in general and Linda Lovelace in particular; whether you believe pornography to be little more than the subjugation of women by a sexually obsessed patriarchal society; or even if you have no preconceived notions about pornography, Linda Lovelace or anti-pornography feminism, it's my sincerest hope that you'll enjoy what you read in the following pages.

Cheers,
Eric Danville
New York City
November 2013

# Chapter 1: INDECENT EXPOSURE

## America Reads All About It

**It wasn't just Linda Lovelace's talent for fellatio that caught the public's eye. More than anything else, Linda Lovelace was created by a press corps starving for something new and exciting to write about. There were plenty of reasons why she whetted the appetite of the media from around the world, and here are some of them.**

# ... 1972 ...

## June 5, 1972

# *Screw*
# "Gulp!"

by Al Goldstein

Linda Lovelace often said that if *Deep Throat* hadn't made her famous and helped her to be around more people in public, she wouldn't have escaped from Chuck Traynor, the man she says kept her captive for almost three years of physical, sexual and psychological abuse. Ironically, the person she owed her freedom to was the only person she hated more than Traynor: Al Goldstein, publisher of *Screw* magazine, self-described as "The World's Greatest Newspaper." "Gulp!" is the article that, as has been said many times before (mostly by Goldstein himself), started the buzz that made *Deep Throat* a national sensation and set the porn industry in motion.

*Screw* was the first underground/over-the-counter mag to review dirty movies—and take the act of reviewing them seriously—in a weekly column called "Dirty Diversions." In addition to writers who could spew forth knowingly about a porn flick's cinematic, technical and erotic appeal, "Dirty Diversions" also had a gimmick. Instead of a four-star rating or an A through F grading system, "Dirty Diversions" had the Peter-Meter, a phallic bar graph that grew according to a film's combined cinematic, technical and erotic quality. A rating of 100 percent on the Peter-Meter was, like, the coolest, and that's exactly what Goldstein gave *Deep Throat* after getting a sneak preview.

Saying that Goldstein loved the flick would be the kind of understatement not usually associated with him. He ranted ("I was seized with yearning by the greatest on-screen fellatio since the birth of Christ"), he raved ("The star of the film has fine legs, firm tits, a not-unattractive face and the greatest mouth action in the annals of cocksucking"), he ranted again ("I was never so moved by any theatrical performance since stuttering through my own bar mitzvah"). And before you could say, "Shtup the presses," *Deep Throat* was on its way to becoming porn's first blockbuster.

Goldstein's horny hagiography lauds the film's "wit, wild humor, fine acting and hilarious story," and even recommends that readers unable to catch the film on opening day check out its trailer, which has "a hard-rock soundtrack" and "fine animation." But it would be a few weeks until Linda Lovelace's 15 minutes of fame officially started ticking. So spectacular were her on-screen talents that Goldstein didn't even mention her by name.

## September 1, 1972

# *Women's Wear Daily*
# "Linda and Her Magic Larynx"

by Rosemary Kent

America's formal introduction to *Deep Throat*'s starlet comes when reporter Rosemary Kent meets Linda Lovelace, Chuck Traynor (identified here by name before briefly appearing in later interviews as "J.R.") and bodyguard Vinnie Peraino for an interview that hit newsstands the same week that *Deep Throat* hit number 35 in *Variety*'s list of America's 50 top-grossing films.

Kent reports as much on the experience of meeting the world's first porn star as on what they discuss. After setting the scene—an "incense-filled room" in a "seedy" hotel—Kent explains the scope of the film's appeal, noting that "United Nations dignitaries, judges, Broadway stars, high-society celebs and off-duty cops" are among those flocking to see Linda do her thing. The mention of the off-duty cops is particularly relevant; given a minimum one-week lead time and the fact that weekly papers are dated a week after they go on sale, their talk must have occurred right after the film's first, albeit botched bust.

Thanks to New York City Mayor John V. Lindsay's election-year campaign to clean up Times Square, which was thanks to the crowds going to see *Deep Throat*, which was thanks to Goldstein's review, police swooped into the New Mature World Theater on August 11, 1972, and arrested the theater's manager and cashier. Kent writes that despite the arrest, "the film continued to roll," but fails to mention the reason why: The arrest warrants were incorrectly dated. The police returned a few days later, though, and carried out an arrest that stuck. In recalling the first raid, Kent does mention that *The New York Times*' reportage of the bust—publicity you just couldn't buy—gives the film's title in full, while ads for the film in the Old Gray Lady, which were presumably paid for in full, referred to it only as *Throat*.

So what was the first quote from the most famous throat in America? "I don't know what Mr. Perry means by that remark," Linda's reaction to the first quote about the most famous throat in America: *Deep Throat* producer Lou "Perry" Peraino's assertion that, "She's a weird chick. Linda can be very difficult. She always has to have her boyfriend hanging around with her." Kent didn't seem to find Linda particularly weird, referring to her, Traynor and even "beefy, bouncer-type" Vinnie as "very pleasant."

If Linda really was a weird chick, you couldn't tell judging by what she said about herself, either. "I'm not out to be anyone famous or important," Linda told Kent. "I'm just a simple girl who likes to go to swinging parties and nudist colonies." When the still-in-discussion-stage sequel to *Deep Throat* is mentioned, Linda states that she'd like to do it, but if she can't then she'll just "go back to being me. I'm not changed at all, one way or the other." The fate of a sequel, which you'd think would be a no-brainer, really might have been up in the air, judging by Vinnie's assertion that *Deep Throat* distributor Vanguard Films might not push Linda as America's newest sex symbol, but might instead go back to its other line of business: making horror movies.

Despite publicity from the bust and the film's place as a top money-maker, the people involved apparently had no idea what they had in Linda, especially considering the way this interview was handled. Even Traynor, his later status as a "porno Svengali" notwithstanding, showed his naiveté in turning Linda out to the press when he said, "She sews a lot." For better or worse, that naiveté wouldn't last long.

Even more interesting than the interview—which would prove unremarkable by Linda's later standards, aside from being her first—was the review of *Deep Throat* accompanying it. *Women's Wear Daily*'s Mort Sheinman liked what he saw, and he saw it from a unique perspective. He didn't just wonder if director Jerry Gerard might be a budding Orson Welles, providing "a bold thrust forward in the history of contemporary cinema, plunging deeply into areas seldom if ever explored on screen," he lauded Len Camp's set designs for giving the film "the proper ambiance," and noted that "the clothes, by Royal Fashions, are as much a part of the script as anything else."

---

**October 9, 1972**

# *Screw*

# "A *Screw* Exclusive: An Interview With Linda 'Deep Throat' Lovelace"

by Jim Buckley and Al Goldstein

*Screw* magazine scores the second published interview with Linda Lovelace, which results in one cover line, two ridiculous illustrations (one featuring an open-mawed Linda with a pussy in her mouth, the other with that orifice sprouting a penis) and four pages of free advertising for *Deep Throat*. But at least the magazine finally mentioned her by name.

The questions aren't credited to either writer, but the interview was, like most things *Screw*-related, probably dominated by Goldstein, whose unique Q&A technique always sought to uncover the more nuts-and-bolts aspects of human sexual relations: "What's the average time it takes a guy to come?", "The angle of approach to the cock, does that make it easier or harder?", and in what would become an almost prophetic burst of inspiration, "Would you give head to an animal?"

Linda's answers are almost as outlandish and, in retrospect, unbelievable as the questions. She made some of her most incredible sexual claims in this interview, a raunchy discussion the likes of which was *Screw*'s trademark:

# AN INTERVIEW WITH DEEP THROAT, P.4
AN INTERVIEW WITH DEEP THROAT, P.4

## THE GREAT HOMOSEXUAL BANK ROBBERY, P.12

# SCREW

50 CENTS | THE SEX REVIEW | NUMBER 188

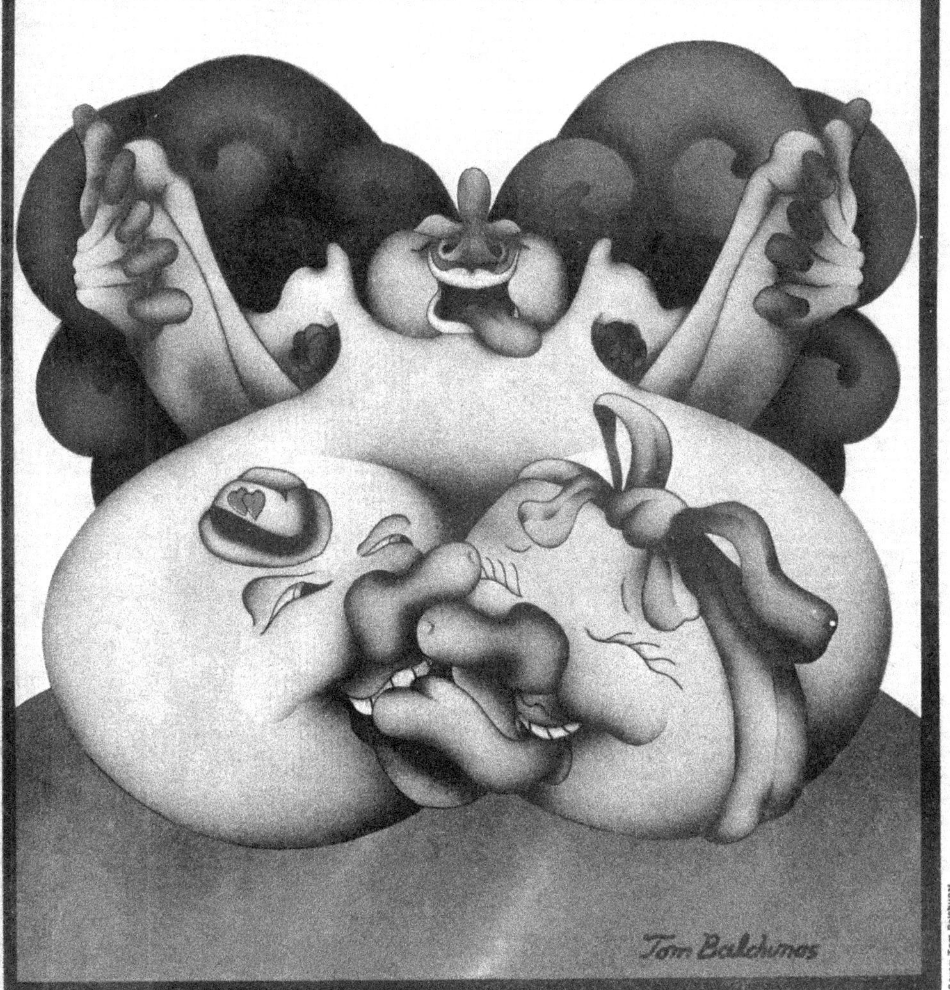


Cover: Tom Balchunas

> ***Screw*:** Do you come even though your clit isn't being worked on?
> **Linda:** Yeah, I do. I have an orgasm every time I get screwed in the throat.
> ***Screw*:** Do you prefer it if a guy eats you while you're eating him?
> **Linda:** Oh yeah. I can get into that. Or I like somebody in my throat and someone in my cunt at the same time. That's nice.
> ***Screw*:** Do you enjoy the taste of sperm?
> **Linda:** Oh yeah, I do. I can't understand why other chicks get so turned off by it. I never spit it out! Oh no! Unn-unnhhh!
> ***Screw*:** How would you describe the taste?
> **Linda:** I really couldn't describe the taste... you'd have to taste it. Try it. Or ask me after I've got some in my mouth and I could tell you. But right now I can't. It just tastes *good* to me. But when a guy comes down my throat I don't taste it. And I feel cheated.
> ***Screw*:** Are you a size queen?
> **Linda:** Oh yeah... I get turned on by that. Sure, the longer they are the further it goes, and I like to see how much I can take.

The importance of this interview, as literally in-your-face as the film it hyped, can't be understated; if his "Dirty Diversions" column had an incredible impact on *Deep Throat*'s boffo box, this interview had at least the same effect on Lovelace's public image. But it's most notorious for Linda's legendary post-gabfest gobbling of Goldstein. As she wrote in her autobiography *Ordeal*:

> Goldstein was asking more and more questions about the act itself—how did it taste and how did it feel and how did I think it made a man feel and so on. Since I wasn't taking the hint, Chuck did. "Well, why don't you find out for yourself?" Chuck said. "You want a free sample, help yourself." The editor of *Screw* almost tripped over his own feet racing over to the bed. As I did it to Goldstein, I could hear Chuck ask Buckley whether he'd like a sample, too. "No thanks," Buckley said.

As it turns out, neither Linda nor Al enjoyed the exchange very much. A few months later, Goldstein wrote in *Screw* that the blowjob didn't excite him and actually made him feel less-than-adequate in the dork department.

The better to preserve this Plimptonian exercise in participatory journalism—and since Buckley wasn't doing anything at the moment anyway—Goldstein had his partner take photographs of the act in progress. The pictures would appear in the pages of *Screw* for years, and not always in the most flattering context—if there's a flattering context in which to be photographed with Al Goldstein's cock down your gullet in the first place.

## December 18, 1972

# *Screw*
# "Deep Throat Fulfilled"

by John Milton

After *Deep Throat*'s rise to fame, it was only a matter of time before the press discovered what Linda did before Dr. Young untangled her tingle. The first member of the press to make the connection was *Screw*'s pseudonymous John Milton, whose "Mail Order Madness" column reviewed mail-order sex products.

Milton mentions that people who weren't able to see *Deep Throat* in theaters are searching high and low for 8mm copies of the flick. Unfortunately neither the film (nor the men who wanted to see it) would come for a while, but Milton reports on rumors that Linda's past included a number of low-budget, hardcore stag films—and those rumors are true! Milton describes the first such loop directly linked to Linda Lovelace, a two-parter released in the New York-based "M" series, catalogued as No. 81 and No. 82 and available for the bargain basement price of just $30 per reel, or $55 for both, from Abco Toys (a ticket to see *Deep Throat* in a theater would set you back $5, more than admission to a straight flick like *The Godfather*).

## December 31, 1972

# *The New York Times*
# "Obscenity: What's Really 'Deep' Is the Logic"

by Lesley Oelsner

Linda Lovelace is in the middle of a *cause célèbre*—and in the middle of the layout for this article, which explains the New York City *Deep Throat* obscenity trial.

The film's fate hinges on the court's interpretation of 15 years' worth of litigation and decision concerning three influential obscenity cases:

*Roth v. U.S.* (1957), which states that material is obscene when it has no socially redeeming value and asserts that obscene material is not, repeat *not* protected by the First Amendment. This case ruled that the mere inclusion of sex in a work does not necessarily make it obscene, but that the test is "whether to the average person, applying contemporary community standards, the dominant theme of the material taken as a whole appeals to the prurient interest." In the years following *Roth*, the definition of obscenity evolved into a three-pronged one: the work in question must appeal to the prurient interest when taken as a whole; it must "substantially" go beyond community standards in its depiction or representation of sex or nudity; and it must be "utterly without socially redeeming value."

*Redrup v. New York* (1967), which affirms obscenity cases only when materials were "pandered," given to minors or forced upon a "captive audience."

And *Stanley v. Georgia* (1969), in which the First Amendment was ruled to "sometimes" protect obscene materials, such as when they were "willingly" viewed (by people shelling out $5 a head to see *Deep Throat*, for instance).

Although the years following *Roth* seemed like good ones for free speech, a 1971 court ruled that obscene materials were not free from prohibition, even when they were viewed by "willing" adults. Oelsner's article raises the question of whether the New York court will stick to the three-pronged ruling or revert to *Roth*'s simpler, more restrictive definition of obscenity.

# ... 1973 ...

## January 15, 1973

# *Time*
# "Wonder Woman"

With the *Deep Throat* obscenity trial over but with Judge Joel Tyler, also the film's jury and executioner (there was no jury because the defendant was Mature Enterprises, Inc. and not theater owner Bob Sumner—the better to gain a conviction, prosecutors reasoned), yet to return his verdict, *Time* updates readers as to the legal wrangling. Linda is described as a "female Don Juan" and "a *Mad* magazine cloning of Little Annie Fanny and Mary Marvel." The only word Linda gets in edgewise comes courtesy of a quote from a "girlie magazine" about why she does porn: "I'm an exhibitionist ... and I make good money."

Expert witnesses are also quoted. Dr. John Money, Johns Hopkins professor of medical psychology, explains why the film is a valuable tool in sexual education: "[*Deep Throat*] puts an eggbeater in people's brains and enables them to think afresh about their attitudes." Psychoanalyst Ernest van den Haag counters, "Once you regard a person as merely a means to your pleasure, then you will be ready to commit any act for your pleasure or displeasure—putting another person in a concentration camp or exploiting his teeth and hair." Finally, Dr. Max Levin has a breakthrough of sorts with his fear that *Deep Throat*'s reliance on an "anatomical absurdity" for its plot device would back up feminist claims to a clitoral orgasm: "I think that vaginal orgasm is superior to the clitoral." Unfortunately the exact date of Levin's last vaginal orgasm wasn't entered into court transcripts.

## February 1973

# *Oui*

# "My Linda Lovelace Problem (and Yours)"

by Richard Hill

Hill's attempt at Gonzo journalism takes the reader on his excruciatingly personal journey to meet Linda Lovelace. Like most writers, Hill thinks the story behind the story is fascinating, but also like most writers, he's wrong. The story behind his story—making the proper phone calls to secure himself an audience with Linda—is not particularly interesting, and neither is this article, until he finally makes contact with her.

And what contact he makes! His first meeting with Linda takes place after he's downed five shots of Wild Turkey waiting for the call confirming their interview. Finally sitting with Linda in a room along with Traynor, Lou Perry, Phil Parisi and assorted bodyguards and flunkies, Hill claims quite rightly that he needs a little privacy to get the story. Later that evening Hill has dinner with Lovelace, Traynor and Parisi. Unfortunately, he again fails to conduct his interview, but for a different reason:

> Phil seemed worried that I wasn't asking questions. I said something about in-depth journalism, about enjoying the meal and asking questions later. The truth was that Linda and I were groping under the table like suburban infidels and I couldn't think of any more questions. Bourbon, Scotch, wine and anticipation had dulled the journalistic edge.

Later, when Hill still hasn't gotten his story, he arranges to meet the pair for dinner again—this time in Florida, where the journalistic edge is once more dulled. He writes:

> [Linda] gets a little drunk during dinner and now the groping is getting obvious, moving the table now and then. What am I supposed to do—make it clear to Chuck that my knowledge must extend to the Biblical sort? Then I realize what I've done. I've idiotically and unconsciously been pursuing my part of the Linda fantasy—the All-American Lollipop—and she's been responding that way. She's feeding my fantasy of her, like the good little professional she is.

Still without "The Story," Hill meets the pair for breakfast the next day, where he's fed the same old story about the sex machine from Bryan, Texas, that closes out the piece.

## February 19, 1973

# *Screw*
# "Dog Dick Down 'Deep Throat' [Linda Lovelace Eats a 'Hot' Dog]"

by Al Goldstein

Almost as soon as Linda earns household-name status, Al Goldstein—always willing to break both a good story and the chops of anyone who crosses him—exposes the existence of the Linda Lovelace bestiality films.

After crowing in typical Goldstein fashion about being the first journalist to get an interview and a blowjob from Linda Lovelace, he also, in typical Goldstein fashion, elicits pity from readers for enduring it in the first place. The experience, he writes, "transcended third-rate fantasy, it was fourth-rate.... The harder I tried to come ... the more ejaculation eluded me.... I felt strange watching my cock go right down Linda's throat and wondered where the damn thing went. Was I that small? Was she that good? Finally I came after what seemed like half an hour and Linda and the guys in the room all breathed a sigh of relief."

But this article's real hook was found in another room, one in the home of Goldstein's on-again, off-again friend Lyle Stuart, whose name is generally preceded by the phrase "maverick publisher" for a career during which he issued *The Sensuous Man*, *The Anarchist Cookbook*, *The Turner Diaries* and, yes, *Ordeal* by Linda Lovelace. It was there that occurred a private screening of an early Lovelace film that, Goldstein explained, "is titled, poetically enough, 'Dog-Fuck (sic),' a 400-foot color rendition of a love affair between Linda and a beige mongrel. Unlike the famous *Lassie* series, this flick transcends mere petting and foreplay and breaks into virgin ground as Linda gets *fucked* by the rather inept and poorly coordinated mutt. The highlight of this tale of bestiality takes place when Linda starts lapping the pooch's ugly red cock. At this point most of the audience left and only three animal lovers were left to view this peculiar porn."

Goldstein sums up the film's legacy with surprising prescience: "Linda was still not the cocksucker or charmer that she becomes in her later work and in any film retrospective on Linda Lovelace I'm sure that this short will merely be an historic footnote in her thrilling show-business career." He then reprints a still used for the film's box cover that would find a home in *Screw* for years to come. But his usually dependable gut was a little off the mark when it grumbled about the film's future as fuck-film footnote. The exposure of this loop did more to affect America's perception of Linda Lovelace than even *Deep Throat*, all thanks to a man who not only had a nose for a news story but knew when to pick it.

## March 1973

# *The Girls of Deep Throat: The Anatomy of a Cinematic Phenomena*

This heavily illustrated, 48-page specialty mag supplements stills from the film and short layouts featuring Linda's female co-stars with dozens of early vintage photos shot in roughly seven sessions that took place in New York City in late 1971 before the filming of *Deep Throat*, and in Jersey City, New Jersey, once production on *Throat* had wrapped.

Linda's partners in the early photos are a bearded Chuck Traynor, one of only two male partners; her other male costar Eric Edwards, then working under the name Rob Everett; Edwards' wife Chris Jordan, who would appear with Linda and Eric in the stag film *Piss Orgy* and later feature in the big-screen *Deep Throat Part II*; a redheaded woman Linda calls "Brandy" in

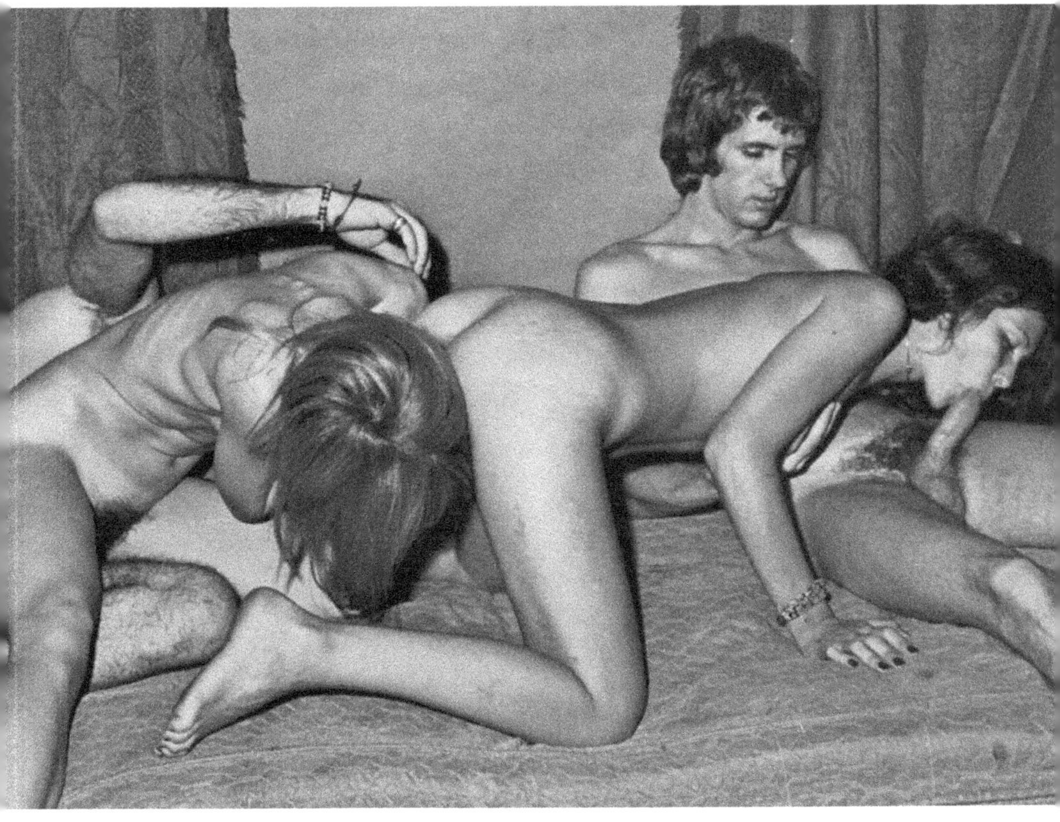

*Ordeal* (her costar in the M-81/82 stag film mentioned above); and a blonde Linda calls "Ginger" in *Ordeal*, who would appear with Linda in the Jersey City loops.

The mag's statement of purpose says, "As we go to press on this first of two special issues on *Deep Throat*, Judge Joel J. Tyler . . . has declared, 'The only theme [of the movie] is hard-core pornography with a vengeance. This is one throat that deserves to be cut. I readily perform the operation in finding the defendant guilty as charged.' Judge Tyler's frank admission of a preference for bloody throat-cutting is indeed the absolute confirmation of our thesis in the article that follows. Those who seek, as the judge did, to substitute violence for love give birth to yet greater acts of gory violence. To you, our readers, we pledge that we shall not be silenced. Violence must not and will not win in this or any other issue. If they drive us underground, we shall still publish and urge you to abhor violence, to MAKE LOVE, NOT WAR."

The magazine makes some heavy-handed points comparing and contrasting the *Deep Throat* obscenity trials with the slaughter of students at Jackson State College and Kent State, and the slaughter of Vietnamese villagers in My Lai and Song My. Those points are illustrated with the only nonsexual images in the mag: photos of social and political unrest in Berkeley, Vietnam and Attica State Prison.

It also includes a few *Deep Throat* trial stories from Binghamton and Chicago (where one newspaper ad said it was "worth the trip to Milwaukee" to see the film) before giving a discourse on the "aesthetics of violence" as they apply to icons of pop culture viz. John Wayne movies and Vietnam. *The Girls of Deep Throat* ends, as more porn magazines should, with a quote from Chinese philosopher Chuang Tzu.

## March 1973

# *The Star of Deep Throat: Linda Lovelace*

This sister magazine to *The Girls of Deep Throat* is another collection of early vintage photos, minus stills from the movie.

The socially redeeming text of this magazine doesn't just cover the asses of its publishers from a *Roth*-ian encroachment upon their right to print pics of hippies humping in hotel rooms. It serves as an utter, direct, damning indictment of those whose inability to see the goodness in what Linda does threatens to wear away the moral fabric of this country and allows those "free to steal from the poor to support their multibillionaire friends of ITT, Lockheed and Penn Central," even as "the war machine goes on in South-east Asia." The anonymous author also posits that "No American POW endured such maltreatment as was inflicted on the Viet Cong or North Vietnamese by the U.S. and the Saigon puppet regime, yet Linda Lovelace is called obscene! What is her crime? Love!" After chronicling the breakdown of the Hollywood star system and the rise of TV celebrity, the magazine sarcastically lauds the usurping of sports stars—those "great behemoths of violence"—by one Linda Lovelace.

The author also tries to tell the reader, "What is Linda Lovelace really like?" The answer: "When Linda and Chuck first came to New York and took up a place at the Loew's Motor Inn, I shot her right away. She was lots of fun, but not like she came off in *Throat*. In *Throat*, Linda was very much into the spoof, the comedy of it all. She's a kick offscreen," he adds, "a sexy kid with no hang-ups about sex and she really digs sex—that's her bag. She is pretty much what you saw in the flick. Other than the comedy of the film, it was Linda herself."

The final answer to that question comes in reference to Nora Ephron's February 1973 *Esquire* article, where it's noted that Ephron "feels she has a right to know Linda's so-called 'real' name. . . . Who really cares what her 'real' name is? To her millions of fans it could mean absolutely nothing for she is, to them, only Linda Lovelace."

**BONUS CONTENT**

Download a mail-order ad for these mags by scanning this QR code or logging onto **bit.ly/LLQR01**

## April 1973

# *Playboy* "Say 'Ah!'"

Although the emphasis in Linda's first major men's magazine pictorial is on Linda as the girl next door, she's still presented to the *Playboy* readership as very much the character she played on-screen. When asked about her deep-throat technique, Linda comes off like a cocksucking coquette: "I had to spend three or four weeks learning how to keep from gagging and how to breathe with the strokes. After the first couple of weeks of practice, I was still choking and turning purple. But now I can really get off that way. That's not the only way, of course." She goes on to explain the ways she gets off in increasingly explicit but increasingly unbelievable detail: "Everything turns me on, actually; my preferences depend on my mood, but I'd say right now I like throat, ass, cunt, one, two, three, in that order."

The pictures are, of course, very *Playboy* and very beautiful, presenting Linda in a light as soft as the focus of photographer Richard Fegley's camera. Linda's shaved pussy is nowhere in sight, although the same can't be said of her abdominal scar, which is visible—passed over, covered up and shot around, but still visible—if you know to look for it. Which, if you'd read an article in *Screw* titled "Lovelace Perils" two months earlier, you did.

## May 1973
# *Esquire*

Linda's first mainstream national magazine cover finds her decked out in puffy sleeves, polka dots and prim white gloves, more than ever in girl-next-door mode. The hyper-polite cover line, "Miss Linda Lovelace requests the pleasure of your company," ushers readers to page 159, where she and Traynor are shown walking down the street. Linda's fellatial fame is described as "an anatomical metaphor for the transvaluation of all values in this decade," and conversely described using Judge Tyler's condemnation of it as "carrion and squalor." But *Esquire* doesn't quite explain everything. "If you don't know yet what the crowds are coming to see Linda *do*," the magazine chides, "we're damn well not going to be the ones to tell you."

## May 14, 1973

# *Screw*
# "The Throat That Swallowed the Heart of America"

For reasons that would be explained in later interviews, Al Goldstein and *Screw* seek to put Linda, if not necessarily in her place, then at least in her proper perspective, attributing her popularity to the comparatively lame cultural events of the day. The uncredited author of the piece (probably the brilliant underground writer Dean Latimer) writes, "Nothing else is happening right now, culture-wise: rock and roll is dead, the war's over, college kids are back to booze and apathy, the progress of domestic Fascism has been stymied by the Watergate scandal and America's in a period of cultural stagnation. Vacuumsville, man." Ultimately Linda Lovelace is dismissed as "an interim fad, like the Hula Hoop back in the Fifties was an interim fad between the sack dress and elephant jokes."

But the writer soon gets read the riot act by *Screw* editor Pete Dvarackas. Chalking Linda's popularity up to "some big artificial Pop Smut fad," Dvarackas tells him, "We can sell *a lot* of issues if we pick up on this Pop Smut horseshit ourselves.... So let's cash in on it, kid, get really shameless and tawdry. Hype the tushie right off her, man. Make Linda Lovelace sound interesting!"

While it fails at that, "The Throat That Swallowed the Heart of America" succeeds at something considerably more valuable to Linda's legacy: lending credence to what she would later say was The Story Behind the Story. Wondering whether they have enough background information on her, the author asks, "Anybody here ever meet her, talk to her, except Goldstein the time she sucked his dork and he couldn't get into it because he felt guilty about exploiting her and sorry for her for having to do it?" When told that they have *Screw*'s interview to fall back on, the author writes, "Yeah, but her manager did all the talking—or bragging might be a better word. He wouldn't hardly let her open her mouth, for some reason."

Despite *Screw*'s usually high journalistic standards, the piece becomes a damn-near incomprehensible tapestry of fact, fantasy, speculation and outright drivel describing the content of Linda's 8mm loops held together with a bare thread of supposition concerning the circumstances under which they were shot.

And wouldn't you know it? The issue also features an ad for the previously unearthed dog film under the banner, "Linda Lovelace, star of *Deep Throat*, Untangles the Tingle of Fido," a tortured take on the *Deep Throat* ad copy "How Far Does a Girl Have To Go To Untangle Her Tingle?" The ad is illustrated with a large, thankfully censored photo of Linda blowing Goldstein, printed upside-down. Whether or not the juxtaposition of Goldstein and Fido was intentional isn't clear.

## May 28, 1973

# *Screw*
# "Inside Linda Lovelace and the Press"

After looking forward to good times ahead (*Screw*'s inevitable attendance at the upcoming press conference for Linda's first autobiography), the editors describe her growing presence in the national press via her appearances in magazines like *Playboy* and *Esquire*; books like the *Deep Throat* novelization and *Inside Linda Lovelace*; and the furor caused by an interruption during her appearance on the *Donahue* show. Of course, the problem that *Screw* has with all the attention Linda's been getting is that lots of people will be making money off her while "the rest of us are going to be bored unto death by the wave of material that is slowly but inexorably beating its subject matter into the ground."

## June 1973

# *Swank*
# "Inside Linda Lovelace: Besides That Infamous *Deep Throat* Clit, What Makes Her Tick?"

by Favia Braun

This good-natured, fawning profile establishes Braun as one of several women who would recount their experiences seeing *Deep Throat* over the years. After allowing that "every feminist knows [porn] is infantile and totally involved with male fantasies of degradation and exploitation," she bravely breaks ranks to admit that watching it really did turn her on.

Not only did Lovelace turn her on in the film ("Hers is the one face in cinema to actually convey the graduated splendors of orgasm"), but in the flesh as well. "First off," she writes, "let me say that she is incredibly and deliriously gorgeous, even without makeup and battling the infamous New York flu germs. If indeed she had dreams up empire, she was superbly equipped for the ascension."

Braun's opinions of and experiences with the film would be parroted for some time, but not because so many women loved the film; actually, most female writers didn't like it. If quotes attributed here to Lovelace and Traynor seemed familiar to the nation's smut readers, it was with good reason: because this was probably written by someone credited later as Diana Helfrecht in *Bachelor* magazine.

While Linda (and, by default, Chuck Traynor) provided the main thrust, another element creeps into The Story of Linda Lovelace: the personae of other porn magazine writers, particularly those who'd recently interviewed the pair for other porn magazines (*Oui*'s Richard Hill and *Screw*'s Al Goldstein, who's cryptically referred to as just your run-of-the-mill "sex guru" when Braun dogs his heels about passing around "pictures of Linda that look like her but aren't"). Indeed the final word in this rather standard interview is for some reason given to none other than Al Goldstein and his claim, "Anything that turns you on must have socially redeeming value."

This issue of *Swank* also features the first known sighting of that rarest piece of technology—the videotape player—through which "charter members" in the Channel X Film Club would be able to view "the most daring and stimulating films in original color and sound right through [their] own TV set[s]," all for the princely (and seemingly ubiquitous) sum of $5. And if you weren't lucky enough to have your very own videotape equipment, no problem: the good, upstanding folks at the Channel X Film Club would hook you up, literally and figuratively, by actually renting you a home videocassette player at a special discount price. Even more surprisingly, none other than Linda herself was set to have profited from this deal, having entered into a contract with Channel X (whether she actually got any money remains a mystery). This wouldn't be the first time, though, that business dealings with or concerning Linda Lovelace would go the way of all good things.

## June 5, 1973

# *The Washington Post* "Linda Lovelace"

by Jean M. White

What starts off as a fairly entertaining profile veers into exceedingly dry journalistic territory when White ponders the commercial trails the queen of porno chic intends to blaze. Her upcoming projects include:

- A $100,000 publishing contract for two books from Pinnacle Books, with Linda earning a 15- to 20-percent royalty.
- A $35,000-a-week guarantee for eight-week stints at nightclubs in Vegas and Tahoe.
- $5,000 a night for one-off shows.
- A $24,000, two-year contract for an advice column in *Oui* magazine.

- Television commercials.
- $300,000 for a new motion picture.
- An adult Linda Lovelace game.

The two-book publishing deal from Pinnacle resulted in *Inside Linda Lovelace* and *The Intimate Diary of Linda Lovelace*; Linda became the first porn star to endorse a non-sex-related product when she shilled for Encino-based footwear company M&J Shoes in a TV spot; and the motion picture was *Linda Lovelace for President*.

The other deals pitched essentially withered on the vine. The advice column for *Oui* magazine evolved, for whatever reason, into a proposed letters column for *Gallery*. When that didn't happen, the letters section from *The Intimate Diary of Linda Lovelace* was serialized to at least two magazines: *Stag* in the United States and *Fiesta* in Britain. There was never a Linda Lovelace adult game, although other Linda Lovelace products—both authorized and unauthorized—sprung up over the years, including but not limited to T-shirts (with Linda's picture and the slogan, "If it feels good, do it!" alongside a fake autograph); posters (a pair of ostriches alongside the phrase "Deep Throat"); and belt buckles.

The worst deal Linda Lovelace made was for her much-hyped but ultimately doomed stage show, which would result in lawsuits for years.

---

## June 23, 1973

# *The New York Times*

# "Decisions on Obscenity Protested by Nation's Media"

by Eric Pace

The Supreme Court's decision in *Miller v. California* upholds the conviction of a distributor of illustrated books and films found obscene, giving individual states the right to define obscenity and creating 50 different and wildly varying sets of community standards. As a result, the nation's book, magazine and motion-picture producers are understandably concerned.

The *Times* gets quotable quotes from those affected by the ruling: Executives at the Screen Actors Guild "envision countless lawsuits" while the managing editor of *Esquire* says, "It's going to be very troublesome for everyone." Playboy Enterprises comments, "We can't comment. Our lawyers haven't had time to study the decision," and *Screw*'s Al Goldstein, ever the optimist, laments, "It's a shame the fights we thought we'd won now have to be rewon," before admitting he and *Screw* are prepared to "soften our photos."

Like the Motion Picture Association of America, which releases no statement about the decision because "no one has decided how it will effect us," Pinnacle Books, the publishers of *Inside Linda Lovelace*, decline comment. But the author of that book, contacted at the Los Angeles offices of Linda Lovelace Enterprises, gives the harshest rebuke on record when she says, "I think the ruling is very bad. It isn't just limited to nudity in films—it takes on everything. The last person that started censorship was Adolf Hitler, and the next thing they'll be doing is knocking on your door and taking away your TV and radio. They're taking away your Constitutional rights."

## June 25, 1973

# *Screw*
# The "Untold Linda Lovelace" Issue

Barely a year after helping Linda Lovelace ascend the porno heavens, *Screw* sets out to bring her back down to earth. This issue combines previously published articles with brand-new musings on America's favorite sex star, all designed to humiliate, embarrass and degrade her. Aside from reprinting Linda's original interview and making mention of her bestiality movies, dirty tricks the mag plays upon its former Golden Girl include shpritzing about her urination film, busting out news of her silicone breast enhancement and printing her real name. The issue also features:

### "Screw You"
by Al Goldstein

The opening editorial of what Goldstein calls *Screw*'s "Special Animal Husbandry Issue" finds him justifiably perturbed about being branded a liar in the pages of *Inside Linda Lovelace*. (Goldstein printed a picture from the dog film in *Screw*; Lovelace denied it was her and called the picture a "composite" in the book.) With Linda no longer the apple of his jaundiced eye, Goldstein declares himself forced to bring a $250,000 libel suit against her and Pinnacle Books.

Goldstein adds Linda to that list of starlets—Marilyn Monroe and Joan Crawford among them—who fucked their way to the top then wanted to be taken seriously as actresses. "The saddest thing of all in this squalid Linda Lovelace episode," he writes, "is that we are losing a cocksucker, and gaining an actress, and the truth of the matter is that we need more cocksuckers, and less actresses."

Showing even more prescience than with its prediction about the dog film's place in cinematic history, Goldstein's gut was right on target when it grumbled, "Linda . . . refuses to admit that which made her famous—her wide-eyed, enthusiastic cocksucking, sodomy and embracing of all that's sexual. Before you know it, I'm sure Linda will be the anti-porn crusader for the Catholic Church and Morality in Media. Stranger things have happened."

THE UNTOLD LINDA LOVELACE

The Etiquette of Fellatio, P.6 Are Dogs Good Lovers? P.8

# SCREW

50 CENTS THE SEX REVIEW NUMBER 225

Cover: Thomas Hachtman

WARNING Sexual material of an adult nature. This literature is not intended for minors and under no circumstances are they to view it, possess it, or place orders for the merchandise offered herein.

## "The Etiquette of Fellatio: Landers & Lovelace Tangle Tongues"
by Sylvia Stern

Blow-by-blow reportage of Linda's appearance on the Chicago-based *Kup's Show* with advice columnist Ann Landers. Not surprisingly, the pair don't exactly see eye-to-eye on most topics they discuss, which not only include whether sex in other than the missionary position is wrong, but whether it would be a good thing to combine the legitimate film-making industry with the porn biz. "No kind of sex is wrong," Landers says, "if it is done between consenting adults, as long as it is not done in public and certainly not on a movie screen.... I don't want to see any sex on the movie screen. It should be a private thing." When the pair's conversation gets to the topic of the film *Deep Throat* specifically, Landers barks, "What seems wrong to me about this movie is that the sex in it is the same as animal sex.... no offense, Linda."

(This comment isn't just a cheap shot, it's also more than a little disingenuous. Years later it will come out that Landers hadn't even seen the film at the time of this meeting. The situation comes to a head when the March 21, 1977, issue of *People* magazine reports that Landers was spotted coming out of a double-feature screening of *Deep Throat* and *The Devil in Miss Jones* in San Francisco. When pressed about why she'd seen the films, Landers confesses she'd been squeezed into seeing her first skin flicks by a group of friends attending a dermatologist's conference. Taking their enthusiasm a little too much at face value, Landers commented, "It was so boring. If Linda Lovelace had even one small pimple I surely would have noticed it.")

Seemingly the only thing Landers and Lovelace have in common is their vocation as advice columnists (Linda's ultimately doomed advice column in *Oui* magazine was scheduled to debut shortly). Landers at one point offers Lovelace an out: "When you want to settle down and have children and return to God and accept all the middle-class values, then good old Ann Landers will be there to help you."

"Thanks, but don't hold your breath," Linda replies.

*Sex Scene*
## "Coming Out of a Cocksucker"

Reporter Bruce David recalls his attendance with Al Goldstein of the *Inside Linda Lovelace* press conference at the Gaslight Hotel, and formally announces the feud between *Screw* and the *Deep Throat* starlet. This was the first place the story would be told in the national press, but wouldn't be the last.

Aside from a few well-placed puns about their success in crashing the press conference (thanks to their "animal cunning") and a clumsy and botched reference to Lovelace turning into a pillar of salt after having lied about *Screw* faking the bestiality pictures, David goes on to tell the story of Goldstein's attempt to "maintain the ethics of the Fourth Estate" by approaching the microphone and saying, "On page 99 of your book you accuse me of having faked a photo of you that appeared in *Screw*. One of us is lying. Did you ever have sex with a dog?"

Goldstein was, at Linda's request, thrown out.

## "Ballad to a Bitch in Heat"
by Fred Leslie

A poem with many references to the dog movies that also lets loose the existence of the *Piss Orgy* loop penned by a *Screw* magazine associate who just happened to be selling copies of Linda's bestiality movies by mail.

## "Deep Throat, Shallow Brain"
by Al Goldstein

*Screw*'s executive editor uses the magazine's "Fuckbooks" column to review the novelization of America's number one sex film, not only branding the publishers hypocrites for not advertising it in *Screw*, but also railing against the book's author, who as it turns out is one D. M. Perkins, a pseudonym for one Michael Perkins, *Screw*'s regular "Fuckbooks" columnist/reviewer.

Since Goldstein would never sully the great name of *Screw* by suggesting he hires hacks, he actually pays Perkins some compliments, left-handed though they might be. "Michael gets all his words in the right order," Goldstein writes, "and his adjectives and verbs connect with an effectiveness that's rare in the fuck word field." (Yes, coming from Goldstein that's a compliment.)

Among the reasons Goldstein gives for his favorable review is his affection for one of the book's characters: Studs Gordon, who Goldstein writes "obviously represents me. [Perkins] very cleverly put me in the book knowing that would be the only incentive I'd have to read any of his crud." So for the most part the book doesn't suck—especially that portion inspired by Goldstein himself.

Goldstein ends his review by urging *Screw* readers to "run out and buy *Deep Throat*, and hope whatever profits Dell gets, they'll piss away."

---

## Summer 1973

# *Bachelor's Best*
# "They Can't Believe She Ate the Whole Thing!"

by Diana Helfrecht

If this interview seemed familiar to readers, it wasn't just because *Bachelor* had already run it in their February issue, which was pulled off the stands and later sold through the mail as the extra-super-special "BANNED!" issue (at an appropriate mark-up in price). It was because this interview was taken almost wholesale from Linda's *Screw* magazine interview with Buckley and Goldstein.

It wouldn't be surprising or unethical or even particularly interesting for *Screw* to have resold the interview to another magazine, especially considering how difficult it could be for less well-connected publications to get an audience with Lovelace, but it is surprising to have it appear under someone else's byline, especially underneath the infamous Lovelace/Goldstein blowjob photo.

While not quite a complete rip-off, the original *Screw* interview is heavily paraphrased. Despite it being possible Linda was asked the same questions by reporters who thought they were being original, the similarities between the two are unmistakable, even despite Linda's later, rightful claims that her interview answers were so heavily rehearsed by Traynor as to seem scripted.

- **From *Screw*, 1972**

***Screw*:** What's the average time it takes a guy to come?

**Linda:** It can go 30 seconds to 30 minutes. One guy was in there for 50 minutes. A regular guy who isn't a fuck-film star takes two or three minutes.

- **From *Bachelor*, 1973**

**Diana:** How long does it take to bring him off, on the average?

**Linda:** Uh, everybody's different. From 30 seconds to 30 minutes, even. Sometimes around cameras guys are nervous, but I can always get to him!

- **From *Screw***

***Screw*:** Are you into orgies at all?

**Linda:** Yeah ... I like to party. I can never get enough! And I like going down on women, too.

**Screw:** Is there anything you wouldn't do in a sex film?

**Linda:** I haven't come across anything yet I wouldn't do.

***Screw*:** Would you give head to an animal?

**Linda:** I really don't know, you know? Probably it would depend on so many things.

- **From *Bachelor***

**Diana:** Are you into orgies or group sex or whatever the current term is?

**Linda:** Oh yeah, I like it any way it comes. It's always good!

**Diana:** Well then, is there anything you wouldn't do on screen? Like, would you give head to an animal, maybe a nice 200-pound St. Bernard?

**Linda:** Oh, I don't know. I can't answer that now. Nothing's come up I couldn't take. I'd have to wait to answer that.

## July 1973

# *Photo Screen*
# "Frank Sinatra: His Secret Hours With *Deep Throat* Star Linda Lovelace!"

by Sally Pickford

Frank Sinatra's lonely. Not only is he lonely, he's so broken up after his break-up with Mia Farrow that he's sworn off women forever. The best Hollywood snoopsters have risked life and limb (no exaggeration, probably) trying to catch Ol' Blue Eyes *in flagrante delicto*, but to no avail. But leave it to the crack staff of *Photo Screen* to answer the question that burns like the loins of a thousand teenyboppers: "Where is Frank Sinatra getting it these days?"

Pickford runs down Francis Albert's résumé for stud-hood (affairs with Garland, Ekberg and Bacall, among others) and follows it up with the story of his failed marriages to Ava Gardner and Farrow. Then she finally wonders What It's All Worth. You know, down in the core of a man's soul, what does getting all that Hollywood pussy really mean?

The answer?

It don't mean nothing, baby. Nada. A big goose egg. All the flings, the floozies, the fun have only left Frank a sad and broken man, a lonely shell of his former self. Here's a man who has loved and lost and will hopefully live to love again. How does he bear it?

No. Not with any of the bevy of starlets anxious to hit the hay with the sexy song stylist. Not with any of the number of Vegas "hostesses" willing to take Frankie's mind off his troubles, for a price. No, these days the only pleasure The Voice can find is in his stolen moments with The Throat, sitting in the dark watching Linda Lovelace chuff choad in his own private print of *Deep Throat*.

That Sinatra whiles away the hours in late-night circle jerks with some boozing Harveys seems to truly disturb Pickford. She certainly must care about Hoboken's favorite son, because she spends almost a quarter of the article begging him to pull himself together, for God's sake, and get over his obsession with this, this whore who's only famous for sucking cock in the movies, where everyone can see her.

Being a shut-in just isn't good for Frankie, she says. "That's why his lark with Linda Lovelace may be harmful to him in the long run. He's opting out for fantasy. What he could really use now is a good dose of reality, like a real woman sitting next to him, a personal contact to the world.... He's one hell of a guy. And that's why we feel he deserves more love out of his life than a couple of secret hours with Linda Lovelace. Come on, Frank," she finishes, "you can do a lot better than that!"

## August 1973

# *Bachelor*
# "Linda Lovelace: II"

by Diana Helfrecht

Lovelace and Helfrecht meet again, and again Helfrecht is highly complimentary of Linda, perhaps a little more complimentary than journalists usually are—even the male journalists Helfrecht delights in exposing as a bunch of sex-crazed hacks on the make for Linda, just like Favia Braun did in her interview for *Swank*.

In this interview Helfrecht, if that is indeed her real name, sounds as much like Favia Braun in *Swank* as she sounds like Al Goldstein in her previous *Bachelor* piece. Not only do Braun and Helfrecht make practically the same parenthetical references to Linda's "dazzling smile" and Blair Sobol's article in *The Village Voice*, but they also (hmmm) ask practically the same questions and (hmmm) get practically the same answers:

- **From *Swank*, June 1973, by Favia Braun**

"I've heard you've had some bad scenes ... with us journalists, like the one who kept talking about how he had to have you, and that large lady from the pretty people's daily who failed to nominate you for sainthood, a couple other sex-gurus who hand around pictures of girls who look like you but aren't ..."

Chuck spoke up. "Oh ... they all come on with her. They try anything to get next to her. Some of them think because they're from big-time magazines they'll sweep this new star off her feet. So they try to hold her hand and give her their cards and call up all the time with new questions they forgot to ask. After a while they wise up and forget it. But they write all about their reactions and you know, once a guy's been put down ..."

- **From *Bachelor*, August 1973, by Diana Helfrecht**

**Me [Helfrecht]:** Tell me about that "new journalist" who did one interview with you and followed you all the way to Miami. He kept saying he had to have "carnal knowledge" of you.

**Linda:** I'm always pretty naive ... he seemed like a regular guy. But he did say something to you in Miami, didn't he, Chuck?

**Chuck:** Oh yeah, he would have liked to ball you. He came down all the way to Florida, thinking he was a big-time magazine writer who's going to sweep Linda right off her feet. When he found it didn't work, he sort of wrote the article around his particular dreams. It was a strange article....

- **Linda, from *Swank***

"I come every time somebody's in my throat. Yeah, I really do. . . . Yeah, I love it! It's me, and it will always be me. When women's lib starts talking about how exploited I am . . . I want to tell them I'm liberated! I've never NOT been liberated."

- **Linda, from *Bachelor***

"I'm so free! Can't you see I love it? I really do come every time somebody's in my throat. How could I be exploited when I was the one out looking for it? . . . I don't really understand women's lib—what do they want to be liberated FROM? I mean, I'm liberated!"

Whatever Helfrecht's relationship to Braun, Braun's relationship to Helfrecht and both of their relationships to Goldstein, the interview has a discussion of Linda's post-hummer relationship with the priapic porn publisher as it relates to *Screw*'s relatively quick turnaround in its attitude towards actively promoting her. The author comes down squarely on Linda's side:

> **Me:** What about that interview you did with them when you went down on their editor, Linda?
> **Linda:** That was another of their fantasies, but I went along with it. I thought they were friends. [*Deep Throat*] had just opened and they wrote really nice things about it. I was just starting out and I was grateful. You can bet I'll never do it again! It was humiliating. I never realized the whole interview was just a pretext for signing me up for their stupid movie [*It Happened in Hollywood*]. Then when I said no, they kept calling us in Miami.
> **Chuck:** That's the whole basis for their digging at her now and trying to degrade her with lies. They wanted her bad. There's a big difference between what happens while you're climbing to the top . . . and what you don't do, when you get up there.

Perhaps tipping her hand, Helfrecht's habit of referencing her various run-ins with Linda reveal that she is, in fact, Favia Braun (or hmmm, maybe Favia Braun is Diana Helfrecht) when she recalls that while meeting Linda in the offices of Damiano Films, she's made an interesting proposition:

- **From *Swank*, June 1973, by Favia Braun**

"Even as I met her at the appointed hour in the office of Damiano Films, she was accosted by two nice folks with a contract for a Linda Lovelace poster to be distributed internationally."

- **From *Bachelor*, August 1973, by Diana Helfrecht**

"This intimate salon repartee is interrupted by two middle Americans, reps from some hotshot poster company. These nice folks want to make a full-color Linda Lovelace poster and distribute it throughout the civilized and perpetually horny world."

Elsewhere the pair discuss the forthcoming *Deep Throat Part II* ("It's not edited yet, so I can't say too much about it. It's pretty funny, though.... The script for this last one is fabulous..."). When the topic of her newly enhanced breasts comes up, she toes the *Inside Linda Lovelace* line, claiming they've grown thanks to mind over matter after another session of hypnotism. The rest of their talk is typical of the time and offers even more similarities between Helfrecht and Braun, which by now are probably as boring to read about as they are to describe.

Helfrecht wraps up this interview on a predictably high note (whoever she is, it's pretty obvious that she likes both Linda and Chuck) by taking a couple of not-too-cryptic swipes at a pair of popular, contemporary sexual self-help books when she comments, "In an age of plastic 'sensuous women' and joyless hustling she is triumphantly, extravagantly, radiantly alive."

---

## August 1973

# *Playboy* "Porno Chic"

by Bruce Williamson

Williamson writes *Playboy*'s first article about the rise of "porno chic" and introduces middle America to porno's heaviest hitters, "a whole new breed of porn-film makers doing what they can to dissociate themselves from the stigma of smut." Considering the number of female porn stars to profile by the time this issue hit the stands—new and interesting and, in their own special ways, talented women like Marilyn Chambers, Tina Russell and Georgina Spelvin—it's not surprising how little column space and how little new information about Linda is given.

The star of *Deep Throat* is only mentioned in terms of Being There First, a Mary Pickford not necessarily because of her appeal but for having pioneered in the industry—and endured the subsequent censorious slings and arrows of the nation's prosecutors. In an offhanded way the bomb is dropped that her next film might be censored: "A striking example is the return of Linda Lovelace in a movie currently titled *Deep Throat Part II*, with a new director and said to have been shot hardcore but re-pruned for an R rating under the Motion Picture Code (though a *Throat* without hardcore sounds rather like a *Lassie* movie without the dog)."

## August 22, 1973

# *Fort Lauderdale News*
# "Films' Linda Lovelace to X-Pand Her Career"

by Jack Zink

Linda returns to Dade County, Florida—where *Deep Throat* was filmed 18 months earlier—for a press conference announcing her plans to star in a live musical nightclub act. Zink calls the affair, held at the Miami International Hotel Airport, "nervous" and "outrageously hilarious," noting that the side-splitting nervous tension didn't come from Linda—who he reports answered questions "better than most politicians"—but from the three dozen reporters and photographers attending the event.

Details of the show, being launched with help from her new friend Sammy Davis Jr., are as sketchy as they are ambitious: It opens for two weeks at Miami's Paramount Theater where Linda will be joined by a pair of no-doubt beefy male dancers, eight musicians and some comedians; her stage time will clock in at about 20 minutes for which she'll earn $25,000; after Linda's chops are honed, her kinks worked out and her act is gotten together, she will take it on the road to the Tropicana Hotel in Las Vegas for the next two months at $50,000 a week; then it's 10 more weeks of touring followed by a triumphant return to the Trop in February.

Other projects mentioned in the piece include commercial endorsements, the forthcoming *Deep Throat Part II* (said to be shot with hardcore but temporarily shelved while legal matters are worked out) and another film that will be rated either PG or R.

In a real show that Linda's handlers had finally learned the value of their starlet, when a photographer asks her to pose for a "cheesecake" shot at the end of the press conference, Linda says, "My cheesecake photos cost between $5,000 and $10,000 apiece now."

## August 29, 1973

## *Variety*

# "Linda Lovelace Tries To Shed 'Deep Throat' Image For Miami Cafe Break-In"

A report on another doomed project: Linda's show at Florida's Paramount Theater in November, which is scheduled to then move to the Tropicana Hotel in Vegas. Traynor says there will be "a minimal amount of dialogue, a lot of dancing and a lot of singing." Mindful that he has to sell tickets but aware of what the recent Supreme Court decision about the *Miller* case could mean to an obscene nightclub act (especially one starring Linda Lovelace), Traynor says that while the revue won't be based on sex gimmicks, it may or may not have some nudity, and that it might possibly make some kind of mention of *Deep Throat* in one context or another, but not necessarily.

## September 1973

## *Daily Girl*

# "Linda Lovelace: An Interview With the Star of the Sexsational Flick *Deep Throat*"

**BONUS CONTENT**

Download the poster from *Daily Girl* by scanning this QR code or logging onto **bit.ly/LLQR02**

by Diana Helfrecht

In addition to reprinting Helfrecht's interview from *Bachelor* (the one hyping *Deep Throat*, not the sequel), the issue includes a 30-inch poster of Linda taken from *Deep Throat Part II*.

THE MAGAZINE FOR CONTINENTAL SWINGERS
SEPT. $1.25
daily girl
THE DEEPEST THROAT ISSUE EVER!!
INTERVIEW
LINDA LOVELACE!
DEEP THROAT, WHAT?
ANWHILE, HOW DO
CHICKS FEEL
ABOUT IT?
AND... THE MALE
ANSWER TO
THROAT!
EXCLUSIVE BONUS:
A PULL-OUT, HANG-UP, WRAP-AROUND,
FULL-LENGTH POSTER OF (WHO ELSE?)
LINDA LOVELACE-THIRTY INCHES HIGH!

## September 1973

# *Playboy*
# "Playboy Panel: New Sexual Life Styles"

This exhaustive and exhausting roundtable discussion of contemporary sexual mores includes Linda; gay-rights activist Madeline Davis; "sexual libertarian," accomplished artist and mother of masturbation Betty Dodson; Al Goldstein; Drs. Phyllis and Eberhard Kronhausen; John Money, professor of medical psychology and associate professor of pediatrics at Johns Hopkins University, who served as witness for the defense at the New York City *Deep Throat* trial; Pastor Troy Perry of the all-gay Los Angeles Metropolitan Community Church; Wardell B. Pomeroy, coauthor of the Kinsey reports; Robert H. Rimmer, author of *The Harrad Experiment*; Dr. William Simon, program supervisor of sociology and anthropology, who was a member of the Institute for Sex Research at Indiana University; and last but not least, Ernest van den Haag, professor of social philosophy at New York University and witness for the prosecution at the New York City *Deep Throat* trial.

In between comments of the type Linda would later say were demanded of her by Traynor (like her claim that an "anal orgasm" is better than the clitoral, if indeed the clitoral orgasm does exist), you can again almost see the seeds whence her story would later sprout. At one point, when discussing how the world would be different if Dr. Money was designing people's sex lives for them, Linda brags, "Nobody plans *my* life for *me*. I've been with my manager, Chuck, for a very long time, and we do have an open relationship. Since we've been together, we've never been apart for more than an hour. He sees other chicks, but when he does, I'm *with* him. And if I'm with other dudes, he's with me, too. I never go off alone into another room with somebody else, and the same with him."

Sometimes her dormant domestic side comes out, despite the fact that she's talking to *Playboy*. When the conversation turns to marriage, Goldstein comments, "When it's bad, I hate marriage. When it's good, it's magnificent." The supposedly liberated (and comparably promiscuous) Lovelace replies, "I think it's ridiculous, Al, to say that when . . . it's going bad you hate it. If you were really into marriage, it would be a magnificent state, however it was going." That wouldn't be the case when she was interviewed by the *Rocky Mountain News* almost 25 years later.

Despite Linda's contributions of the stripe she says were scripted by Traynor, she does ad-lib one great line. When the topic turns to marriage and fidelity, Goldstein throws it into gear with, "I stay with my wife in spite of my sexual experiences with other people, and that my love for my wife has nothing to do with, say, Linda Lovelace's technical virtuosity. You'll excuse me, Linda, but for me my wife is better."

Linda drives her point home saying, "People who own Fords think Fords are the best-made cars."

## September 1973

# *Swingle*
# "After *Deep Throat*, What?"

How does a porn magazine make a *Deep Throat* cover line work when they have no new information, no pictures from the film and no interview with its star? They spend an inordinate amount of time wondering what the future might hold for the film's star, even though they have nothing more to go on than a few rumors and a little speculation. Then they illustrate the article with pictures of the issue's cover model, who is most definitely *not* Linda Lovelace but . . . Rhoda Handel, used here as the humor-delivery device for a not-too-funny gag wherein she wonders why there isn't a version of the movie *Deep Throat* geared towards women, perhaps titled *Deep Tongue*.

## October 1973

# *Ace!*
# "The Big '8' of Movie Erotica"

by Pat O'Reilly

After Linda stops granting interviews to adult magazines on her way to becoming, as she told *Playboy* in December 1974, the "Shirley Temple of sex," there springs up a new crop of fresh-faced young women eager to walk a mile in her shoes. And by the time editors release this "Spectacular *Ace!* Special" featuring fuck-film "Hall of Famers," some of them have already replaced Lovelace in the hearts and groins of America's pornographic press. Georgina Spelvin, for instance, was getting raves in *The Devil in Miss Jones*, Gerard Damiano's follow-up to *Deep Throat* (*DMJ* takes top honors in *Ace!*'s "Big 8," with *Throat* coming in second). Adding insult to injury, where Spelvin is pictured to put a face on *Miss Jones*, *Throat* is represented by Carol Connors, identified as "Carole Kyzer," whom O'Reilly calls "a remarkable creation in flesh and hair." Of course, Lovelace is mentioned too, in the incredibly lightweight article "*Deep Throat*: The Re-Birth of the 'Blues,'" a two-page spread of stills from both parts of *Deep Throat* that show only Connors and Dolly Sharp, and a different Bunny Yeager photo than the one usually printed at the time.

## October 1973

# *Oui*

# "Arf? Arf, arf, arf! (Maybe)"

by Nick Tosches

*Oui* magazine celebrates its first anniversary in grand style with an account of the Gaslight Club press conference for *Inside Linda Lovelace* that sheds considerably more light on the event than even Bruce David's account in *Screw* a few months earlier. While Linda is busy pressing the flesh of bookstore owners, writers and television reporters, Tosches notes, in walks "*Screw* publisher and porn churl" Al Goldstein, carrying an "ominous manila envelope" containing a blow-up of the dog-humping picture recently printed in *Screw*. After a while Goldstein finally asks if Linda had indeed fucked the dog in the photo.

Lovelace's reply: "Please have Al Goldstein thrown out."

But as David failed to report, probably because he was being shown the same door as Goldstein, the *Screw* editor managed to slip the envelope containing the photograph to Tosches. During his later and presumably more tactful audience with Lovelace, Tosches pulls the magazine out of the manila envelope and asks if it does in fact show Lovelace getting boned by a dog.

Linda's reply: "Nope, look at the picture, it's an Oriental girl."

But as Tosches writes at the conclusion of this article, "I looked at the picture. Doesn't look too Oriental to me. I dunno. And so, Goldstein, Linda and yours truly go our separate ways—three humans under retainer to *Oui* in search of truth, or something like that, while somewhere a dog sighs knowingly."

## October 25, 1973

# *The New York Times*

# "Advertising: Vacation Computer"

by Philip H. Dougherty

Once again a prediction made by *Screw* comes to pass, but not the way they envisioned it. The Old Gray Lady chimes in on the virgin foray into testimonial advertising being attempted by M&J Shoes, an Encino, California, footwear retailer. This might not necessarily seem like news that's fit to print until you realize that their celebrity endorser is Linda Lovelace, who becomes famous for being the first porn star to become famous for endorsing a product after becoming famous for being a porn star. (Marilyn Chambers' face graced the front of the Ivory Snow box before she made *Behind the Green Door.*)

As M&J Shoes honcho David Williams tells the *Times*, "It's a good clean commercial, and [Linda] did an excellent job." Williams went on to say that two versions of the commercial were shot, but he wouldn't reveal how much Lovelace was paid.

## November 1973

# *Man to Man*

# "What Next for Linda Lovelace?"

by Raoul MacFarlane

How does another porn magazine make a Linda Lovelace cover line work when they have no new information, no pictures from her film and no interview with its star? According to the Editor's note, with some good old-fashioned reporting. "After considerable legwork and rumor-tracking [MacFarlane's] come up with some rather lively projections about what's ahead for America's reigning sex queen." Which is all true, except for the "lively" part. This puff piece recycles information from *Inside Linda Lovelace* and runs three unexciting pictures.

## November 1973

# *Venus*

# "Jesus Still Loves You, Linda Lovelace"

by Yvonne Postelle

This premiere issue of an adult magazine for women gave the ladies a male centerfold (and a black dude, at that!), a socially redeeming and thereby legally defensible article about hang gliding and a cover line promising, "Erotic Films—Produced by Women, Defended by Linda Lovelace, Viewed by the Hip Elitist."

Did they succeed? Well, occasionally. While she certainly has only the best of intentions, Postelle's attempt at feminist theorizing sometimes draws not only a wrong conclusion but also a blank from Lovelace, such as when they speak of the feminist's reactions to her. Linda says:

> "[S]ome women's libbers are against me because I'm being exploited. Others are for me; they say I'm part of the movement because I'm the first woman in an X-rated film to openly seek pleasure and gratification when that's always been the role of the man."
>
> "That's the way it started in *Deep Throat*," I say. "Do you remember, when the doctor first discovered the clitoris in your throat, they used the [fireworks] to express your orgasm? Near the end of the movie [the fireworks] are repeated; it's supposed to be a visual representation of what you earlier described as 'bells ringing, dams bursting, and rockets exploding.' Only the second time the movie cuts, not to your face, but to the man's face; and there's a complete shift in emphasis. It becomes his orgasm the audience is watching, not yours."
>
> "That was just poor editing. They just probably overlooked it," Linda says.
>
> "Yes, but don't you think they overlooked it because the crew is conditioned to think of sexual orgasms in terms of male gratification?" I persist.
>
> "I see what you mean ..."
>
> There's a silence in the room.

Postelle overthinks things just a little bit, but this is still a winner of a profile in which she manages to see Linda not just as a sex symbol but as a real person. Perhaps because the questions aren't being asked by a graduate of the Helfrecht/Braun School of Sex Journalism, this is one of the most intelligent and least condescending interviews that the early '70s Linda Lovelace ever gave.

## December 1973

# *Mr.* "Linda Lovelace Tells All"

by Allan Starr

After telling who Linda Lovelace is (again), Starr describes his experiences interviewing Lovelace after the Gaslight Hotel press conference. Admitting that "Linda was very polite and hardly uttered a cuss word" (much less a provocative quote), he peppers this piece with quotes from *Inside Linda Lovelace*, written as if they were given in person. The best part of the article is the inclusion of behind-the-scenes shots taken on the set of *Deep Throat*.

## December 1973

# *Penthouse* "The Great American Sex Boom"

by Bruce David

David offers this nasty take on porno chic, again in the context of the Gaslight Hotel press conference. He discusses recent obscenity rulings, as well as Linda, Marilyn Chambers and Georgina Spelvin. Marilyn is the prettiest, Georgina the only actress and Linda is ...

1. accused of hypocrisy for holding a press conference and signing autographs for the mainstream media when all she does is have sex on film
2. described as looking 28 when she's really 22
3. described as a woman "who can't act, isn't beautiful, and who has been accused of having sex with a dog," a seemingly favorite hook for this piece and
4. called a "1970s version of the Beatles."

David conveniently avoids describing his own culpability in the hypocrisy equation as a *Screw* staffer and *Penthouse* contributor, but he does conclude that given the Supreme Court's relinquishing of control in obscenity cases to local governments—whose verdicts they can overturn if those local governments become overzealous in their application of obscenity law—the future may be good for erotica in America. But maybe not.

## December 1973

# *Playboy* "Sex Stars of 1973"

by Arthur Knight

A full-page picture of Linda Lovelace opens *Playboy*'s annual raunchy rundown, confirming her status as the year's hottest sexual celebrity. She's described as one of the country's hottest box-office properties as well, her contemporaries in that regard including Marlon Brando and Burt Reynolds.

Despite the accolades Lovelace receives as the major sex symbol of the year, male or female, Knight's tone is somewhat condescending towards the young starlet. He writes of her performance in *Deep Throat*, "It was the kind of work that, as she has frequently announced, she enjoys. The rest, as the saying goes, is history—some of it recorded in her purportedly autobiographical *Inside Linda Lovelace*." While again more attention is paid to her hardcore porn contemporaries, Knight describes Lovelace's contribution to the recent *Playboy* panel discussion of "New Sexual Life Styles" by recalling one observer's comment that, "She may not have a Ph.D., but she's certainly passed her orals."

## December 17, 1973

# *Time*

## "People" section

Linda, having recently been given the "Wilde Oscar" award by the *Harvard Lampoon*, will soon return to Philadelphia to continue rehearsals for the bedroom farce *Pajama Tops*, scheduled to open on Christmas Day. Speaking about his recent divorce from Lovelace and his own new career course, Chuck Traynor comments, "You gotta trade in your old car when it can't make the hills." Since splitting from Lovelace, Traynor has been kicking the tires of Marilyn Chambers, who tells Linda's ex, "I hope I'm never your old car."

**BONUS CONTENT**

Download a fun fact about Linda Lovelace by scanning this QR code

## 1973

# *Superstars of Porno*

One look at the cover and it isn't hard to see where this one's going, as Linda shares cover space and column inches with porn stars including Rene Bond and Tina Russell. The pictures are of the same vintage as the two Linda Lovelace-specific publications mentioned previously, but feature a few different photo sessions, which you can tell from Lovelace's different hairstyles. The text is of the same caliber as those magazines, written in the same life- and love-affirming hippie-dippy style contemporary with the times. The centerfold is a double spread of two pictures, each getting a separate page.

# ... 1974 ...

**1974**

## *Cinema X*

## "Linda Lovelace: The Whole Truth. Nothing But"

This British film journal dedicates an entire issue to the topic of American porn films. Many quotes from Linda and other sources are pieced together to create the profile of America's favorite cocksucker for the edification of Brits who are yet to be allowed to see *Deep Throat* (they wouldn't legally have that privilege for more than 25 years). After lamenting Lovelace's retreat from hardcore, the author decides she probably won't abandon the genre that made her famous, quoting her thusly: "I'm not gonna sit around and say I'll never do another hardcore film because I was forced into *Deep Throat*, that I needed the money or something like that. I did it because I loved it. It was something I believed in: It was me, I was just playing myself. Greta Garbo studied acting and English to improve with each subsequent film. Same with me. I'm going to fuck and suck better and better as my film career progresses. And if, when I'm 65 years old, they're making an X-rated movie and they need a little old lady to be in it, I'm gonna say, 'Here! I'm right here!'"

**1974**

## *Drag Racing Photo Greats Special Edition No. 4*

Linda is shown in a full-page picture with champion funny car driver Ed McCulloch after he wins the 1973 Northwest Open in Seattle. The accompanying caption mentions that Linda is in town "to promote her movie," but glosses over who Lovelace is and the fact that the movie she was using the photo-op to promote was *Deep Throat Part II*.

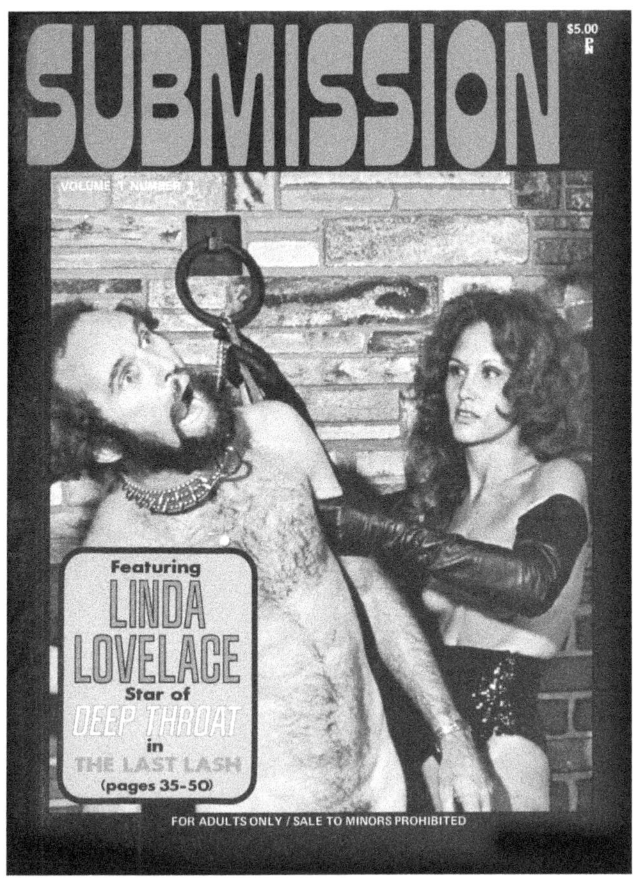


## 1974

# *Submission*

These are likely the "ketchup on the back" S&M pictures Linda describes in *Ordeal.* "Brandy and I had done several tricks together in Florida," she wrote, "and our first job in New York was for a still photographer. This was in a studio that was used exclusively for sadomasochistic photos: chains hanging from the walls, strange medieval torture devices, a full selection of whips, a jumbo-sized bottle of Heinz ketchup. . . . Brandy and I stripped down, then took turns pretending to whip and torture each other. It was all so absurd. What kind of a man would get turned on by seeing a woman with ketchup smeared on her back?"

*Submission* features 16 pages of Linda, Chuck Traynor and the fabulous firecrotch Brandy (female costar of Linda's first two loops) in a layout called "The Last Lash" that's more Irving Klaw than the Marquis de Sade. Traynor appears as "Harvey," a horny mook who's gettin' it on with "Paula" (Linda) in his "sex-trap pad," until the "dynamic Karen"

(Brandy) shows up and turns him into a "whimpering whelp." Traynor mugs his way through whip-strikes, dog collars and a knee to the balls administered by Linda herself with wide-eyed, open-mouthed terror. In other words, he loves it.

This is probably the sexiest Linda Lovelace ever looked in a photo spread. Once she's shed her button-down shirt and beat-up zippered boots, she's outfitted in opera gloves, sheer black stockings, a black garterbelt (high-waisted enough to hide the scar on her tummy) and a pair of pointy-toed black pumps that must be rocking a good four- or five-inch heel. Brandy's overcoat looks like it could have come from the wardrobe of *The Ten Commandments*, and in some shots she's wearing thigh-high boots and a garter and stockings that show off her burning bush beautifully. The fetish fashion statements alone make this spread a total turn-on, despite the fact that the only one getting ketchup smeared on their back is Chuck Traynor.

## January 21, 1974

# *Soul Newspaper*

# "Smokey and Linda on the Couch, Please..."

It was a miracle indeed when Linda Lovelace made the cover of this black music newspaper to illustrate one of her more interesting television appearances: a guest slot on *90 Tonight*, an interview show airing out of Burbank, California, and hosted this night by Smokey Robinson. Other guests on the show that evening include the Lockers (the "hip" dance troupe that featured Fred "Rerun" Berry from the popular sitcom *What's Happening?*); Gene Bell (the dancer who recently appeared with singer Josephine Baker) and Toni Basil (the singer, actress and choreographer whom America could later blame for Paula Abdul).

The article's title refers to the stage manager's request for the pair to get their bad selves onstage and start to conversating, which they did, about how Linda got her role in *Deep Throat* (she started out as "script girl") and whether it was true she had to come a certain number of times in a day. Her answer, of course, was yes, but the home audience may have been left hanging themselves, as the question was bleeped out for broadcast.

Smokey shows himself to be a total class act when he told the audience that anyone who thought Linda was a bad girl was wrong, calling her "charming" and one of the nicest people he ever met.

## February 13, 1974

# *Variety*
# "Deep Throat Part II"

Hollywood's most influential newspaper reviews the sequel to *Deep Throat*, warning all potential theatergoers (and theater owners thinking of booking the film) that "*Deep Throat Part II* is in the shoddiest of exploitation film traditions, a depressing fast-buck attempt to milk a naive public. Audience ire is likely to be aroused."

And just what is likely to arouse audience ire? "Amateur-night quality . . . from truly awful performances from Lovelace and a cast of N.Y.-based hardcore regulars, through [director Joe] Sarno's hackneyed script and direction to a number of raunchy tunes on the soundtrack, all keyed to remind viewers that the leading lady can do something special, even if she can't do it with an R rating."

If that's not bad enough, "La Lovelace can do one thing, but she doesn't do it in this pic, in fact she doesn't do much of anything but mug as she stumbles through a witless plot about espionage and randy psychiatrists." *Variety* also decrees that Gerard Damiano "should be grinning from ear to ear" after having been shoved aside from the chance to direct this film.

The review finishes by saying, "Pic is being distributed by Bryanston Pictures but is going out through a Damiano Films pseudonym. When a distrib won't put its own name on a feature, refuses to screen for critics and opens showcase in N.Y. on a Friday, the trade raises its eyebrows. The public may take a bit longer to catch on."

## February 22, 1974

# *The New York Times*
# "Notes on People"

by Albin Krebs

Linda Lovelace is back on the market, having been granted a divorce from Chuck Traynor in Santa Monica, California, in which "She relinquished all claims to alimony or division of community property assets." Other notable events of the day include Lieut. (jg.) Barbara Allen becoming the first woman flier in military history; Democrat Richard F. VanderVeen taking new Vice President Gerald Ford's chair in the House of Representatives; and the announcement that the next mayor of the great city of Cincinnati will be one Gerald N. Springer, later known to a nation of afternoon television addicts as "Jer-*ry*! Jer-*ry*! Jer-*ry*!"

## March 1974

# *Rascal*
# "Deep Throat"

by Allan Starr

This review of the "hard-sex comedy" celebrates the film's light-hearted approach to the topic of explicit sex, unlike previous films that suffered censorship problems. Starr's article once again recalls the film's plot for the benefit of those who haven't seen it, using that friend of overzealous prosecutors everywhere—badly paraphrased dialogue—before putting it in this interesting nutshell: "Imagine, if you can, the Galloping Gourmet working out of Masters and Johnson to the music of Hot Tuna and you have some idea of what to expect." The article is illustrated with lots of photographs from the film as well as additional shots that were taken on the set during the filming, some of which accompanied Starr's earlier piece in *Mr.* magazine.

This issue later features a large photo of Lovelace illustrating Dorothy Allen's review of the movie *The Suckers*, which doesn't count Linda among its stars.

## March 11, 1974

# *Women's Wear Daily*
# "A Bird in the Hand"

Linda Lovelace returns to the fashion paper that got her first by shopping for a pair of parakeet cages at Kreiss' Ports of Call, a store in California. Despite having pulled up in front of the store in a maroon Rolls-Royce, Lovelace is asked to produce identification to back up a check and whips out . . . her driver's license. When the clerk asks her for another piece of ID, she whips out . . . a nude photograph and signs it for him. This story was later told as happening to porn starlet Sharon Mitchell.

## March 24, 1974

# *The New York Times*

# "Sex Week Is Quiet at U. of Alabama"

by Wayne King

A mere 11 years after Governor George Wallace denied entry to two black students, the University of Alabama throws open its doors to a bunch of blue moviemakers. The show's syllabus includes an appearance by Al Goldstein; a performance of the gay-themed student play *Boys Will Be Girls, Girls Will Be Boys*; a lecture on rape prevention; a screening of the Russ Meyer film *Cherry, Harry & Raquel!*; and a show-stopping lecture by Linda Lovelace. While the *Times* reports that there were few protests, Baptist minister Reverend Dr. Allen Watson called the presentation "almost totally useless if not harmful." Another minister asked, "What of any significance is Linda Lovelace going to be able to say to an academic community that will be any aid in understanding human sexuality? She's just a porno chick," he explains, "and that's what will pack the arena." To back up that point, program chairman Philip Rawls notes, "Frankly, it makes me a little angry. We had the Lipizzaner stallions here and only drew 2,500 people in a 16,000 seat stadium. We showed Chaplin's *Modern Times* and 100 showed up. Then we booked a Swedish porno film and filled the house for two shows."

## April 15, 1974

# *Screw*

# "From Head to Eternity"

by Al Goldstein

The director of the world's first crossover porno gives his first interview to The World's Greatest Newspaper. By this time the fix was in with regards to destroying Linda in the eyes of her fans; despite the fact that *The Devil in Miss Jones* had already been released to great reviews, that Damiano was readying the release of *Memories Within Miss Aggie* (referred to here as *Memory*) and that he was scouting talent for an unnamed flick to be marketed with the William Morris Agency, Damiano spends most of his time fielding questions from Goldstein designed to make Linda Lovelace look like a cunt.

Damiano claims he met Linda casting for inserts (hard-core clips used to spice up soft-core films) for the movie *Changes*. "She knocked me out the minute she started going down on a cock," he says, "doing her 'deep throat' thing. [So] the insert I made did not get into the film. It went right on the cutting-room floor because I realized she had too much potential to throw away on merely an insert into another film.... I was so knocked out over what she did that I went home and wrote *Deep Throat*, the whole screenplay, over the weekend. And we went into preproduction work that Monday."

Damiano's recollection of his initial meeting with Lovelace would go through some changes itself. In the article "A Throat Is Born" (*High Society*, January 1977), an excerpt from the proposed but unreleased autobiography *Getting Deeper*, Damiano writes that he was casting for inserts, but goes on to tell Linda, "Come around tomorrow morning at 11:00 and I can use you in the loop."

While trying to figure out exactly what kind of relationship Linda and Traynor enjoyed, if that's really the right word, Damiano ultimately supports the claims Lovelace would make five years later with the publication of *Ordeal*. "When I first met her she was with Chuck," he says, "and after 10 or 15 minutes I wanted to speak to her alone, so I asked Chuck to leave the room. She was nervous. But when Chuck left, she almost crawled up the wall. I couldn't understand it, so I had Chuck come back in again. It wasn't until a while later that I realized their relationship, that she wasn't allowed out of his sight. He held such a close rein on her that if she was away from him for more than five minutes, then he would beat the shit out of her."

Considerably later in the conversation, Goldstein picks up on what Damiano has just said. Sorta:

> ***Screw*:** Did they hold hands? Were they romantic? I heard that he often beat her up. Is that a fact?
> **Damiano:** I've often tried to pinpoint the psychology of Linda. She seemed to have a distinct sadomasochistic relationship with Chuck, to the point where he constantly dominated her. They were never anywhere where she was not holding him, touching him. There was always a physical closeness, or contact. Even in total exhaustion. One night we were driving back from a shooting. Chuck was driving and Linda was sitting in the back seat and she leaned forward at the edge of her seat just to touch Chuck on the shoulder for 45 minutes. She had to be physically uncomfortable. There was this strange need all the time. And he acted as if he wasn't even aware of it. It was an amazing thing to see their relationship. As close as they were in the daytime, I knew that Chuck would bang Linda off the wall all night. And the next day she'd appear on the set black and blue.

Later, Goldstein decides that he still hasn't heard enough:

> ***Screw:*** Tell us more about her masochistic relationship with Chuck.
> **Damiano:** In Miami he made her wear these cut-down jeans

that were so short and so tight that the lips of her pussy would hang out the sides. She did have nice long legs and anyone passing by her would have to notice that her pussy lips were hanging out of this costume. But in Chuck's mind, anybody who did look at her was grounds for taking Linda back to the hotel and beating the shit out of her.

***Screw*:** Well, what about the way he was peddling her ass? He did want her to do it, and he didn't?

**Damiano:** She was damned if she did and damned if she didn't. Obviously in her case, she was supposed to do it, but not enjoy it.

***Screw*:** When Linda was sucking my cock, Chuck was there with a photographer during her first *Screw* interview. So, this is not a big deviation from her behavior. Chuck was pushing power.

**Damiano:** Linda wanted that situation. Regardless of the way he treated her, she stayed with him. She must have encouraged him.

***Screw*:** Was she more masochistic than other people in the fuck-film business?

**Damiano:** More. There are very few relationships that I have seen in the porn syndrome that rival hers with Chuck. Most of the girls work on their own. They are their own bosses. They do what they do because they want to do it. It's very seldom that I see relationships like Linda's.

On the topic of how much money Linda made during her time with Chuck Traynor, Damiano concludes, "Chuck made out better because, after he broke off with Linda, he hooked into Marilyn Chambers, who is really Avis. She's Number Two. Chuck mystifies me. He's innocuous, he's no continental lover, he couldn't get it up on the *Deep Throat* set, but you have to admit the man must have something. It mystified me then and it still does."

It would become obvious over the years that Damiano liked Linda, and maybe had a bit of a crush on her. Even after the publication of *Ordeal* (which, in addition to the release of his other films, gave him several more opportunities to be interviewed by the adult press), Damiano would admit no small affection for the woman he helped make a star. In the September 1981 issue of *Genesis*, he spoke about Linda's description of her relationship with Traynor as realized in *Ordeal*; he calls her claims of abuse on the *Deep Throat* set "bullshit," despite earlier confirming them in *Screw*:

**Damiano:** Whenever I was in their company, she doted on him. She loved him, she was close to him, she was never out of his sight. Actually, I was kinda jealous of him, because I liked her. She would have done anything he asked her to.

***Genesis*:** You never got involved with Linda Lovelace, did you?

**Damiano:** Personally? Sexually? No. Not that I would not have. I tell you, I loved her; not in the sense that I wanted to marry her and be with her forever, but she was such a wonderful person that if things had been different and the situation had arisen, I would have been very happy to have had Linda be my lady.

Speaking to *Hustler* in March 1975 about how porno stardom had affected his various leading ladies, he said, "I think Linda's one of the most beautiful people I know. She's filled with contrast. She's honest, shy and sexy—every man's dream. Unfortunately she's prone to being used, as events since *Throat* have shown. It's too bad because I think maybe her best quality is her total openness and honesty."

## April 29, 1974

## *Screw*

# "Exclusive Interview With Chuck Traynor: How Linda Lovelace's Hubby Taught Her Deep Throat—Part One"

by Al Goldstein and Peter Brennan

Chuck Traynor tells The World's Greatest Newspaper how he created The World's Greatest Sex Symbol. The interview begins with Goldstein trying to dispel the last remaining myths surrounding Lovelace, getting Traynor to reveal her true age, her parents' location and vocation and, for anyone who missed it a few months earlier, her real name. If anybody had doubts about Lovelace's claims in *Ordeal* and couldn't be swayed by the Damiano interview, this interview would have done it. Traynor all but admits that what Linda would later write in her book is true:

> ***Screw*:** In Gerry Damiano's interview with *Screw* he said that while he was shooting *Deep Throat* there was some talk about a lot of banging around going on in your motel room. Did you beat her up? Or is it just gossip? We want to get it out right now.
> **Traynor:** Yeah. Right. Well, yeah. I wouldn't bullshit anybody. I've always tried to deal with people two ways: I talk to them as long as I think I can talk to them, and then I hit them. With Linda, you know, if she and I got into a hassle, it wouldn't be beneath me to backhand her or bend her over my knee and beat her ass. Linda dug it, you know.

Those same circumstances would be confirmed a second time in *High Society* (February 1981) after *Ordeal* was published:

> ***HS***: You say you loved her. But when did you start beating her and how did that happen?
> **CT:** Well, that's kind of stretching it. I was raised in the country and still live in the country. I don't consider it beating if you slap your old lady for something. To me that's almost a sign of feelings, of closeness. When your old lady does something wrong or when she's giving you too much lip or something—I don't really consider that beating up. Of course, Linda did in her book and she stretched that point unbelievably. The marks on her legs—I think they were from her car accident. I didn't beat her legs with chains or anything.

Traynor also confirms that it may not have been as easy for her to leave him as he wanted people to think:

> ***HS***: During any of this period of time—before or after you were married—if Linda was unhappy, was she free to leave you?
> **CT:** No, not in the normal sense. First of all, I'm very possessive. Secondly, I'm probably a lot more physically capable of threatening people than most. Of course, if you care about somebody and if you're involved with them in the film business and they say they're going to leave you, I think a normal reaction would be, "You better not or I'll bust your ass." I just would not say to anyone involved with me professionally or emotionally, "Yeah, you can walk out the door any time you want to." Whether I would or wouldn't "bust their ass" would depend on the particular situation. But she was not kept prisoner, nailed to the wall. I would tell her not to leave, probably forbid her to leave, just as I would imagine most boyfriends or husbands or managers or pimps from the South would do. If she actually left and stayed away, I would be very pissed off about it, but it would have died. She appeared before a grand jury, she appeared before district attorneys and all kinds of legal people and she could have walked out then. She could have walked out any time prior to that because of other legal complications I had—that marijuana hassle she talks about in the book. At any time she could have walked out and I couldn't have done anything.

That's as close as their two stories meet, though, in terms of their relationship. Traynor confirms several incidents that were later brought up in *Ordeal*—meeting the one-time Linda Boreman while she recovered from her 1970 car accident; the turkey raffles at his Las Vegas Inn topless/bottomless club in Miami—but he tells far different stories about such things as their breakup (which Linda would later come to refer to as her "escape"); and his reaction to them.

Elsewhere in the *Screw* interview, a bitter-sounding Traynor, who by this time was well into his relationship with Marilyn Chambers, also claims that Linda broke things off with him, as she could have at any time, after being chatted up by David Winters, the choreographer who was helping put together Linda's proposed stage show; Mel Mandel, who was writing the music; and Lee Winkler, who would go on to stage the production of *Pajama Tops* in which Linda appeared.

Traynor also gives a logical reason for giving up his presidential position in Linda Lovelace Enterprises: the various shows for which Lovelace was contracted obviously weren't going to happen, and that was going to leave some club owners very, very unhappy. Knowing it was Linda Lovelace Enterprises that would be sued, he gladly gave the business to Winters, who Traynor felt had given the business to him.

---

## April 30, 1974

# *The Boston Phoenix*

# "The Devil Behind 'The Devil in Miss Jones'"

by Bill O'Reilly

Much of the big debate about the Linda Lovelace story is whether she was beaten into submission to hook and pose for dirty pictures and fuck on film or whether she did those things because she was a horny hippie chick who got off on public sex with hairy guys. This article settles that debate once and for all, and the winner is ... Linda Lovelace.

Back in the early '70s, O'Reilly was a journalist working for local publications including the *Boston Phoenix*, for which he interviewed Gerard Damiano. The occasion for this meeting of the minds, this battle between America's nascent culture warrior and a whoremongering merchant of smut, was the release of *The Devil in Miss Jones*. Not only does O'Reilly use coverage of the Boston University film screening/Q&A session to describe Damiano's platform shoes, his "lecherous smile" and his platinum-blonde wife... not only does he report on Damiano spouting "the usual banalities and well-rehearsed answers concerning censorship"... not only does he send readers scrambling for their dictionaries by using the word "grumous" (it means "lumpy"), O'Reilly decides there are un-A'd Q's from the Q&A, so he grills Damiano at the Aegean Fare restaurant in Kenmore Square.

Damiano indeed gives what seem like well-rehearsed answers, mainly because the questions O'Reilly asks are so fucking dull: *Deep Throat* was written in a weekend; porn's about the art, not the money; and no, Damiano still won't talk about how the Perainos bought out his investment in *Deep Throat*. But O'Reilly really hits pay dirt when he asks Damiano about Linda Lovelace. And fuck it! He does it live!

Quoth Damiano:

> "Linda changed, she became affected by what she was. She demands a very high salary and she can't perform. She never had

any talent as an actress. She just had one unique quality of being the most sensually turned-on person I have ever met. She had this innocence. No matter what she did she came across as not being dirty. She doesn't have this quality anymore.

"In *Deep Throat Part II* she was awful—god-awful. Whatever she had the new people who are handling her have no way of bringing it out. I taught her how to walk, how to stand, how to project herself and lose her shyness.

"I thought she might progress when she got rid of her husband, Chuck Traynor, who then went over to manage Marilyn Chambers. That man was a nothing. He had no personality, no charm, no brains. He was just a user of people and he used Linda. He gave her nothing and abused her. He was very brutal with her. She was supposed to do what she did but she wasn't supposed to enjoy it, and if she enjoyed it he beat her up. Many times she'd come on the set completely black and blue."

## May 1974

## *Movie World*

# "Roger Horrified As Porno Star Tries To Take Over Ann-Margret's Act!"

by Hillary Kain

After crowing about the undeniable beauty of singer/dancer/actress Ann-Margret, "the most gorgeous creature to come out of Sweden and to be discovered since 'the blonde,'" Kain contributes a cruel recollection of the night the swinging Swede almost met Linda Lovelace.

It's obvious from the first sentence that Kain could have had a good career in porn journalism. Writing about the Ann-Margret performance she had attended, she notes, "Her full breasts, straining against the skin-tight top of the silver bugle-beaded gown, heave sumptuously as she goes whole-heartedly into her flawless act. The long, slinky dancer's legs, clearly visible beneath the skirt slit up to the waist, flit across the stage in one erotic, hip-swinging dance after another. . . . The audience is ecstatic. They jump to their feet, wildly proclaiming her the queen of her art. But every queen has her rival—some pretender to the throne. And so it was that a usurper arrived on the scene."

That usurper was, of course, Linda Lovelace, who at David Winters' prodding dared speak to the former "Kitten With a Whip," who went on to gain her legit acting cred with her star turn in *Carnal Knowledge*. (Winters had an in with the Swedish beauty, having choreographed several of her films and stage shows.) Kain practically crucifies Lovelace, whom she says is "intent on furthering her career" with her "competitive inclination" for daring to want a photo taken with A-M.

Kain takes a series of merciless, prejudiced swipes at Lovelace, mentioning that the sequel to *Deep Throat* is titled "cleverly enough" *Deep Throat Part II*, while conveniently failing to mention that the Ann-Margret show Lovelace had attended the night of this debacle bore the equally clever title of "The Best of Ann-Margret."

## May 20, 1974

# *Screw*

# "An Intimate Interview With Harry Reems: Super Stud of the Silver Screen"

by Al Goldstein

The most famous man in adult film takes this, his first-ever interview, seriously. After confessing he doesn't care for life as a porn stud ("Pornography is . . . a thing I do for an income. I don't pursue the way of life [Tina and Jason Russell and Georgina Spelvin] have chosen, which is pornography. They're the revolutionaries, but I'm not a trailblazer"), the discussion goes from what he does get out of his involvement with smut—a little money, a little pussy and a little stroking of his actor's ego—to Lovelace's incredible fame:

> ***Screw*:** Linda Lovelace is one person who's broken out of this field.
> **Reems:** She's gotten notoriety the likes of which nobody else ever had. She became the first person to get pointed out. As far as a personality, Linda has got that magnetic ability to draw an audience or anybody in a room directly to her, that twinkle in the eye, that real smile without phoniness or presumptuousness. I don't know about now, I haven't seen her since *Deep Throat Part II*, where she became scared of certain things. She suddenly hit a financial plateau where she had to watch what she did and said. She's a beautiful person.
> ***Screw*:** How was she in the film? And how do you view her relationship with Chuck, her boyfriend/manager?
> **Reems:** At first I thought they were into an open sexual relationship, but I felt a certain resistance whenever Chuck was present. While we were doing a sex scene she would get uptight. She

> didn't want to reveal to Chuck that she was enjoying herself. Indeed she was. As soon as Chuck went out of the room—and Gerry would ask him to go out and get cigarettes just to get him out of the room and get her free emotionally—the scene was five times better.

Asked whether he had any special sexual memories of Linda, Reems recalls his meeting with her on the set of a loop they shot for Damiano prior to *Deep Throat.*:

> **Reems:** I was not supposed to act in the film, but after six days watching everybody fuck and suck while I'm putting lights up and rigging cameras, I'm getting horny. Linda and I had worked in New York two weeks previously in those loops, so I kept eyeing her and she kept eyeing me. At this point Damiano was looking for a guy to play the doctor, so ultimately I played the part. At the hotel, when Chuck wasn't around, Linda and I would say, "I can't wait until we can get it on." We never had a chance to have sex off the set, however.

---

## June 1974

## *Bachelor*

# "Lovelace—The New Liz?"

by Marsha Van Leyden Deane

Deane starts out wondering what Linda Lovelace will do with a shitty *Deep Throat Part II* in release and a lawsuit from Al Goldstein narrowly avoided. At least this time she has an answer. And it is? The bedroom farce *Pajama Tops*, *certainement*!

Although a review of Linda's stage debut in Hollywood tabloid *Screen Star* was less than kind, reporting gleefully that she was "literally laughed off the stage," Deane enjoys her performance, although she found the play somewhat stale and predictable. She writes that "[Linda] runs around in flimsy baby dolls playing the mistress of a philandering husband.... *Pajama Tops* is ... chockfull of ze ancient French witticisms, ze antique grimaces and innuendos, ze twisting of le moustache and ze lifting of les eyebrows and ze subtlety of V-E Day in Paris ... but ze nudity? *Mais non*! So *naturellement* much of ze audience split at intermission."

Linda's burgeoning comedy career comes no thanks to Traynor, whom Deane mentions Lovelace dropped like *le chaud pomme de terre* for "re-routing her physical flagrancies into an Ann-Margret nightclub [act]," adding that "Linda Lovelace is not Ann-Margret and we should all be grateful, as the world needs many more lovely libertines and many fewer carrot-brained hooflets doing the shim-sham to the Vegas Philharmonic."

The titular comparison to Liz Taylor comes with the revelation that after Linda divorced Chuck he shacked up with Marilyn Chambers, who moved in with him at the Beverly Wilshire Hotel and began divorce proceedings on her own husband in a move that "reeks of [the] Liz & Debbie and Eddie-ism that characterized the Hollywood '50s ... back when we could still be shocked."

But apparently there is still opportunity for shock in Deane's eyes. People will no doubt be shocked, she muses, when they see *Deep Throat Part II* and see no hardcore sex. It is to avoid such shock, she concludes, that people should flock to see *Pajama Tops*. While Linda's no Mae West or Judy Holliday, Deane declares her "the best sex comedienne the sorry '70s have to offer. The very last thing we need is one more sex goddess to take herself seriously."

## June 12, 1974

## *Variety*

# "Lovelace: Fame But Not Fortune"

Hollywood's bible reports on Linda's attendance at the Cannes Film Festival's showing of *Deep Throat*, which by then had grossed an estimated $20,000,000. Linda's had a hard time getting on television shows lately—she was denied a spot on the *Jerry Lewis Muscular Dystrophy Telethon*, described here as a "benefit show for retarded children"—but her highly anticipated upcoming film appearances include the Hollywood-based film *Linda Lovelace for President*, and a possible Andy Warhol production about a porn star who comes into contact with British society—which could actually be an interesting case of art imitating life, as one of Linda's escorts for the Cannes Film Festival is Jimmy Vaughan, Warhol's London distributor.

## July 1, 1974

# *Sports Illustrated* "People"

The magazine for athletic supporters compares Douglas Fairbanks Jr. not quite "los[ing] his shirt" when his Kentucky Derby bet finished out of the money to Lovelace's appearance in top hat and tails (but no blouse) at the Royal Ascot Racecourse. She wasn't in danger of losing her shirt, they joked, because she already had!

Linda's day at the races was less than humorous, though: acting as goodwill ambassadress for the National Coordination Committee Against Censorship, a decidedly ad hoc coalition that included Linda's paramour/manager David Winters, whose primary objective was opening England up to the possibility of showing *Deep Throat*. Such an event would not happen; after a review, British authorities refused permission for the film to be shown. *Daily Mail* film critic David Lewin wrote, "Miss Lovelace is a spearhead of an intense campaign to make hardcore films acceptable.... However much the clever publicity may confuse things, this isn't porno chic, a new art form.... It is about making money out of sex. And there is another word for that." *People*'s coverage of Linda's uncoverage also notes that, despite her penchant for wearing see-through blouses to England's "snooty combination racetrack and fashion show ... no Bobby has been shortsighted enough to arrest her."

## August 1974

# *Rona Barrett's Hollywood* "Hollywood's Big Night—The 1974 Academy Awards!"

The legendary gossip queen's report on the annual Tinseltown gala opens with a picture of the horse-drawn carriage that squired Linda to the ceremony, and like Hillary Kain's article offers a condescending opinion of Linda's attendance. The caption under the photo reads, "Linda Lovelace tried to bring her unique 'touch of class' to this year's Oscars by showing up in a carriage drawn by horses. Don't worry, Linda was *not* a nominee—for anything!" But she was one of two starlets *The New York Times* credits with bringing some animal charm to the event. In addition to Lovelace's steeds, actress Edy Williams, dressed in a leopard cape and bikini, arrived with a Great Dane in tow. The dog had to sit outside.

## October 1974

# *Playboy*
# "Playboy Interview: Al Goldstein"

The Mouth That Whored gets his moment in the sun as the subject of the infamous *Playboy* interview. The magazine recaps Goldstein's journalistic career—being fired from the sensationalist tabloid the *National Mirror* and the heretofore unexplainable celestial convergence that ultimately resulted in the first issue of *Screw*—before Al expounds on his influence in making *Deep Throat* a hit. And like any Good Samaritan, he was "just doing his job," man:

> I went to review the film, and I was suddenly confronted with Linda Lovelace on-screen. She had a lot going—or should I say coming—for her. She was lovely, thin, young and fresh.... *Deep Throat* was cute; it moved along. It had music. It had wit. But mostly it had Linda as a brilliant cocksucker.... Her enthusiasm and her vitality were wonderful. I got so hung on that film that I got 11 hard-ons.

Of course, he also gets to relive his infamous Linda Lovelace blowjob, which he seems to wish he could just forget:

> The guy who owned the World Theater asked me if I wanted to interview Linda. I said, 'Jesus, sure, I'd love to meet her.' We met in a small, cold $17-a-night hotel room, and it was the most difficult interview I ever conducted, because she's really inarticulate. Chuck Traynor, then her husband and 'manager,' did most of the talking. After the interview, I said, 'Listen, I'd really like you to suck my cock.' I figured she was just a hooker anyway, so I wasn't embarrassed. She said fine, Chuck said okay and she blew me.

The resulting "paradigm of personal journalism" left the poor Goldstein feeling, as he put it:

> [V]ery alienated. There I was with the world's greatest cocksucker, and yet it was a very lonely experience. I was sweating. She was hot. But it was false, because it was not spontaneous. I have an average cock of about seven inches and the fact that it disappeared down her throat interfered with my concentration.... My con-

> centration kept wandering. She was sitting on my face in a sixty-nine position, and as I was eating her, I knew I wasn't bringing her any pleasure. I was feeling very selfish, so I asked, 'You don't really come this way, do you?' She said, 'Yeah, I come.' It finally dawned on me that this was a nonmonetary gift from the distributors for my review. So then I was able to come in a detached sort of way.... It was like working. I felt like a hooker faking an orgasm with a john. I left there feeling sad.

In a moment damn near approaching genuine reflection, Goldstein describes his seeming obsession with the porn starlet:

> I began running everything I could find about Linda. She was my star. She was my Marilyn Monroe. If I had been a faggot, she would have been my Judy Garland. Only in America could a cocksucker go so far. But I'm thrilled at being party to her success.

Maybe Goldstein should have used a more appropriate phrase, like "tickled pink," because it seems that maybe Lovelace *was* Goldstein's Garland. Speaking of some other journalistic successes he was party to, he confesses to some true undercover reporting:

> I once wrote about my experiences in a movie theater where you can get blowjobs. It's a sleazy joint in New York only frequented by men.... Nobody looks at the films, but up in the balcony you can find whatever sex you want. I participated. One guy who blew me was an old man who took his teeth out first. It was fantastic, better than Linda Lovelace. Most guys are better cocksuckers than women anyway.

If that isn't good enough, Goldstein's *Playboy* interview finally reveals the truth behind his greatest literary flub. "I never mentioned her name in the review [of *Deep Throat*]," he admits, "probably for the same reason I bought Rolls-Royce stock before it went into bankruptcy. I didn't realize Linda would be a star."

# ... 1975 ...

### 1975

## *Cropped Crotches*

"Linda was one of the first to shave and smile," reads the girl copy for yet another repackaging of pre-*Deep Throat* Linda Lovelace photos sets by Eros-Goldstripe Publishers, this time catering to the bald-beaver crowd. "She is . . . famous in esoteric circles for her famous shaved look, a style that seems to be catching on more and more with hip femme lovelies."

Many of the photographs here are previously unpublished but come from the same five or six sessions that Linda did in late 1971—and that Eros-Goldstripe reprinted *ad nauseam* for years after—presented here in the context of her hairless hoohah, including a few stragglers from her S&M session with Brandy and her foursome with Chuck, Eric Edwards and the always adorable Chris Jordan.

### January 1975

## *Gallery*
## "Christmas Goosings"

*Gallery*'s gift to their readers during the holiday season of the mid-'70s? Parody Christmas cards, including one from Linda Lovelace, which, ironically, is shown on the same spread as greetings from two people with whom Linda would share some eventual facetime on the public stage: Gloria Steinem and kidnapped college student Patty Hearst.

Linda also makes an appearance that ostensibly led people to buy the magazine in the first place. A cover blurb on this issue announces, "Linda Lovelace Is Coming!" and while that was certainly front-page news at one time, it seems as if the only thing that's coming is Lovelace's career, and it's coming to an end. The magazine explains the cover line by means of an ad trumpeting her upcoming advice column, which, once again, never happened.

Hell having no fury like an editor scorned, that much-discussed-but-never-seen advice column might have led *Gallery* to commit an unusual snub to porn's formerly shining star. When the mag published its list of "Who's Who in Sex: 1975" in April, Erica Jong, PONY founder Jean Powell and corporal punishment advocate John Elliott Brooks are there with porn queens Marilyn Chambers, Georgina Spelvin and Andrea True. Lovelace is conspicuous by her absence, appearing only in a photo from *Deep Throat Part II* celebrating the fame of... Harry Reems.

## February 1975

# *Playboy*
# "Linda Lovelace for President!"

If only the motion picture vehicle it was hyping had been as good as this photo layout and discussion of Linda's upcoming film, *Linda Lovelace for President*. Ken Marcus' photographs are considerably better than those of Fegley's "Say Ah!" layout, his focus being a little more sharp in both interpretation and technical style. His use of light rivals Fegley's use of soft focus, Linda's mons being skillfully hidden from view by clothes and sometimes her own hands, even in the set's tightest close-ups. Some stills from the movie itself are included, such as Lovelace's waterfall skinny-dipping scene and her semi-nude romps with actors Skip Burton, who plays Olympic swimming champion Huck Phlegm (a takeoff on Mark Spitz) and John F. Kennedy impersonator Vaughn Meader, who plays the Right Reverend Oral Sacrifice and eventually performs a quick dry-hump of his own with Lovelace.

Linda is still obviously in Hef's good graces at this point; positive mention of the film is made (even though they admittedly hadn't seen it, since it opened "within a week of this issue's hitting the newsstands"), and a nice nod is also given to the previous year's book *The Intimate Diary of Linda Lovelace*, which they describe as "an account of Linda's experiences—sexual and otherwise—with various people, some of them unnamed but easily identifiable celebrities."

Including the book's "King of Sex" himself, Mr. Hugh Hefner.

**BONUS CONTENT**

Download a fun fact about Linda Lovelace by scanning this QR code

## March 6 – 13, 1975

# *Georgia Straight* "Ooooh Linda"

by Bob Ness

Otherwise unremarkable, this interview gives us Linda in Canada and in full-on PR mode, being wrangled by a personal manager who personally manages to provoke the same fear and loathing in the press that Chuck Traynor did.

Ness' story begins with a lengthy (again), Gonzo-tinged (again) tale of being woken from an otherwise sound sleep to be hustled by limo (a "26-foot long Black Whale") to the $350-a-day room at the Bayshore Hotel before rushing headlong into the revelation that Linda's manager/coordinator Larry Marchiano not only got her into town a day late, but he's a real pain in the ass: "He's new with Linda and trying to impress her with what he can do. Extremely fussy and dictatorial."

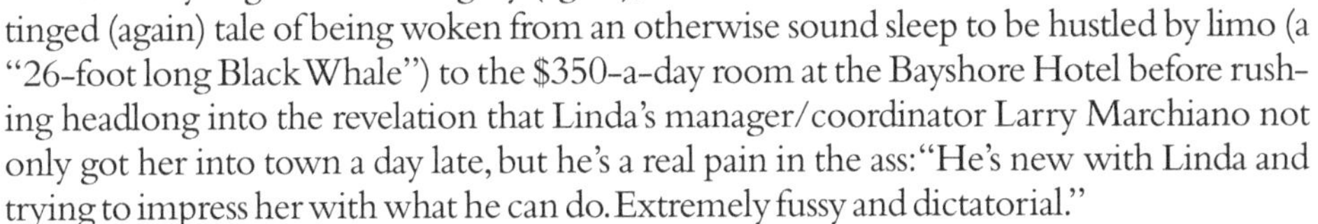

Linda, on the other hand, he likes. "As soon as we're alone I tell Linda that I like her already," he writes, because she's not the hard-boiled New York broad he expected to meet.

"That's right," Linda says. "I'm honest and up-front and I hold nothing behind. I say what I feel and people can either like it or dislike it."

Linda gives a short history of her history with *Deep Throat*:

> "[Damiano] wanted a 'fresh face' and not the typical porno actress, the bleached blonde with large breasts and every other word is a four-letter word and loud and boisterous.
>
> "I don't think there's anything wrong with sex and I don't think it should be hidden. Most people hide sex, they can't talk about it. When a kid comes into the world he's breast-fed and then he gets older and he's told he can't look at that, it's sinful and it's dirty and if he does he gets smacked. I don't think people should be hung up about sex—so I made the film. I felt like it and I had a great time."

Linda describes the film as lighthearted in its dealing with sex then says she's over porn. "To me so-called pornographic or X-rated films with hardcore sex are boring. I get very bored watching something going in and out, in and out, in and out. And how much can you watch of it—an hour and a half? It's not a turn-on to me. If anything, it turns me off."

This leads to a discussion of Linda's teeth—nice in the front, Ness says, full of cavities in the back, she says—at which point Larry busts into the room, bringing Ness' fantasies of giving Linda's choppers a little look-see back down to earth. Linda is then squired off for a B-12 shot and Ness is squired back to the bowels of the Black Whale.

## May 5, 1975

# *Miami News*
# "Life for Linda a Legal Bust"

by Ian Glass

Push comes to shove as Linda is asked to shit or get off the pot, put up or shut up, or do *anything* by Leroy Griffith, proprietor of the Paramount Theater, where Linda was to start her much-hyped nightclub career. The shows never got past the planning stages, and Linda is in town to give a deposition in the case. Joining her are her new Miami attorney, Joel Hirschhorn ("The first lawyer I've had who handled my legal problems ethically and efficiently," she says) and Larry Marchiano, her personal manager. The difference between being Linda's business manager as opposed to her personal manager, according to Marchiano, is that he only takes care of her personal matters—"and she has many personal matters."

Griffith is seeking, and is later awarded, a $32,000 judgment against Linda.

## ... 1976 ...

## April 5, 1976

# *Time*
# "The Porno Plague"

Displaying the type of perspective that comes with the three years' worth of hindsight they've exercised since first mentioning Linda, *Time* offers this cover story about the rise of porn in America and America's resulting downfall. Lovelace is just one of a number of once socially acceptable players (including all the usual suspects like Harry Reems and John Holmes) whose very social acceptability is called into question in no uncertain terms.

The slant here is that the commercialization of sex has destroyed once-vital liberal urban centers of metropolitan life and turned them into the red-light districts peppering Santa Monica, Chicago, Minneapolis, San Francisco and, of course, New York City, citing such factors as profit motive ("the markup on dildos is 600%") in what was, as the mag's cover story, probably responsible for selling a few copies itself.

With Santa Monica Boulevard given as a "typical" example, porn consumers who were once described as chic and included in their numbers U.N. dignitaries and the social elite are replaced in *Time*'s mind by "carnival barkers with army-ant tenacity who pounce on passersby; cellulite-scarred ladies with bad teeth who strut, pose and eventually curse their embarrassed admirers; and bemused, disdainful deputy sheriffs who randomly cruise the area in black-and-white AMC Matadors."

After describing U.S. obscenity law from 1815 to the present and preaching about the downfall of the American Empire, the magazine introduces new ammunition in the fight against smut, specifically the Memphis *Deep Throat* trial that was being spearheaded by the ambitious district attorney Larry Parrish, who at the time boasted an impressive five-and-two record for obscenity convictions. An upcoming case against another Damiano product, *The Devil in Miss Jones* "and its horizontal heroine, Georgina Spelvin," is being watched by those ever-independent thinkers at the Justice Department, who are willing to prosecute similar cases depending on whichever way popular public opinion sends the winds of change blowing.

# ••• 1977 •••

## 1977
# *Superstars of Porno*

If there are any more photographs left from Linda's pre-*Deep Throat* photo sessions, then Eros-Goldstripe has just about used them up in this magazine, one more retread of the sexy but by now well-overexposed nudes. Maybe this will be the last we see of these pictures, but then again, maybe not....

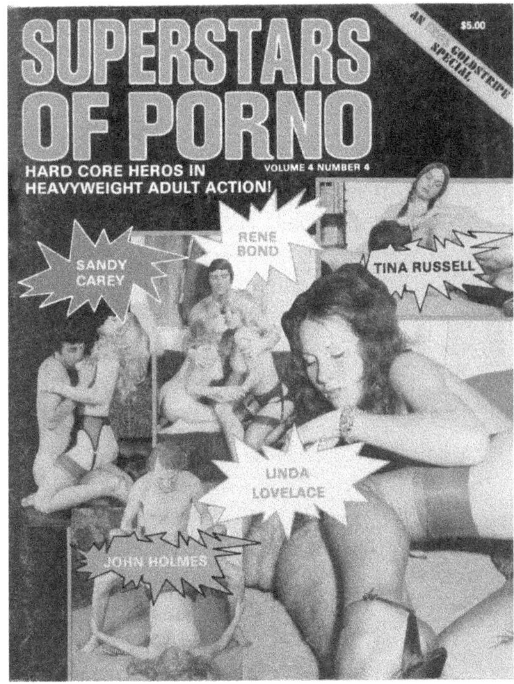

## May 1977

# *Cinema Blue*
# "Mr. Blue: Porno Traynor"

By John Rimington

Chuck Traynor's interview in this British adult film journal is, surprisingly enough, almost wholly bullshit except where Linda is concerned, in which case his comments seem disarmingly honest. Among his personal claims: He once shot a 35mm nudie-cutie for $2,000 and turned it around for $6,000. "Investors" dug *The Foot*—which he says was made before he met Linda Lovelace—but they thought it was far too ahead of its time, man! Gerard Damiano got the idea for *Deep Throat* after Traynor told him an oral-sex movie would be a good idea. And people had no clue Linda was the star of *Deep Throat* for almost a year after it came out.

Regarding Linda, Traynor admits he wrote *Inside Linda Lovelace* (which had just recently been declared not obscene in a landmark British obscenity case before the Old Bailey court); Linda was shy, a lousy lay and better at housework than sex; and her various live appearances and stage show tanked because she can't sing, dance or act.

Probably the most honest thing Traynor says regards his business dealings with Linda once her contractual obligations start going unfulfilled:

> "Linda soon heard that I had found another girl [Marilyn Chambers]. I planned to promote her. So [Linda called] her lawyers. They called me saying that Linda wanted to buy Linda Lovelace Enterprises, in which we still both had a 50-50 shareholding. My lawyer informed me that because it was Linda who had actually broken the contracts during the previous six months, the company would very soon be buried in lawsuits. He therefore advised that the smartest thing to do was to *give* Linda the company, which I duly did.
>
> "As far as I know, she now has over a million dollars worth of lawsuits against her. For all the contracts she broke were in the company's name. If she hadn't taken it over she could simply have resigned and I would have been the one to be sued. But she didn't. She took over the company and I resigned. Then I began working to build Marilyn's career."

# ... 1979 ...

## 1979
## *Bizarre Stars*

This S&M themed magazine features 15 pages of Linda, Chuck Traynor and Brandy in more of the domination setting previously seen in *Submission*.

The girl copy, penned by some anonymous porno wage slave doing a little healthy projecting, concerns Linda leading on the hapless Mack, played to perfection by one Chuck Traynor, who seems to think "he's the super stud of all time." (In a lovely bit of wordplay that helps make a porno job easier to get through, the word "Mack" is also slang for pimp.) Just when Linda and Mack are about to get down to it, enter the bitch Jorrine. It seems that Jorrine is jonesing for Linda too, and wins her over, dressing her up in fetish finery to ... dominate the worm Mack! Some of the layout's funniest photos, in retrospect, anyway, show Linda leading Traynor around on a leash and menacing him with a long, slim riding crop while he begs for mercy until "with Linda's help, [Jorrine] utterly humiliates him."

## November 30, 1979
## *The Washington Post*
## "Personalities"

by Robert Samek

The shape of things to come is revealed in this short piece announcing that court-appointed lawyer Ira Block is investigating Linda's financial situation. What has Block discovered? He has discovered that "who[ever] took over her money management during her movie career apparently abused the privileges and her monies."

The article adds that according to a recent court affidavit, the former Linda Lovelace, now married to cable-television installer Larry Marchiano (who it is duly noted "does not have sufficient financial acumen to assume the [financial] duties" mentioned above), claims to have been "beaten severely in and about the body continuously" to perform in *Deep Throat*. "It would also appear," the piece concludes, "that these acts that were performed by her in that picture were involuntarily performed by her as a result of the beatings."

# ... 1980 ...

## January 28, 1980

## *People*

# "Mrs. Marchiano Calls Herself 'A Typical Housewife': The World Knew Her as Linda Lovelace"

by Karen Payne

The mag that once sniffed about Linda's Las Vegas cocaine bust introduces the world to the new Linda Lovelace, who describes her porn years as full of "nightmarish ... sexual perversion and enslavement" in one of her first public appearances after the release of *Ordeal*. "I'm a woman with a lot of courage and a lot of strength," says she who once told the world she could come by being fucked in the throat, ass and cunt, one, two, three, in that order. "I would say I've learned my lesson. I don't think anything like that could ever happen to me again."

Linda says of her life with Traynor, "At first he was really nice, very gentle and understanding. He would open a door for me and light a cigarette. And then he suddenly changed.... If I showed the least amount of independence, I would get beaten for it. I was not allowed to have any money, because he felt if I did, I could get away. He threatened to kill me or my parents if I escaped." Linda also recalls her second meeting with Marchiano, an old New York friend whom she ran into years later on a beach in Florida and who is now her husband: "When we saw each other, that was it, like in a fairy tale."

This article helped form a picture in the public's mind that would survive for years, mentioning Linda's financial woes and medical problems, including leg veins damaged by years of beatings and a possible double mastectomy due to illegal silicone injections she'd gotten in the early '70s. This first chapter of The New Linda Lovelace Story closes with her advice to women caught up in a world of prostitution and pornography (but not, interestingly enough, domestic abuse). "You can get back your self-respect and live a normal, decent life," she says. "I did. It takes a lot of strength and, for me, a lot of belief in God—but you can survive."

## July 1980

# *Elite*

# "Goodbye Linda Lovelace: Porno's First Superstar Goes Straight"

by Richard Lafferty

Sandwiched between ads for some "Super 8mm Sex Flicks" and photographs featuring the hirsute haunches of "Sam," this Canadian sex magazine contains one of the most positive post-porn profiles of Lovelace, notable most especially because it appeared in an adult magazine. Despite its positive spin, that's the article's main point of interest. Quite possibly she didn't know it would wind up in an adult magazine; if Lafferty had merely identified himself as a freelance writer, Linda would have no definite idea where the interview would finally be printed.

Lafferty reports the new side of Lovelace's story the same way porn magazines had once believed what Linda Lovelace the porn queen said. At points, though, Lafferty's respect for Lovelace and her story approaches the bombastic—"[*Deep Throat*], which has grossed millions, may be said to be one of the all-time jinxed films. No one connected with it was fully immune from its sting—a poison that may be traced to its star and her owner." Lafferty manages to get Lovelace to describe exactly how she made the break from Traynor:

> "What really undid Traynor was his own egomania and non-control of his overestimated power. He constantly interfered with David Winters and the other members of the [song-and-dance] act during rehearsals, just as he had bugged Gerry Damiano during the *Deep Throat* filming. Only this was big legit business. They took no shit from Chuck Traynor. *I* was the star and *he* was the nuisance. They all turned on him. Chuck lost his grasp. The strength of David and the others to defy him became my strength. I could now see the light at the end of the tunnel.
>
> "Then I moved in with Winters. Traynor went berserk. He threatened everyone. Chuck told Peraino, the mob guy from *Throat*, that I had been kidnapped, so the Mob guy sent his bodyguard to assist Chuck in my 'recovery,' which was actually my recapture. It failed. I talked to all the people Chuck conned. Suddenly Traynor's power-pack fizzled. He no longer threatened to kill people, their wives, their kids, their relatives. He tried to plead for my return. Fat chance! It was over."

The remainder of this piece, an in-depth print interview of the post-porn Linda Lovelace, recalls what readers would soon find out on their own when they read *Ordeal*.

Which they would, by the millions.

# ... 1983 ...

## February 1983

# *Playboy*
# "The Year in Sex"

To show how "Time Flies When You're Having Fun," *Playboy* looks at "A Decade of Decadence," tracking down *Deep Throat* stars 10 years after the rise of Porno Chic. Harry Reems is shown in a scene from *Society Affairs*; as if her stint on *The Gong Show* had never happened, buxom blonde Carol Connors is shown in a scene from *Desire for Men*; a somewhat dour Gerry Damiano is mentioned as having just made the sex documentary *Consenting Adults*; and the former Linda Lovelace is shown standing next to actress Valerie Harper in an anti-porn picket line protesting the showing of *Deep Throat*.

# ... 1985 ...

## June 1985

# *The Breast of Expose*
# "Linda Lovelace: Sucked In Again?"

Condescending and tasteless twaddle abounds in this excuse to print antique pictures of Linda after the publication of *Ordeal*. "If Linda's mind is so . . . susceptible to every passing suggestion, how are we . . . to know that she is not in the grip of her new husband's mind control. . . ? And what of the feminists who are now using her famous image with such success? Our more militant sisters have long proclaimed that the end justifies the means in their battle against demon porno; would they stop at enslaving the feeble mind of this human sump pump? The possibilities are terrible to consider, so let's forget 'em and just jerk off to these vintage shots of ol' Linda in better days."

All that condescending and tasteless twaddle aside, it's interesting to note that the editorial drone responsible for it may not have been too far off the mark when you come down to it.

# . . . 1986 . . .

## July 20, 1986

## *The Newsday Magazine*

# "Linda Lovelace Doesn't Live Here Anymore"

by Mike McGrady

Unlike Richard Hill's doomed attempt at Gonzo journalism in *Oui* almost 15 years earlier, McGrady's recollections of having worked with Lovelace since 1977 do succeed, if not as completely as he would have liked.

To coincide with the release of *Out of Bondage* (in the newspaper that paid his salary), McGrady recalls the day he first heard that there was something new and provocative to be told about the life of the former Linda Lovelace. While dining with Long Island attorneys Anthony V. Curto (who represents writers) and Victor Yannacone (who brought about the first Agent Orange cases and the first successful DDT case), he was told that the former porn queen claimed her life before the cameras was the result of beatings and coercion. His interest piqued, he requests and receives a meeting with her—after warnings of what a potential partnership could do to his career. He takes the meeting anyway, and his "reporter's instincts" tell him she is telling the truth.

McGrady describes Linda and her blue-collar husband Larry Marchiano as strong, proud people who have lived on welfare after declining offers for more hardcore films (one for seven figures cash to be deposited in a Swiss bank account). Larry is described as being something of a prude, but understandably so, who once walked out of the prison masturbation scene in the film *Midnight Express*, which he and Linda attended with a group of their friends.

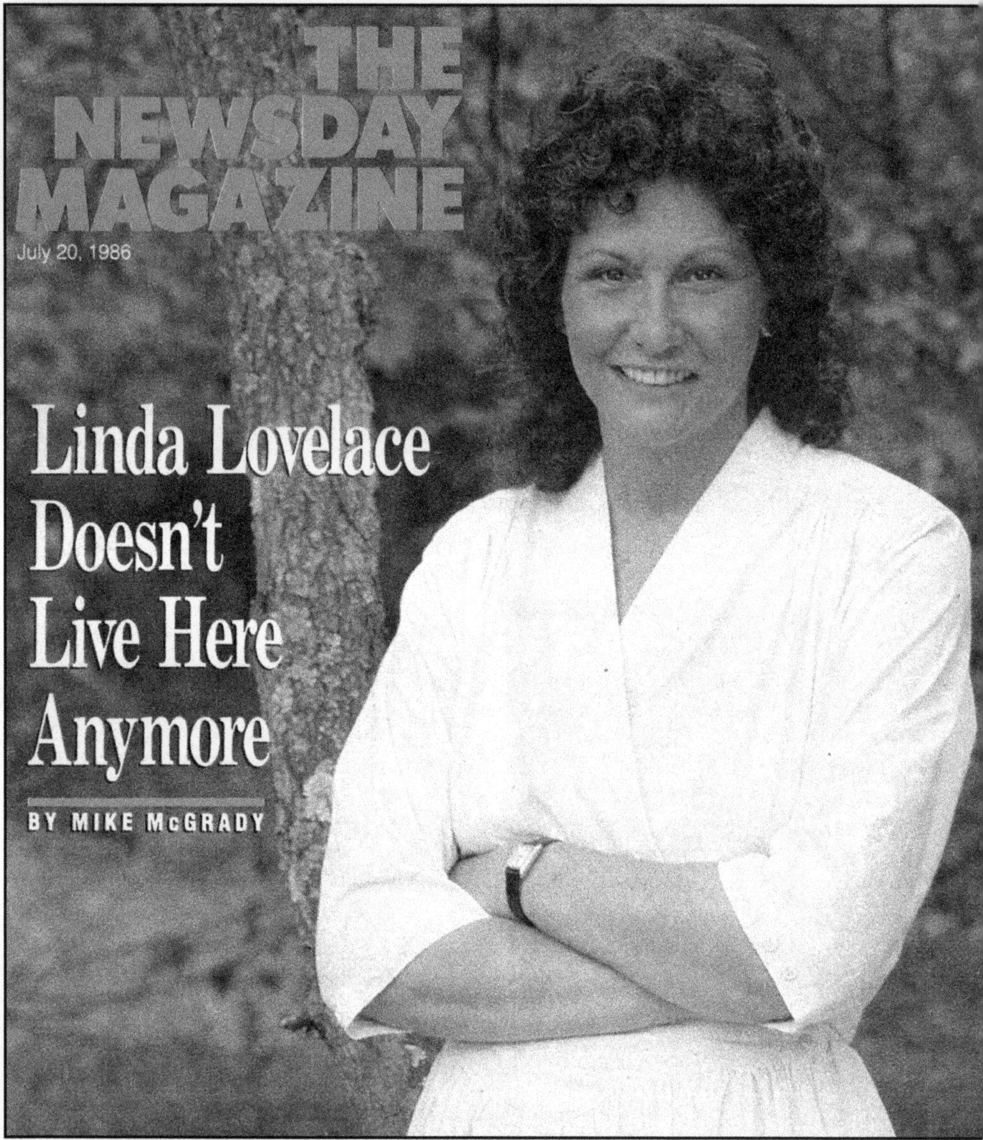


The first time that they met, McGrady says, Marchiano's arm was in a cast, the result of a run-in with some men who made unsavory comments about his wife. Ultimately though, his own personal story is not as interesting as the somewhat flowery insight he gives about his working and personal relationships with Linda, which is indeed quite touching.

McGrady's tale ends with the news that doctors are now debating whether Linda Lovelace will need a double mastectomy to reverse damage done by a series of illegally performed loose silicone injections performed in the early '70s. "The result [of the injections] this year," he writes, is "a massive, lingering, upper-body infection and at this moment, a debate among several surgeons on the advisability of removing her breasts. Biopsies are being taken now, and the debate will be decided within the next few weeks."

## November 1, 1986

# *New York Post*

# "Linda Lovelace: I Need New Liver or I'll Die"

The world learns that Linda needs a transplant due to an "unknown hepatitis," unidentified at press time but later revealed as Hepatitis C, which Linda contracted from a blood transfusion after her 1970 automobile accident. Insurance won't cover the bill, expected to be approximately $200,000, because liver transplants are still considered experimental. Linda, who has just published her fourth autobiography, *Out of Bondage*, must have the operation within four to eight months.

Even though the operation is incredibly expensive, Linda refuses help from the pornography industry. "I don't want anything to do with any of those people," she says. "I escaped from them and was finally able to begin my own life. They already took two-and-a-half years away from me." One porn star, who requested anonymity on the matter, confided to this writer a decade later that she had made a cash donation to help pay for the surgery. That porn star was Marilyn Chambers.

Linda got help from several distinctly different groups of people. The Long Island PTA to which she belonged raised $600 on her behalf. "That was a proud moment. This isn't a rich community," she beamed. Women's groups, whose ranks she has joined with her anti-pornography crusade and her recent book, have been "very supportive."

Lovelace's refusal to accept help in the form of monetary donations from the porn community wasn't shared by at least one family member. Linda's sister Barbara wrote a letter to *People* magazine that appeared a few weeks after they published the story "Awaiting a Liver Transplant, Linda Lovelace Marchiano Struggles To Close the Book on Her Past," saying that "If the millions of people who viewed the movie *Deep Throat* would contribute even 25 cents each, it would certainly insure that she will reach the $200,000 necessary to perform this surgery."

Linda's liver transplant would be covered in newspapers, magazines and on television until March 16, 1987, when she underwent a 13-hour operation at Presbyterian-University Hospital in Pittsburgh. Like all liver transplant recipients, she continued to take anti-rejection medication—when she could afford it. As a testimony to her strength, Linda outlived all the members of her survivors' group.

# ... 1991 ...

## January 15, 1991

## *Weekly World News*

# "Sammy Davis Had His Way With Me—AND MY HUBBY!"

This article reprinted from Australian *People* magazine exploits one of the most sensational claims in *Ordeal*: that Sammy Davis Jr. was so close with Linda Lovelace and Chuck Traynor that he not only had an affair with Linda, but one night, as the *Weekly World News* puts it, "seduced" Chuck, who couldn't believe he was "getting together" with Mr. Bojangles himself. Not that Linda was calling the Rat Packer a fudgepacker; anyone who'd read *Ordeal* knew that "seduced" and "getting together" meant "sucked the pimpin' dick of" and "having the Candy Man gobble your one-eyed trousersnake."

# ... 1995 ...

## July 2, 1995

## *The Washington Post*

# "The Sharon Stonewall"

by Richard Carlson

While telling of his experience seeing Sharon Stone address the National Press Club on the topic of holistic cures for breast cancer, Carlson offers this snotty diatribe about the media's penchant for forgiving famous people the embarrassing things that made them famous in the first place. Stone's fame finds its roots in most of the public's mind thanks to an incidence of what Carlson calls "wookie-flashing" from the film *Basic Instinct* (and if you don't know what people saw Sharon Stone do, I'm damn well not going to be the one to tell you).

Making his anecdote a wee bit more personal, Carlson recalls sitting in the green room at the ABC television show *A.M. Los Angeles* in 1974, where Lovelace had a run-in with motorcycle daredevil Evel Knievel, who was carrying a cane with a large brass ornament on the head. "Say Linda, think you could handle this?" he asked. A not-amused Lovelace called Knievel a pig and retired to a neutral corner. While he claimed to be embarrassed at Knievel's tactless display, Carlson concluded that Lovelace had no right to be offended by it. "Evel Knievel, boorish as he might have been," he wrote, "was a fellow of comparative good taste in the professional world of Linda Lovelace, who had previously, on film, performed coitus with a dog."

At the time this article appeared, Richard Carlson was the president and CEO of the Corporation for Public Broadcasting.

# ... 1996 ...

## June 18, 1996

## *The Independent*

# "Do You Know Who I Am?"

by William Hartston

Hartston tells the tales of the people, from blue bloods to blue-movie stars, who have famously been denied admission to the Royal Enclosure of the Royal Ascot Gold Cup thoroughbred race in England, which requires a badge that must be worn for entry. Princess Anne and Joan Collins were among the ladies who had forgotten to wear theirs; Linda, on the other hand, had her badge but little else: she was in definite violation of the racetrack's dress code for wearing a see-through dress when she attended the event in 1974. The choice of frock was probably meant to have her denied entry, which could be parlayed into more than a few column inches in the British press.

## July 7, 1996

# *The Daytona Beach Sunday News-Journal*

# "'Deep Throat' Star Figures in Keys Sheriff Race"

by John Fernandez

Sex scandals involving American politicians and sex stars are nothing new. In the '50s there was Blaze Starr and Huey Long. In the '70s there was Fanne Foxe and Wilbur Mills. And in the '90s there was Linda Lovelace and Phil Mandina, the lawyer she accuses in *Ordeal* of using drugs, taking part in orgies with her and Traynor—where the female participants were hypnotized—and suborning perjury that resulted in Chuck Traynor's acquittal on marijuana possession and trafficking charges.

When Democrat Mandina launches his bid for Sheriff of Monroe County, Florida, his Republican opponent Richard D. Roth introduces Mandina's 23-year-old association with Lovelace into the campaign, using six copies of *Ordeal* bought by staffers for, well, *research purposes*.

Discussing that tactic, Roth said, "I had no intention of publicly distributing the book. I was just getting some insight from close advisors on who I was up against. I didn't mean to start this [scandal] up. Of course, now I can't stop it." Of course you couldn't, Dick. After all, fanning the flames of a good old American sex scandal is no way to run a political campaign, is it?

Mandina countered, "What does Linda Lovelace have to do with the sheriff's race? I'm trying to run a campaign on the issues. That's what people really care about." Especially when those issues include Roth's admission of drinking alcohol before a car accident in which he rear-ended a motorcycle driver (he passed a field sobriety test given by the Florida Highway Patrol, but wasn't given a Breathalyzer) and a sexual harassment case in which Roth was accused of telling dirty jokes to women, for which he later apologized. Understandable, Phil. Dishing dirt on your opponent is no way to run a political campaign, either.

Asked by the *St. Petersburg Times* about the possibility that Mandina may one day be the new sheriff in town, Linda said, "I don't want him in the legal system. Unless it's behind bars." Linda got at least half her wish. Mandina lost the election, garnering just one-third of the vote.

# ... 1997 ...

## April 20, 1997

## *Rocky Mountain News*

# "Linda Lovelace's New Life in Colorado"

by Fawn Germer

The former Linda Lovelace, now the single mother of two, discusses the end of her 22-year marriage to Larry Marchiano. "I prostituted myself so I could have kids. They were the most important thing to me. They were all I ever wanted .... I look in the mirror and I look the happiest I've ever looked in my life," she says. "Full of confidence, full of self-esteem. I'm not ashamed of my past or sad about it. And what people might think about me, well, that's not real. I look in the mirror and know I've survived."

# ... 1999 ...

## August 26, 1999

## *Long Island Voice*

# "Porn Island: An Oral History"

by Bill Jensen, Stacy Albin and Jon Hart

This story chronicles Long Island's impact on the world of mainstream pornography, after the business shifted from New York City and before it moved to the West Coast, in the words of those who were there. In addition to Linda and coauthor Mike McGrady, interviewees include Radley Metzger (who directed the film version of McGrady's gang-novel *Naked Came the Stranger* and other classic porn flicks); actresses Veronica Hart, Sharon Mitchell, Gloria Leonard and Shane; and gay porn star/North Shore native Mark Pulver.

McGrady describes the difference between porn "then" as opposed to porn "now." He discusses the "then" type of pornography, his novel *Naked Came the Stranger.*

> "Pornography, even in the late '60s, was nothing like it is today. All there was really softcore, like *Valley of the Dolls*. In 1968, I interviewed Harold Robbins and Irving Wallace, two of the worst writers who ever lived. But they were making millions. It was driving me crazy that there were so many decent writers who couldn't make a living. I do remember saying, 'Hey, we can do this if we each wrote a chapter.' There would be an unrelenting emphasis on sex."

After mentioning the "somewhat negative" reaction his book got from his friends—and conveniently forgetting to mention why it's okay for him to cash in on art meant to appeal to the prurient interest, but not okay for anyone else—he describes the dire straits Linda was in when they began *Ordeal.* "Linda was living on welfare," he says, "opening a can of dog food for the occasional meal. . . . I put her through lie-detector tests to see if she was telling the truth, and she was. When I met her she was in desperate fear that the Mafia would find her. . . . That book took six months to write. It was the most exhaustive writing job I ever had, including Vietnam. I was writing it at home in Northport. I would do interviews with her at the office of her lawyer in Bay Shore. An hour a week taping her. It was emotionally gut-wrenching. I couldn't believe the shit she was telling me."

Aside from discussing her life on the Island, Linda gives her own recollections about the decision to write *Ordeal* as well as people's reaction to the book—and to her:

> "One day I was watching *Donahue*, and Susan Brownmiller [radical feminist author of *Against Our Will: Men, Women and Rape*] made a comment like, 'LL [Lovelace's euphemism for Linda Lovelace] did this to become famous in the movies.' And it just made me angry. And I said, 'I'm writing the book.' Michael McGrady was the first person that I ever told what really happened to me. It was pretty powerful. But it was good therapy for me. 'Cause I couldn't trust doctors or anybody else, psychiatrists. There was something about Michael. Until the book came out, no one knew the real story. When the book came, people in the neighborhood reacted by thanking me for my courage and my strength. The lady across the street—who I thought was really not even going to talk to me anymore—had two daughters and she said 'the book really helped me with my two girls.'"

When the topic gets to her former home, she says, "I miss Long Island. I miss everybody there. I miss the ocean."

## December 1999

# *Playboy*
# "Who Changed Sex?: A Hundred Years of Heroes and Villains"

by James Petersen

The author of *A Century of Sex* counts down the most influential sex people of all time. Out of 38 places, Linda Lovelace shares number 23 with none other than Marilyn Chambers. Further proving what an incestuous place the sex biz can be, the pair are sandwiched between "J," author of *The Sensuous Woman*, published by Lyle Stuart, and Catharine MacKinnon, co-author of the Dworkin/MacKinnon Anti-Pornography Civil Rights Ordinance, which Linda helped promote.

**... 2001 ...**

## January 2001

# *Leg Show*
# "Linda Lovelace: The Ordeal Is Over"

by Eric Danville

Linda Lovelace returns to porn, and yours truly is there.

This came about as a complete fluke. The night before I left New York City to interview Linda in Colorado, I had dinner with *Leg Show* editor-in-chief Dian Hanson and her then-boyfriend (now husband), novelist Geoff Nicholson. We were sitting around laughing at the idea of a Dirty Rotten Pornographer winning an audience with the original

Porn Queen when Hanson said, "Ask Linda if she'd pose for *Leg Show*." She said the absolute top-dollar she'd pay for the session and took another sip of wine.

"Yeah, right," I said, half-pissed that Dian wanted to horn in on My Linda Experience and half-grateful for the chance to ask Linda a question like that. "Sure. Yeah, I'll ask her," I said, figuring I'd wait until after the interview to invite Linda Lovelace back to the world of adult—unless I didn't and just told Dian I did.

After our interview, Linda and I were having dinner at her apartment when the chance came up to make good on my promise. "Linda," I said, "if you got 'X' amount of dollars and didn't have to show anything, would you model lingerie for *Leg Show* magazine?"

After explaining to Linda what *Leg Show* magazine was, since obviously she had no idea, Linda smiled and said, "Yeah, I'd do that. Would you like some more pasta?"

And that was pretty much that. I don't think we mentioned it again for the rest of the night, but when I got back to New York the first thing I did was call Dian to tell her that the flight was okay, the interview went fine and oh, by the way, you're officially on the business end of the single greatest exclusive in adult publishing: The Return of Linda Lovelace. A little intermediary work and one short introduction later, Linda was New York City-bound and preparing for her first adult-magazine layout in a quarter century.

I arrived on set at the tail end of Linda's makeup session to find a very upbeat but slightly nervous Linda sitting in a chair getting her hair and makeup done. She didn't seem worried about posing for an adult magazine—she wasn't cowering in a corner wondering what people would think of her afterwards—but she did ask how she looked a few times.

Two of the four costume changes Linda made for the shoot were used in the published spread. The first part of the session had Linda lying on a mattress with stylishly rumpled gold sheets, her hair appropriately tousled and a red pump dangling from her toe.

Photographer Warren Tang stood on a ladder maybe eight or 10 feet above her, shooting straight down. The final effect in the pictures was unusual because shooting from directly above distorts the subject, so all the photos from that part of the shoot were scrapped except for one printed on the back cover of the December 2000 issue of *Leg Show*—with a big black dot over Linda's face and ad copy teasing her upcoming layout.

Linda's other outfits included a glittery silver corset and silver lamé stockings, a flowery corset with sheer seamed stockings and a long evening gown and cigarette holder.

From the moment she stepped in front of the camera, I was amazed. At one point Tang asked her to "do something" with her hands. Linda barely missed a beat and asked, "Like this?" and started voguing. Tang chanted, "Yes! Yes! Yes! Yes!" in that way photographers do when they're getting something great.

Then I realized I was finally in the same room as Linda Lovelace, not the lady who played her on-screen or relived her life on TV talk shows and in Congressional halls. It was interesting knowing I had a hand in bringing it about. It was bizarre seeing a woman whom I'd become friends with in such a context, watching her do what most people had only read about. And it was cool to do something I'd fantasized about since I was 16 years old: Meet Linda Lovelace.

Linda Lovelace Collector's Issue
LEG SHOW
JANUARY 2001
NUMBER ONE IN THE WORLD!
LINDA LOVELACE NOW!
A LEG SHOW EXCLUSIVE
THE ORIGINAL Sex Star's 1st Photos IN 20 YEARS!
"I'M STILL A FEMINIST, I STILL HATE PORN, BUT . . ."
$5.95 U.S.

## April 24, 2002

# *The New York Times*

# Linda Boreman, 53, Known for 1972 Film '*Deep Throat*,' Dies

by Douglas Martin

Special people get their obituary printed in *The New York Times*. Unfortunately, people never know how special they are until after they've made the cut. Martin's memoriam boils Linda's life down to less than 500 words, covering the history of *Deep Throat* and Linda's relation to it (with a relevant quote from Vincent Canby); her involvement with the women's movement in the '80s; her marriage and divorce in the '90s; and her relationship with me and the public appearances we made to promote *The Complete Linda Lovelace*. Unfortunately I was misquoted when it came to my involvement with Linda watching *Deep Throat* for the first time. She didn't watch it with me but with a friend in Colorado, although Martin accurately quoted her reaction—"I don't see what the big deal was."

## May 14, 2002

# *The Globe*

# "Porn Legend Dies, Broke and Lonely"

by David Thompson

This tawdry send-off from one of publishing's tawdriest rags contains at least one libelous statement that, if made when Linda was alive, would be actionable in court, and Linda would sure as shit win.

Thompson writes that Linda "had to sell her body to support the family [when she was married to Larry Marchiano in the '90s]," using as proof a quote from her 1997 interview in the *Rocky Mountain News*. "I prostituted myself so I could raise my kids," she told journalist Fawn Gemser. "They were the most important thing to me. They were all I ever wanted."

That quote is obviously metaphorical in the context of the original article—obviously, that is, to everyone but Thompson. Even the slightest amount of reporting would have found that Linda had not gone back to prostitution. She was not hooking. She was not working as a whore. She was not selling her body. And men weren't paying her to have sex with them. She was commenting on the fact that she had to compromise things in her life to have a family, that she had to accept the trade-off of being with someone she ultimately didn't love in order to have children. The ability to wring anything else from that quote shows why *The Globe* is the mainstay of supermarket magazine racks that it is.

---

**December 29, 2002**

# *The New York Times Magazine* "Pop-Porn"

by Daphne Merkin

Special people get their obituary printed in *The New York Times*. But *very* special people get their obituary printed in *The New York Times* twice, their postmortem curtain call appearing in the year-end *New York Times Magazine* feature "The Lives They Lived."

Merkin (heh heh) gives a reasonably even-handed account of Linda's life and death, although it reads like a longer version of Douglas Martin's obit. She even gets most of her facts straight too, but ultimately blows it with her last two lines.

She writes:

> "In the sort of narrative symmetry that would seem to be implausible if it didn't happen to be true, [Linda] had been gathering material for the Linda Lovelace display for the opening of Manhattan's Museum of Sex this September."

If that seems implausible, that's because it didn't happen to be true. The person gathering said material wasn't Linda, it was me.

She goes on to state, "No doubt the biopic that is currently being planned will attach a heartwarming moral to her irredeemably sad and sordid tale." Comments like that usually come from people who profess the greatest kinship or empathy for Linda "Lovelace" Boreman. Those same people—invariably women who identify as feminist—conveniently forget that it was Linda who said her story ultimately had a happy ending, because she had survived years of domestic abuse.

In the last two years of her life, when I knew her, Linda Boreman was able to make some money and accept the admiration of people she met from both sides of the porn debate. She was also able to put the Linda Lovelace part of her life in perspective, if not completely behind her, by embracing—and exploiting—the Linda Lovelace character. One night when we were talking about the dog movies, she admitted that they were shot 30 years ago

The New York Times Magazine

DECEMBER 29, 2002 / SECTION 6

The Lives They Lived

Geraldine of Albania: A One-Act By Tony Kushner • .406 By John Updike
The Ethicist on Ann Landers • Mr. Television By Frank Rich • The First Modern Terrorist By Gershom Gorenberg
Armistead Maupin on The Ultimate Gay Dad • The Day Cyrus Vance Called It Quits By Douglas Brinkley
Adolph Green's Last Supper By Adam Green • Daphne Merkin on Linda Lovelace's Liberations
How Inge Saw Me By Arthur Miller • The Arledge Team By Peter Jennings, Ted Koppel, Barbara Walters, Diane Sawyer
The Brilliance of Lite By Rob Walker • How Johnny Unitas Changed Football By Stephen J. Dubner
James Traub on The Brief Death of Osama bin Laden • And more.



and maybe it was time to get over them. By admitting it was even possible to put what she called the most horrific event of her life behind her, Linda continued towards the heart-warming moral of her irredeemably sad and sordid tale. Merkin and most feminists don't like to admit that's possible, though, because that doesn't fit into their narrative of what the Linda Lovelace story should be. That narrow and ultimately exploitative mindset was what helped make Linda Boreman a prisoner of Linda Lovelace more than anything else.

# Chapter 2:

# TOKEN GESTURES

## Linda Lovelace's 8mm Canon

**Considering the impact she made on pornography, you'd think Linda Lovelace made hundreds of stag films before starring in *Deep Throat*. Where other porn starlets left behind hours and hours of 8mm loops, you could watch Linda Lovelace's entire catalogue of stag films in less time than it takes to watch *Titanic*, but you'd see almost the same amount of semen go down.**

Through research and interviews conducted for this book; Linda's recollection of the loops in *Ordeal*; a Zapruderan analysis of the wallpaper and sheets in the films; and some plain old journalistic good luck, it seems that Linda's 8mm films were shot in three different locations: the first seven in New York City apartments or loft studio spaces, either on 42nd Street or 14th Street, and connected with either Bob Wolfe, Ted Snyder, Carter Stevens, Chuck Vincent, Gerard Damiano or some combination thereof; the final two in a Jersey City, New Jersey, hotel room rented by Chuck Traynor. The New York City loops were done in late 1971, before Linda and Chuck went to Florida to film *Deep Throat*; the Jersey City stags were shot after they returned from Miami in early 1972.

Whether it's the passage of time, faded memories or a deliberate rewriting of porn history, the people involved with Linda's brief pre- and post-*Throat* porn film career all have different tales to tell about her first appearances on the silver screen.

Linda, for her part, would rather have forgotten they ever happened, but usually spoke freely about what she remembered.

Eric Edwards, Lovelace's only male human 8mm costar other than Chuck Traynor, remembered making "about a dozen" stags with her. When told by this writer of Bruce Williamson's tally in *Playboy* that Linda made nine loops (my own accounting of eight in the first edition of this book was incorrect) and he was in four of them, Edwards said, "Well, your memory's probably better than mine." He also said his first loop with Linda was directed by Ted Snyder, although it's generally attributed to Gerard Damiano. Snyder was unavailable for comment for this book, having been gunned down on his front lawn by his cocaine dealer in 1989, but he was most likely the cameraman.

In their respective autobiographies, Linda (in *Ordeal*) and Harry Reems (in *Here Comes Harry Reems!*) claim that the second doctor/nurse sex scene in *Deep Throat* was shot by Damiano (urban legend says for either the film *Changes*, *The Truth About Blank* or *Sex USA*) and later inserted into *Deep Throat* "without rhyme or reason," as Linda described it. When asked by this writer, once and for all, whether that was her first performance with Reems, Linda said it wasn't.

Discussing the number of loops Linda made, Chuck Traynor told Al Goldstein in his 1974 *Screw* magazine interview, "Probably between 10 and 15, something in that neighborhood. It's really hard to say, because with someone like [director Bob] Wolfe, who shoots with two cameras, you never know how many you've made."

Paula Damiano relayed facts and figures from hubby Gerard, who politely but in no uncertain terms refused my original request for a few minutes of his time in the late '90s because he was literally on his way out the door to play golf. Gerard told me, through Paula, that the second doctor/nurse sex scene in that film was not the first time he worked with Linda. According to Gerard, he only shot one stag with her: again, the first in which she appeared and the first mentioned below. End of story.

These loops became widely available as "starring Linda Lovelace" within six months of *Deep Throat* becoming news. Almost all of them remain available through vintage video companies. The few that don't conform to the majority of community standards across the country are traded among small networks of people who possess one or more of the kinks Linda was kind enough to satisfy.

This chronology, based on the time frame given by Linda in *Ordeal*, may have been the course of human (and not-so-human) events, or an example of Linda and coauthor Mike McGrady showing the loops becoming increasingly more lurid to heighten their dramatic effect. If that's the case, it definitely worked.

**BONUS CONTENT**

Hear a reading of ads for these films by scanning this QR code or logging onto **bit.ly/LLQR07**

# M-65/M-66

## DIRECTED BY GERARD DAMIANO
## ALSO STARRING CHUCK TRAYNOR, ERIC EDWARDS AND "BRANDY"

Eric Edwards is an Adult Video News Hall of Fame performer who worked either in front of the camera or behind it for almost 30 years. The self-described "horny kid" answered an ad in *Screw* magazine for actors to make fuck flicks. His callback would give him an interesting credit in a career full of them: "Linda Lovelace was my first partner [in sex films]. I remember being impressed with her deep-throat ability, but that's about it. She wasn't much of a looker, but she was enthusiastic about what she did. We worked well together." Then he gives Lovelace a credit she'd probably consider dubious at best: "If anything, Linda Lovelace brought *me* into the porn world," he laughs. "She was always the one who made the calls, not Chuck. She'd say that she had some work and would ask if I wanted to do it. I usually did.

"The place we shot my first loop was some loft on 42nd Street. It kind of looked like some bedroom/studio set with one cameraman and with an 8mm wind-up camera. I was scared shitless, shaking up a storm, because I had no idea what I was in for. The cameraman was Teddy Snyder and the girl was Linda Lovelace, only she wasn't Linda Lovelace yet—she was just Linda Traynor, Chuck's wife.

"It was Linda and Chuck and some redhead. Chuck couldn't perform, so I was brought in to perform with these two other girls. I started feeling fine. I had two women who were kind of cute, and I was gonna make $40, so I thought, 'Wow!' We were there for about two hours."

During his interviews in the '70s and '80s, Gerard Damiano maintained that he directed this film—only the details seemed to change. In his 1974 *Screw* magazine interview, Damiano recalls, "I was casting for a sex insert, which is a short segment of a full-length movie [usually put in at the request of distributors who wanted more sex

scenes]." The director saw Linda take in Eric Edwards' cock and was floored. Damiano said then that the stag he was shooting never saw the light of day, much less the inside of a grindhouse, because he scrapped the footage. "It went right on the cutting-room floor because I realized she had too much potential to throw her away on an insert to another film." Exactly why Damiano would throw away such apparently valuable and jaw-dropping footage remains a mystery, unless this part of his story is a bit on the hyperbolic side.

In an article excerpted from his planned autobiography *Getting Deeper*, published in *High Society* magazine three years later, Damiano claims the loop didn't even see the inside of a darkroom much less the light of day because he actually stopped filming after he saw Linda sucking dick. "It was the most fantastic thing I'd ever seen," he wrote. "Right down her throat. 'Do that again!' I said, and she slurps it right down her throat again. I filmed for a few minutes, then made the actors stop. 'Hey,' I said, 'let's forget this. I want to do a film with you, not this shit.' "

When asked if Linda had done porn before *Deep Throat*, Damiano disingenuously claims, "I don't know if [her 8mm films] were made before or after *Deep Throat*," even though he used the same room to film the loop that Bob Wolfe used for his—and if you're rehearsing the star of your upcoming feature film you better know what she's doing during the day, and who she's doing it for, so it's odd, considering how valuable he knew her to be, that he would let her work for other directors for three weeks.

What Damiano describes as a transcendent moment in porn, one of those vintage, virgin performances in which you see the emergence of a true star, couldn't be any less the case, because like the young starlet whose career it started, this loop sucks.

It opens with two couples casually passing a joint around; Edwards plays bongos while Traynor strums a guitar. The joint makes its way around a few times and the mellow-yellow foursome start loosening up. Linda, her blonde wig held in place with a hippie-ish headwrap, loosens up Traynor's belt and unlooses his uncircumcised cock. Brandy and Edwards get naked, too, and soon all four folks get down.

As mentioned by both Damiano and Edwards, Traynor's otherwise impressive unit indeed has some problems, despite Linda giving him head (the first cock she sucks on-screen is Traynor's, and she looks like she's about to suck it right off his body). Brandy proves herself almost as accomplished (if not as flashy) a fellatrice as Lovelace when she goes down on Edwards.

Traynor's dick is only useful when it's being sucked, which becomes obvious after Brandy, who's been licking Linda, starts trading off blowjobs between the two men. Then Traynor and Edwards switch partners. Since he's got to do something anyway, Traynor starts giving Brandy head while Lovelace almost immediately crams Edwards' cock down her throat.

They fuck in a few different combinations for the next few minutes. Linda definitely gets the most face time, and it's easy to see what Damiano saw in her. She also spends a considerable amount of time with Edwards' cock stuffed up her ass in reverse-cowgirl (porno-speak for woman-on-top, facing-away), sometimes while fucking herself with a thick blue dildo, sometimes while being eaten by Brandy. When Brandy fucks her with the dong, Linda bucks her hips and tries to gobble Traynor's dick. Brandy then pops Edwards' cock from Lovelace's butt and sucks it down before sending it back up Linda's ass. A truly creepy moment of male bonding comes when Traynor and Edwards, standing face-to-face, put their hands on each other's shoulders while they're getting blown.

Then it's suck some dick, lick some pussy, suck some dick, lick some pussy until Edwards fucks Brandy missionary style. He pulls out for the come shot and Linda jumps into frame and takes his cock in her mouth again, sucking him down then wiping his prick on her face and licking Brandy's bush clean. Traynor, a painful look on his face, finally makes his nut in Brandy's mouth before flopping down on the bed, where a joyful Lovelace takes his flaccid fuckstick into her mouth.

And the rest is history.

# M-81/M-82

**DIRECTED BY BOB WOLFE**
**ALSO STARRING ERIC EDWARDS AND "BRANDY"**

Edwards and Brandy are back for more in this, a loop worth seeing for more than just its pornocological significance.

It begins with Porn Plot-Advancing Device No. 1: Linda is lying in bed caressing her stocking-clad legs, getting ready to masturbate. She looks beautiful. The blonde wig from her first loop is gone and her wavy hair flows freely. Linda's playing with her breasts and pulling her nipples, then grabs two dildos: one hollow and flesh-colored, the other thick, solid and blue. The flesh-colored dildo, a hilariously old-school strap-on with large harness snaps, is stuffed into her pussy first, then she starts fucking her ass with the thick blue one.

Then Linda finds herself distracted by Porn Plot-Advancing Device No. 2—"The Knock at the Door"—and looks up to see a young man and a his female companion enter the room. Covering herself with a pillow, she feigns embarrassment, but in deference to Porn Plot-Advancing Device No. 3 ("Giving in to Lust") welcomes the inevitable threesome.

Brandy puts the dildo in Linda's cunt and Edwards sticks his cock into her mouth. Linda fucks her own asshole and sucks Edwards' balls before swallowing him with the technique that would become her trademark, then takes Edwards out of her throat and

mounts him for a cowgirl anal. Every few strokes, Brandy takes Edwards' cock out of Linda's butt and aims it at her pussy until it's ready to go back in her asshole—and so on and so on and so on, except when Brandy pulls it to the side and gives it a quick suck herself. (So no, Max Hardcore did not invent ass-to-mouth.)

Assuming what is one of the six or so Basic Porn Sex Positions, Linda spins around for a reverse-cowgirl anal and Brandy licks her pussy until the director calls for another position.

The film winds down when Edwards mounts Linda for some doggie-style anal and Brandy pulls up the rear—at least as much of it as she can get to—licking Linda's cunt from below. After a few more minutes of Edwards buttfucking Linda, her ass riding high and her face on the mattress, he stands in front of the pair, blows a considerable load onto Brandy's face, then rolls over so she and Linda can worship his spent pecker.

This is what a good stag film should be. It's well-shot, moves quickly and boasts a good-looking cast enjoying lots of exciting sex. Having the future star of *Deep Throat* as one of its performers is just icing on the cake. Future smutmongers are more than welcome to use the blurb, "If you only see one Linda Lovelace stag film this year, make it this!"

# UNTITLED

## DIRECTED BY BOB WOLFE
## ALSO STARRING CHUCK TRAYNOR

Despite my original assertion in the woefully Out of Print edition of this book that, "If *Deep Throat* is Linda Lovelace's best work, this reel ranks as her rankest," I've come to really love this loop for one reason. It looks dirty. Sure, it lacks the one thing even the most fuzzily focused fuck-flicks have—sex—and true, seldom have two porn actors seemed less interested in what they're doing and less convincing while doing it. But if you want to watch a stag film that, as Johnny Rotten said about the first edition of this book, looks like something you're not supposed to see, this baby's for you.

Linda's legs part to reveal a tight close-up on her pussy, shaved somewhat smoothly as ever. A pan up to her face shows her half-smiling and half-sneering; what should be a sensuous pout is really a snide smirk as she leers narcotically.

At least she's trying. Even more miserable than Linda's feeble attempt at seduction is the reaction it elicits from Traynor. Linda looks neither excited nor interested as her husband clumsily gropes her tits, but still responds with stereotypical porn-film enthusiasm . . . fake. After Traynor's meager attempt at foreplay, Linda plays with her twat and then starts jerking his joint. He starts nuzzling her nipples, finally licking the long pink scar on her belly in the only real show of excitement he displays. In light of Linda's later claims about Traynor, it's not surprising what he considers an erogenous zone.

Traynor never goes near Linda's pussy, instead rubbing his face over her belly in mock joy as she tosses her head in mock orgasm. After feigning cunnilingus, he gets on his knees in front of her as she writhes and moans, her wails of ecstasy incapable of seeming any more put-on. For some reason the pair get down on the floor, but their attempt at sixty-nine is really a big zero. Linda doesn't get anywhere near sucking Traynor's cock, even though she does graze his thigh before straddling him for some fake insertion.

The rest of the clip shows little more than two sad, stoned hippies grinding their hips. The "sex" is in this loop doesn't go much beyond second base and there are no hardcore shots at all, which isn't surprising because Traynor's dick doesn't get hard for a second. If anyone looks like they're doing it with a gun to their head, it's him.

# PISS ORGY

## DIRECTED BY BOB WOLFE
## ALSO STARRING ERIC EDWARDS AND CHRIS JORDAN

According to Edwards, this is the only film featuring him with his wife, who weren't quite the career porn whores Linda portrays them as in *Ordeal*. "My wife and I were swingers," he remembers. "Those were the days of free love and all, so it was a natural turn of events that we would do some films together. She made [the piss] one, but she didn't care for making movies and didn't do any more." Chris was in about a dozen other sex films in non-sex roles and was featured in *Deep Throat Part II*.

Edwards apparently had no idea what a groundbreaking piece of erotic cinema they were all creating. "I didn't know this would make such a splash when we did it," he laughs. "Jesus, did I say that?"

Lovelace writes about *Piss Orgy* in *Ordeal*:

> The movie began with what I suppose is a fairly standard porn opening: the old girl-meets-girl-meets-boy formula. The three of us were in bed and after we had done everything that three people could do to each other sexually, the director decided that the movie would come to a socko ending with the actors urinating on each other. . . . All I know is that the director had about five minutes of film left when the inspiration hit him.

Edwards has a considerably less dramatic memory of the filming. "I don't recall exactly how the pissing part got into it. I may have just said something like, 'I have to pee,' and Bob said, 'Let's get it on film.' "

Linda also writes, "Even when my mind was numb to everything, my body seemed to know it was insane. When it came my turn to urinate on [Chris], I couldn't do it." When Wolfe offers to let her assume the role of pissee, "All of a sudden it became easier. I was standing there, still aware of the sheer insanity of it all, but doing it nonetheless. I guess I was still strong enough so that I would rather piss on than be pissed upon."

Sorta. Linda does piss on Chris, but only after she's pissed upon by Eric first.

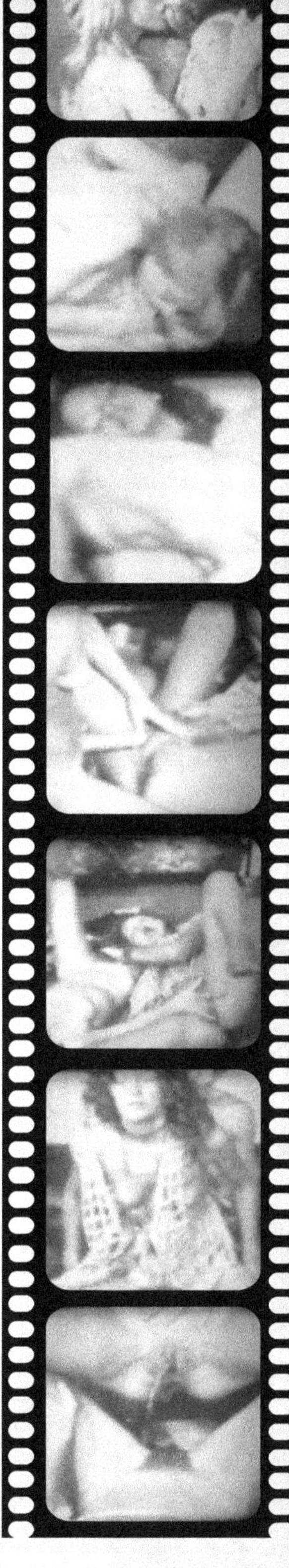

# DOG 1

### DIRECTED BY BOB WOLFE
### ALSO STARRING ERIC EDWARDS AND NORMAN

# DOG FUCKER (AKA DOGARAMA)

### DIRECTED BY BOB WOLFE
### ALSO STARRING NORMAN

These are the most notorious loops that Linda Lovelace or any adult actress with the possible exception of Candy Barr ever made. They were the films Linda and Chuck were most worried would get out following her rise to fame, and by denying their existence in *Inside Linda Lovelace*—before admitting their existence in *Ordeal*—Linda assured their place in porn history.

Once Al Goldstein exposed these dogumentaries in *Screw*, they were mentioned (or at least alluded to) in the porn and mainstream media for decades. Goldstein crowed about them for months, taking every opportunity to mention them when the topic of Linda Lovelace came up.

If Linda and/or Chuck had just admitted she'd made these films when *Screw* first mentioned them, these loops might have just faded into fuck-film obscurity and not become the career-defining moments they did. When this writer asked Linda why she denied it all back then, she said Traynor told her to. That's entirely likely, considering the way Traynor himself handled the question of the dog-fuck films when it was posed by Diana Helfrecht (or whoever) in *Bachelor* magazine in August 1973:

> **Helfrecht:** How about those lowdown articles in that sex newspaper, and some of those weirdo photos?
> **Linda:** They weren't me! You notice you never saw the face too clearly.
> **Chuck:** They're all bullshit! Anyone who knew her knew that right away. . . . [Goldstein and Buckley] wanted her to star in their film that just opened. She refused to do it and that alienated them right away. So they began writing this bunch of lies, so people would be turned off to *Deep Throat* and go see their movie instead. But it never worked!

Less than a year later, Goldstein asked Traynor point-blank:

> ***Screw*:** Why did she deny the dog-fucking picture we printed in *Screw* in her book? Why did she do such a dumb thing as accuse *Screw* of making a composite picture of her when we had the original photo in our hands?
> **Traynor:** Well, Linda never realized that people were interested in her as a freak. Linda figured, if the dog-fucking comes

> out, I'm dead. Probably one of the only reasons Hefner was interested in her was because he's got all those movies and he looks at them 10 times a night, you know? So consequently I think that's where her head was at when she did the book. Because she believed that a rumor about the dog-fucking would destroy her in Hollywood.
>
> ***Screw*:** Why didn't she just ignore *Screw* in the book? It would have been smarter. Why say it's a phony photo when obviously it's not, when she can't sustain it? Didn't she know *Screw* would sue her?
>
> **Traynor:** Well, it would have been smarter to ignore it, except, see, she was getting a lot of heat out in California. The local papers out there were saying, "What about this thing with Goldstein?" Every interview she did, people would say, "Is it true what we read in *Screw*? Did you really ball a dog? Was that you in the movie?"
>
> ***Screw*:** The damn thing's being sold mail-order in every paper across the country.
>
> **Traynor:** Sure, but somebody told her, "If you deny it, they'll never prove it was you. It could be a look-alike."

Linda gave that explanation to reporters more than once, but Traynor fails to mention that not only had he written *Inside Linda Lovelace*, he was managing her affairs at that point, and he doesn't come across as the type of guy who takes kindly to being told what he—or someone he's working with—should do.

The ever-litigious Goldstein threatened to sue Linda, Traynor and Pinnacle Books for libel to the tune of $250,000. Surprisingly, although he most assuredly would have won, the case never went to trial. Explaining his decision to drop the matter in his October 1974 *Playboy* interview, Goldstein claimed Traynor told him he and Linda were expecting some big-money movie contracts in Hollywood but were having legal trouble because of the bestiality films. For once Goldstein let his cooler head prevail and called off the dogs.

It's pointed out in many discussions of the dog films that adult historian Jim Holliday interviewed the principals involved, all of whom denied any coercion occurred on the set. (Holliday also wrote, in his book *Only the Best*, that this loop was shot in 1969; Linda didn't even meet Chuck Traynor until 1970.) Holliday's claim, while almost undeniably true, is also undeniably laughable. Does anyone in their right mind think they'd admit forcing a woman to have sex with a dog at gunpoint? Twice?

Further clouding the issue, Sharon Mitchell recalls in Legs McNeil's *The Other Hollywood: The Uncensored History of the Porn Film Industry*, "They were shooting up in Carter Stevens' studio, and I walked in and Linda was having sex with these dogs. It didn't look like they were forcing her to do anything. It looked like they were forcing the dogs! I was really young and new and going up there to shoot a scene with Chuck Vincent. When I walked in there and saw that, I was like, 'Okay, I'm out of here.'... So I ran down the stairs. It scared me. It was just too weird—because nobody was holding

anybody anywhere. Nobody was forcing her to do anything."

Mitch's recollection is double-dog dubious. Linda's dog films were shot in 1971, and by Sharon's account she entered the industry in 1975. It is true that if she had been on the set of the dog film, she would have been young. Like, really young. Born in 1956, Sharon would have been 15 years old.

*Dog 1* opens with Edwards and Linda fucking on a bed. A short oral-sex scene leads to a short anal scene, neither of which are too remarkable by either of their standards. Edwards pulls out of her butt, comes on her ass, gets dressed and walks out the door. Linda, still unsatisfied, flips him the bird.

Enter her next costar, who thinks she looks just fetching.

"I did my scene with her, and that's when they brought Fido in," Edwards recalls of the shoot. "I sat down off to the side, behind the camera, watching, and my jaw just dropped. That dog didn't need any coaching at all. He knew what to do. I don't remember if Chuck was even there during the shoot—I don't think he was—but I remember there was no coercion going on, and certainly no gun. And when it was over, I was just like, 'Wow.' "

Traynor's comments in *Screw* to the contrary, *Dog Fucker* doesn't contain the same footage as *Dog 1* shot from a different angle. It's a completely different film and shows only Linda and the dog; one widely distributed European print edits the two films together.

# DEEP THROAT

**DIRECTOR UNKNOWN**
**ALSO STARRING CHUCK TRAYNOR**

Judging by Linda's big hair and the Christmas tree in the background, this is most likely the last stag film she made before heading off to Florida to film *Deep Throat* in January 1972—but judging by the loop's title, it was almost certainly released after the big-screen film became a hit.

The scene opens to show Chuck Traynor in red bell bottoms tending a fireplace then offering a mini-skirted, go-go-booted Linda a drink. The room is chock full of Christmas cheer and not much else, except a single stereo speaker and a pair of large pillows the pair will soon defile with their oral-centric antics. After Linda takes a quick sip, the suave pimp-in-training takes the drink from her hand and they begin making out. But this time all porn convention is thrown out the window; there's no knock at the door, no surprise appearance by a couple of horny friends, not a drop of piss or a canine in sight. Chuck, ever the sly dog, unzips Linda's dress and the pair are soon naked and ready for some sixty-nine action.

Much more so than their previous one-on-one reel, Linda and Chuck seem a little more together and a little more turned on this time around, although you can still tell that Chuck, never the master of foreplay, isn't even erect as Linda gobbles his knob, which bounces and bobbles in Linda's fist the way a kid shakes a pencil so it looks like it's made out of rubber. Whoever's working the camera must have been getting a case of vertigo watching all this because the production immediately goes into Shak-E-Cam™ , bobbing and weaving from side to side and up and down for about 10 seconds until the cameraman's DT's subside or he gets his diazepam or something happens to make the *mise en scene* a little less *mise er able*.

The pair's sixty-nine starts with Chuck tonguing Linda's clit, fingering her puss and splaying her brown-ringed asshole until a much appreciated edit offers an impressive view of Linda performing the title act, huffing Chuck's dork down to the balls, up to the head, down to the balls, up to the head, flicking her tongue across the tip of Traynor's cock and handling his balls like Captain Queeg on the witness stand.

After Chuck pulls her off his joint, something interesting happens that certainly hasn't happened too often when the pair, uh, worked together: he's finally able to stick his dick inside her—for all of 45 seconds. Then he slithers out, frigs her clit, and something even more interesting happens: Linda crosses her legs yoga lotus-position style, reaches to the side and grabs an empty Coke bottle, with which she fucks herself while leaning backwards on Chuck's chest.

This is interesting not just for the Tarantino-esque cinematic reference—an homage, if you will—to the classic stag film *Apple Knockers and Coke Bottle*. It's also intriguing because Linda fucks herself with the bottle three times longer than Chuck could manage with his dick, making Linda's soda jerk a fitting side trip in a fuck session that's awkwardly executed, amateurishly shot but good for a laugh—especially when Linda sideswipes Chuck's face with her foot after she's enjoyed the pause that refreshes.

Then it's back to a little more cocksucking—during which a huge rope of snot slides out of Linda's nose and down onto Chuck's cock, which she dutifully keeps huffing—until, the director's hope of a come shot obviously dashed, a hand-drawn title card declares "The End."

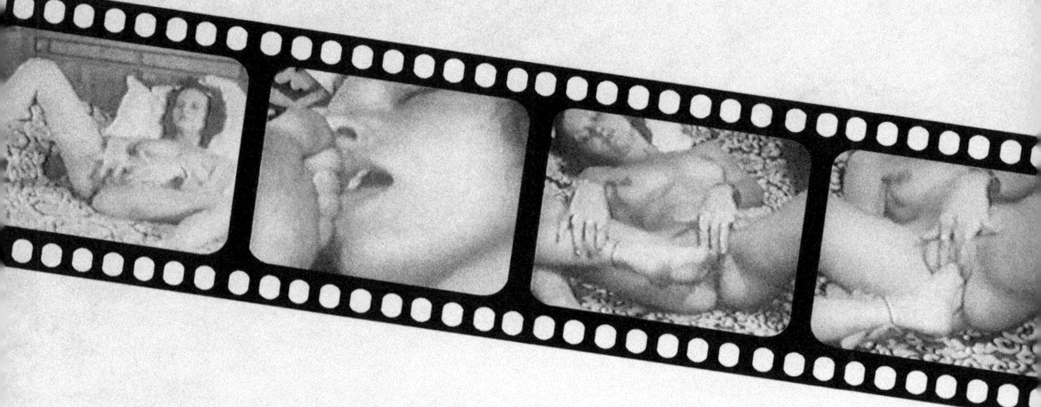

# THE FOOT

**DIRECTED BY CHUCK TRAYNOR**
**ALSO STARRING "GINGER"**

When *Deep Throat* finished filming in Florida and the gang headed back north in late January 1972, Damiano and crew hit New York to begin post-production. Always on the hustle, Chuck Traynor says he borrowed a camera from Lou Peraino, rented a Jersey City hotel room and the services of a girl Linda dubs "Ginger" in *Ordeal* and directed the last two stag films Linda Lovelace would ever make. Despite Linda's claim in *Ordeal*, this is the only loop she made with an "appendage as john" scenario. Despite Traynor's later claim that the appendage was Linda's, it actually belongs to Ginger.

Traynor walked *Hustler* magazine through the making of *The Foot* in a January 1975 interview. "I went to work doing loops," he said, "8mm balling films. I did a few and then I went to the guy who owned the joint and I told him that I could do much better films, but I wanted $1,000 a print for the master. So he said, 'Do one, and if it's any good, we'll take it.' So I did *The Foot*. And they freaked over it."

As Traynor remembers, "It was a dynamite film. It was about a chick that balls a foot. Now, my foot had a character. It had a smiling face, an ankle bracelet and painted toenails. There were two girls involved, but you never saw one of the girls. All that you saw was the foot, and that was the whole deal. All the way through the film you kept thinking that when the foot arrives at the other girl's house, the camera would pan up and you'd see these two chicks balling. But it never did. The camera stayed on the one girl's foot and the other girl's pussy. And this chick with the pussy was large enough for this foot to get in her. . . . [Linda] was the foot."

Traynor says the response to his film suffered only when other people stepped in. "[*The Foot*] was very, very underground. I was invited to the Cannes Erotic Film Festival with it, but by that time the company I sold it to said it was too freaky for the dirty old man with the raincoat that buys 8mm films. They had cut it up and cut the story right out of it. They just went for the erotic scenes."

*The Foot* kicks off with a typically innocent- but typically horny-looking Linda (here we go) lying in bed masturbating before she (wait for it) hears a knock at the door! Linda welcomes Ginger, who, despite Traynor's explanation, is seen briefly

enough to let the viewer know that the visitor is a girl. They make some small talk before Lovelace slyly accepts a few folded bills and places them underneath her pillow. After the deal is struck, the foot steps out of its boot and gets ready to get into it.

And does it ever.

The action starts with an erotic bout of toe-sucking. Linda lies back and dines on digit after dirty digit, snaking her long, pointy, sexy tongue between each blackened little piggie, at one point practically taking half of Ginger's foot in her mouth. Then the foot moves down to Linda's pussy and gets ready for penetration. The foot points skyward, erect for all symbolic and practical purposes, and the real action begins.

Linda mounts Ginger's foot to within an inch or two of the ankle, her pussy lips distending as she pumps up and down, up and down like she's fucking a size-five cock with stubby pink French ticklers. The depth and breadth and height that sole can reach are amazing, as are Linda's sexual gymnastics: At one point she spins around to get a better camera angle with the foot still lodged inside her, not missing a beat.

If nothing else, *The Foot* shows that Traynor understood fetish psychology by keeping the foot and the pussy as the main *objects de tart*. Linda's cunt and the jane's disembodied foot dominate the show until the climax, which will go down in history as one of the dumbest come shots to appear in a stag film.

As Traynor explained in *Hustler*, "For the come shot I took a piece of neoprene tubing and ran it down the back of the girl's leg, under her foot and up under her big toe. Then I took a rubber syringe and filled it with Carnation milk and egg white. The foot was balling away and then pulled out of the pussy and came [out of] the big toe."

# THE FIST

**DIRECTED BY CHUCK TRAYNOR**
**ALSO STARRING "GINGER"**

*The Fist* opens with Ginger sitting alone on a hotel bed reading a paperback book titled *I, Pervert*—and probably thinking about masturbating, since the only reason people read in porn loops is to start jerking off.Then . . . she hears a knock at the door. The visitor is Linda Lovelace, sporting her *Deep Throat* ho 'fro and carrying a large shopping bag. Ginger lets her in and they sit down on the bed and examine the bag's contents: three big dildos and a jar ofVaseline.

Linda stuffs a double-headed dong up Ginger's cunt. Ginger doesn't look too good at (or too interested in) what's going on (and in), but they go through the motions, joking and exchanging directions before some pretty standard lesbo-scene choreography, like both mounting the dong at the same time and meeting in the middle. (So no, Darren Aronofsky did not invent ass-to-ass.) Ginger laughs at the modest amount she can absorb herself, then they switch places and Ginger penetrates Linda. In a matter of seconds her eyes bulge, impressed at how much of the dildo Linda takes in.

Ginger slowly inserts a finger and massages Linda's muff. One finger becomes two, two become three, and thanks to a glob ofVaseline Ginger stuffs her whole fist an inch or two past the wrist.After a few minutes of hands-on loving Lovelace comes—and it looks like she comes hard—before Ginger pulls out and Linda pats her on the head, pausing to catch a well-deserved breath.

# Chapter 3: COMING SOON

## A Porn Star Is Born

**In the years after the release of *Deep Throat*, the only thing more valuable than a gallon of gas was Linda Lovelace's name on a marquee—which was sometimes much easier to find. Although Linda only made three feature films, she appeared in several others thanks to some judicious editing and what can only be called an early exercise in product placement.**

GERARD DAMIANO'S
DEEP
THROAT
HOW FAR DOES A GIRL HAVE TO GO
TO UNTANGLE HER TINGLE?
EASTMANCOLOR (X) ADULTS ONLY

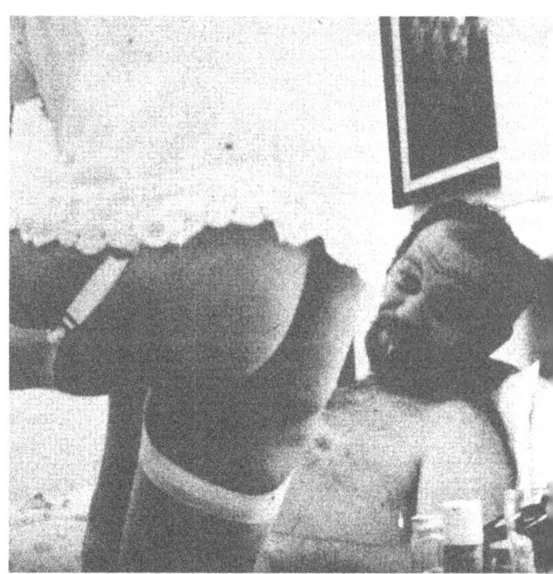

# IN THEATERS

## DEEP THROAT

**Directed by Gerard Damiano**

**Also starring Harry Reems, Dolly Sharp and Carol Connors**

There is absolutely nothing new to be said about *Deep Throat* in regards to its technical skill (passable), its erotic content (outstanding, at least as far as Linda's blowjobs go), its effect on the pornographic arts (minimal, aside from introducing the world to Gerard Damiano), its effect on the pornographic industry (massive), its place among the most influential films (low on the totem pole), its place as one of the most profitable films ever made on a dollar-for-dollar basis (high on the totem pole, but not as high as people would have you think), the fellatio technique of its star (incredible) and its place in people's hearts (warm, cockle-wise, considering that it was the first porn film most people ever saw).

But I will say this. *Deep Throat* is not a particularly great film—it looks like the collection of stag loops it ultimately is—but it's not just a piece of cheap smut either. It's a good-natured dirty little comedy made at a time when there was nothing wrong with making good-natured dirty little comedies, a piece of blue burlesque that lucked into its place in history when it became a *cause célèbre*. It's extremely doubtful that the Perainos or Damiano thought they were creating something with "socially redeeming value" because they had no reason to think that. They couldn't have known it would get busted any more than they knew it would make hundreds of millions of dollars.

The most high-profile trials took place in Binghamton, New York (where it was declared not obscene); Memphis, Tennessee (where the Perainos were found guilty of trafficking in pornography and Harry Reems was convicted but later cleared on appeal); Tucson, Arizona (where it was found not obscene); and New York City, the one city out of all the cities on the planet—a planet that includes the cities of Binghamton, Memphis and Tucson—to find it obscene.

The New York City trial began on December 19, 1972, just a few weeks after a jury in conservative upstate Binghamton declared that the film is not obscene. It lasted 11 days. In a nutshell, witnesses were called, objections were made and Judge Joel J. Tyler found that the film isn't just obscene, it's really, really obscene. Really.

# JUDGE TYLER DECISION RE: DEEP THROAT

**JOEL J. TYLER, Judge**

We are again thrust into the overexplored thicket of obscenity law. The defendant is charged with promotion, or possession with intent to promote obscene material, knowing the contents and character thereof, all in violation of Penal Law §235.05 Subd. 1, a class A misdemeanor. It was tried before the Court without a jury.

What is involved is the showing in a public theater, at a $5.00 per admission charge, the film *Deep Throat*. The case has engendered some public interest here and elsewhere, however it is not unique. Many cases dealing with depiction of the same or similar deviate sexual behavior have been reported but few have had such a full measure of directed publicity.

**The Film**

The film runs 62 minutes. It is in color and in sound, and boasts a musical score. Following the first innocuous scene ("heroine" driving a car), the film runs from one act of explicit sex into another, forthrightly demonstrating heterosexual intercourse and a variety of deviate sexual acts, not "fragmentary and fleeting" or 10 minutes out of a 120-minute movie as in *I Am Curious (Yellow)*; but here it permeates and engulfs the film from beginning to end. The camera angle, emphasis and close-up zooms were directed "toward a maximum exposure in detail of the genitalia" during the gymnastics, gyrations, bobbing, trundling, surging, ebb and flowing, eddying, moaning, groaning and sighing, all with ebullience and gusto.

There were so many and varied forms of sexual activity one would tend to lose count of them. However, the news reporters were more adept and counted seven separate acts of fellatio and four of cunnilingus. Such concentration upon the acts of fellatio and cunnilingus overlooked the numerous clear, clinical acts of sexual intercourse, anal sodomy, female masturbation, clear depiction of seminal-fluid ejaculation and an orgy scene—a Sodom and Gomorrah gone wild before the fire—all of which is enlivened with the now famous "four-letter words" and finally with bells ringing and rockets bursting in climactic ecstasy.

The performance of one sexual act runs almost headlong into the other. One defense witness thought 75 to 80 percent of the film involved depiction of explicit sexual activity and another viewed it as over 50 percent. A timekeeper may have clocked a higher percentage. Nothing was faked or simulated; it was as explicit and as exquisite as life. One defense witness said he saw "realism and genuine sexual experience." No imagination was needed, since it was intended to appeal to the imbecile as well.

The defense expert witnesses testified that the film possessed entertainment value and humor. The court appropriately answered that tedious and tenuous argument often, but conscientiously, made in obscenity cases which have nothing to redeem them:

"Presumably the Romans of the First Century derived entertainment from witnessing Christians being devoured by lions. Given the right audience, the spectacle of a man committing an act of sodomy on another man would provide entertainment value. However, neither this spectacle nor the activities described in the instant case are invested with constitutionally protected values merely because they entertain viewers. However chaotic the law may be in this field, no court has yet adopted such an extreme result."

In passing, it should be noted that the defense "expert" witnesses were unpersuasive in the main. For example, a defense psychologist testified that he would use films like *Deep Throat* as classroom sex-educational material not only in colleges but for certain high school students as well.

The alleged "humor" of the film is sick, and designed on a level to appeal especially to those first learning that boys and girls are different. Drama critic Vincent Canby characterizes the jokes as "dumb gags, [which] cannot disguise the straight porno intent." This, the defense experts here maintain, helps redeem the film as worthwhile. As to plot, there is none, unless you exclude the sexual activity, which is the sole plot. And as to character development, a desirable and necessary concomitant of meaningful film, stage or book, again there is none, unless, of course, one means that the progression (or retrogression) of multiple and varied nymphomania to a singular form (fellatio) is evidence of this attribute.

Oh, yes! There is a gossamer of a story line—the heroine's all-engrossing search for sexual satisfaction, and when all sexual endeavors fail to gratify, her unique problem is successfully diagnosed to exist in her throat. She then seeks to fulfill the doctor's prescription by repeated episodes of fellatio, which Nora Ephron euphemistically characterizes as "compensatory behavior." (*Esquire*, Feb. 1973)

The defense experts testified that they see the film legitimatising woman's need and "life right" (as one put it) for sexual gratification, equal with that of men. They also see in the film the thoughtful lesson that sex should not be unavailingly monolithic (usual face-to-face relationship), but should take varied forms, with complete sexual gratification as the crowning goal, or as the film seems to advertise in its plebeian fashion—

"different strokes for different folks"; or as others, less articulate, might say, "there's more than one way to skin the cat." These unusual and startling revelations are of social value, they say, not only for the bedroom, but necessary as an object lesson for a public forum.

The alleged story lines are the facade, the sheer negligee through which clearly shines the producer's and the defendant's true and only purpose, that is, the presentation of unmistakably hardcore pornography, where "imagination has gone to work in the porno vineyards"—a quotation by a newsman, and adopted by the defendant in its newspaper advertisements. One defense expert actually, but unwittingly, confirms the charade when he says that the "plot" of the film "provides a thread on which the various sequences of sexual acts would be hung."

Movie critic Judith Crist characterizes the production "idiot moviemaking" and the actors "awful" (*New York* magazine, 2/5/73, p. 64). I agree, except to add that a female, who would readily and with apparent, anxious abandon, submit to the insertion of a glass dildo container into her vagina, have liquid poured therein and then drink it by means of a tube, as was done here to and by the "superstar," is not a reflection merely upon her thespian ability, but a clinical example of extraordinary perversion, degeneracy and possible amentia. Whatever talent superstar has seems confined to her magnificent appetite and sword-swallowing faculty for fellatio.

In this court's view, the film and its genre have a significant meaning and impact, transcending this case, for all society (including for those who have seen the movie).

**When All Is Said**

*Deep Throat*—a nadir of decadence—is indisputably obscene by any legal measurement, and particularly violative of Penal Law Section 235.05.

It goes substantially beyond "the present critical point in the compromise between candor and shame at which the [national] community may have arrived here and now." It is another manifestation of the refusal to use words as emotional symbols unrelated to the purely physical. There is no effort, by word or conduct, to cut through the imponderable barriers of human understanding to the defense of human integrity. It, in fact, denigrates that integrity of man and, particularly, woman, the expert witnesses notwithstanding. It does this by objectifying and insulting woman, as Anthony Burgess, the author, puts it, by "making woman the sexual instrument come before woman the human being." Thus it supports the misogynist's view.

Its dominant theme, and in fact, its only theme is to appeal to the prurience in sex. It is hardcore pornography with a vengeance. Quoting Burgess again, speaking of pornography generally and well applied here: "It creates an abstract paradise in which the only emotion is lust and the only event orgasm and the only inhabitants animated phalluses and vulvae." It is neither redeemed nor redeemable, lest it be by the good camerawork, editing, clarity, good color and lack of grain, which defense witness, a movie critic, was seemingly impressed with. But that is hardly enough to remove it from the pale of obscenity.

It does, in fact, demean and pervert the sexual experience, and insults it, shamelessly, without tenderness and without understanding of its role as a concomitant of the human condition. Therefore, it does dirt on it; it insults sex and the human body as D. H. Lawrence would describe condemnable pornography. It "focuses primarily upon what is sexually morbid, grossly perverse and bizarre. It smacks, at times, of fantasy and unreality, of sexual perversion and sickness." Justice Jackson says he knows hard-core pornography when he merely sees it. We have seen it in *Deep Throat*, and this is one throat that deserves to be cut. I readily perform the operation in finding the defendant guilty as charged, as to both cases.

Tyler's decision helped create one of those rare porn artifacts: a sex film without the sex. Just because Tyler ruled *Deep Throat* obscene, distributors and theater owners figured, didn't mean that people couldn't see it. They'd just have to see it without the sex. Hence the "revised" version of the world's most famous sex film.

The revised version actually runs longer than the original, despite a lack of hard-core footage (*Screw* and *Variety* both mention that scenes from *Deep Throat Part II* are edited in). The substitution is laughable unless you've actually paid to see it: Still frames are animated into soft-core stop-action footage like a child's flip-book. The opening cunnilingus scene is reduced to two shots played over and over while the soundtrack blares; the orgy scene shows Linda's head bobbing dangerously close to Jack Byron's penis without touching it.

One way people were able to see *Deep Throat* with the hardcore footage intact was through the sale of 8mm versions that could be shown in the privacy of one's own home. Dialogue cards replaced the audio, but even if you couldn't hear what Lovelace said, at least you were able to see what she did.

Two decades later, Tyler would take back the tongue-lashing he gave both Linda Lovelace and that deep throat of hers. *Entertainment Weekly* celebrated the twentieth anniversary of Tyler's decision by asking if he'd do anything different after viewing the film today. An apparently mellowed Tyler told the magazine that, given the same situation, he probably wouldn't have ruled the same way. Better late than never, huh?

**BONUS CONTENT**

Download a fun fact about *Deep Throat* by scanning this QR code or logging onto **bit.ly/LLQR09**

LINDA
LOVELACE
IS BACK!
DEEP
THROAT
PART II
(ALL NEW)
COLOR · FROM DAMIANO FILMS
R
RESTRICTED
Under 17 requires accompanying
Parent or Adult Guardian

## DEEP THROAT PART II (1973)

**Directed by Joe Sarno**

**Also starring Harry Reems, Rick Livermore, David Davidson and Chris Jordan**

The plot of *Deep Throat*'s notorious sequel goes something like this: A group of American FBI agents (played by Jamie Gillis and Marc Stevens, among others) try to recruit Nurse Linda Lovelace to learn the secrets of patient Dilbert Lamb, a bespectacled computer programmer (played by Levi Richards, billed here as Richard Livermore) being treated for an incestuous crush on his Aunt Juliet (played by Tina Russell), who has recently developed but plans to soon destroy an ultra-intuitive surveillance supercomputer named Oscar (played by a large pile of plywood and Plexiglas).

Meanwhile, Russian agent Sonya Toroscova (played by Chris Jordan) and her foils are also hot on Linda's tail just as consumer advocate Ken Whacker (played by David Davidson) sends one of his band of Whacker's Attackers (played by Andrea True, billed here as Inger Kissen) to seduce Dilbert, with whom she ultimately falls in love. In the end, Linda gets the gratitude of her country, she gets the love of Ken Whacker and she gets a pie in the puss during the film's slapstick ending.

The plot goes "something like" that because *Deep Throat Part II*, written and directed by Joe Sarno, is a sometimes rambling, occasionally confusing mess of a film, not necessarily unwatchable but not necessarily deserving of a spot on someone's bucket list of cinematic rarities, either.

On the one hand, you could be benevolent and say the film is Sarno's attempt to expand upon the original *Deep Throat* by fleshing out its two main characters, giving them depth and purpose and bringing them to life in a Richard Lester-esque piece of vaudevillian social satire appealing simultaneously to aficionados of erotic cinema and people anxious to enter a dialogue about human sexuality, censorship and international politics. On the other hand, you could just be honest and call the film an obvious attempt by the producers of *Deep Throat* to once again turn the name of Linda Lovelace into so much money they wouldn't bother counting it, they'd just weigh it.

Considering its reputation, the film doesn't fall to an Ed Woodian level of cinematic incompetence; it's the criminally inept editing—credited to George Thomas, although Sarno denies knowing the real perp—that turns what might have been a good idea between the time it entered Sarno's brain and the time it hit the big screen into a film whose main historical importance remains its casting a Who's Who of Big Apple porn talent and the absolute critical crucifixion it got upon release.

After *Deep Throat Part II* disappeared from movie screens in 1974, it was presumed (and no doubt hoped) lost forever, but like the secondary stage of syphilis, it returned years later to an otherwise innocent and unsuspecting world. Arrow honcho Ray Pistol planned to unveil a then-recently unearthed print at the 2004 Adult Entertainment Expo in Las Vegas, a year after Linda Lovelace was inducted into the Legends of Erotica exhibit, maintained by William Margold and Pistol at his Pure

**BONUS CONTENT**

Download the *Deep Throat Part II* press release by scanning this QR code or logging onto **bit.ly/LLQR10**

Pleasure bookstore in Sin City. That screening didn't happen, but *Deep Throat Part II* has since been released on DVD in at least three different versions.

Surprisingly, the version issued by Alpha Blue Archives on their *Linda Lovelace Collection* disk is the best quality and the one to watch just for the sake of watching it. The picture shows little of the wear and tear customers know to expect from ABA product (the company maintains that it would rather issue a scratchy, spliced and shitty copy of a rare fuck flick than none at all, the better to preserve the heritage of America's erotic cinema, blah, blah blah). I for one agree with them on this point, frustrating though it can sometimes be to watch their films. *The Linda Lovelace Collection* presents the film without any *Deep Throat Part II*-specific extras alongside a typically chewed-up print of *Linda Lovelace for President*, a few fuzzy, pixilated stag films and the trailer for the original *Deep Throat*.

After Hours/Pop Cinema issued the true obsessive's version of the film through their Secret Key Motion Pictures imprint in a two-disc, three-film "Deep Throat Sex Comedy" collection of Sarno softcore howlers. This slightly lesser quality but still highly watchable print is supplemented with an interview with Sarno and an additional audio commentary track in which Sarno scholar Michael Bowen interviews Livermore and Sarno, who walks into the room about a third of the way through. They speak about Linda briefly and politely, summing her up as nice girl with a bit of a diva streak who, as Sarno says, "always had to have her boyfriend around."

The audio commentary provides an interesting first-hand look into the early-'70s New York City stag film scene; Bowen's main interest is Livermore's history in that elusive era of dirty filmmaking, although their conversation is peppered with talk about the action taking place onscreen. Sarno, however, still maddeningly insists that no hardcore was shot for the film; Livermore concurs, claiming that he and Linda most likely kept their clothes on during their dry hump scene, although Sarno does admit that if the talent wanted to fuck, he'd let them but wouldn't film it, allowing the penetration to take place out of frame.

Livermore and Sarno's claims are puzzling, to say the least. One can understand why a porn actor would do softcore scenes when his real stock in trade is fucking on film (that reason would be money), and even why a producer would pay porn performers to *not* fuck on film (that would be the access to marquee name value and the avoidance of jail time). But why wouldn't a director presented with people who want to fuck during a scene film it as hardcore and edit it down to softcore later? If Livermore and Sarno's claims are something else, that something is bullshit. For proof of the existence of hardcore footage from *Deep Throat Part II*, one need look no further than *The Confessions of Linda Lovelace*, where some of it is indeed included.

The most complete and apparently first release of the film was issued in Italy on the Cult 70 label, dubbed in Italian and containing a few minutes of extra softcore footage, some of which is ridiculously innocuous but apparently edited out of the American version to avoid a visit from *la polizia*.

Early in the film, perpetually horny Dr. Jayson Young pursues the comely and come-friendly Nurse Lovelace, but this time he's come (or is about to) with a special friend in tow: his fiancée Bonnie Smiley, played by the adorable Helen Madigan (misnamed in the end credits as Tina Russell). The trio move from the reception area to a back room where they're soon on a couch, the hardcore edited out, with Linda sitting next to Reems, eyes closed and an intense ecstatic look on her face as Madigan bounces up and down on Reems' lap.

Other quite possibly watered-down sequences are shown later, captured by surreptitiously placed cameras and being monitored on closed-circuit screens by the KGB agents and FBI agents: Linda and Livermore humping and bumping in the office; Linda caught later in the same flagrante delecto; and Reems getting friendly with FBI Agent Tanya T. Tickler, whom he originally assumes to be a guy with tits. Also included is a brief sequence in which Linda slobs the knob of Oscar the talking computer and a gratuitous throwaway sight gag at film's end when she swirls her tongue around the end of a hot dog she just bought from a street vendor.

Ultimately, *Deep Throat Part II* is a poor follow-up to the then-groundbreaking *Deep Throat*, and it's doubtful that even the inclusion of the legendary, long-lost hardcore footage—at least one scene of which, again, still exists—could have saved the film. Had the film been made with a different title and a different cast (or more specifically without the notable names Linda Lovelace and Harry Reems), it may have actually been more fondly remembered, if not necessarily in regards to the rest of Sarno's canon, but against other, similar sexploitation comedies of the time.

**BONUS CONTENT**

Listen to a *Deep Throat Part II* radio ad by scanning this QR code or logging onto **bit.ly/LLQR11**

## LOVELACE MEETS MISS JONES (1974)

**Directed by Angelo Spaveni**
**Also starring Georgina Spelvin, Darby Lloyd Rains, Harry Reems and Ellen Smith**

With no new Lovelace product forthcoming, producers released this piss-poor collection of water-sports loops. Linda appears in the *Piss Orgy* loop and no, she never meets Miss Jones. The same scene is in *Exotic French Fantasies* featuring Andrea True and John Holmes, whom Lovelace also doesn't meet.

## THE CONFESSIONS OF LINDA LOVELACE (1974)

**Directed by Michael McDermott**
**Also starring Harry Reems, Dolly Sharp, Carol Connors and other people from a couple of porno movies you've probably already seen**

If there was ever a porn equivalent to *Plan 9 From Outer Space*, this is it. Like Ed Wood's anti-classic, *The Confessions of Linda Lovelace* gets around its lack of a flesh-and-blood star by replacing Lovelace with an actress whose face is obscured by a large hat and black veil and whose voice is several notches lower than Linda's (this is explained later when she credits Dr. Young's medical technique). Like *Lovelace Meets Miss Jones*, *Confessions* relies mainly on previously existing material to justify Linda's name on the marquee.

The wraparound footage shows "Linda" applying for a job guarding the daughters of a Middle Eastern sheik who are making their first trip to America. During her job interview, Linda recalls various life events—moving in with her cousin Helen; her first, futile attempts at finding sexual satisfaction; and her decision to use her talents to help mankind once she does—all illustrated with every sex scene in *Deep Throat*: edited, sometimes in the wrong order and set to different soundtrack music.

This film's humor is bottom of the barrel with not only fewer but lamer jokes than *Deep Throat*. Come to think of it, the funniest lines in this movie are *from* the original *Deep Throat*. The sole reason *The Confessions of Linda Lovelace* deserves a look is its inclusion of an all-too-short four-minute medley of scenes from none other than *Deep Throat Part II*.

In that footage, the scar running up Lovelace's tummy is, of course, hidden, but this time by Harry Reems' head. Reems is lying on his back being ridden by Helen Madigan while Linda sits next to them (all together now) masturbating. Lovelace is so caught up in the moment it looks like she's trying to get her whole hand inside herself.

The other clip from *Deep Throat Part II* shows Lovelace fellating Reems in what is almost a carbon copy of their first scene in the original, the camera angle maybe 10 degrees to the side. Occasionally the camera cuts to reaction shots that duplicate Harry's mugging as well.

Linda and the Sheik later discuss his daughters' trip, an innocent jaunt that turns into an all-out cooze cruise shown in aquatically erotic scenes from the film *Lovewitch* (which also featured Al Goldstein). Illustrating Linda's tale of the girls taking part in "a local poetry reading" is an orgy scene that starts out with a burlesque comic lip-synching the song "Stickball," a rowdy, raunchy rarity written by P. Vert—aka Tony Bruno, whose musical career is similarly linked with Lovelace in a way that again proves, to quote someone or other, it really is a small world, after all.

*The Confessions of Linda Lovelace* ends on a supposedly humorous note as Linda and the Sheik celebrate the successful completion of her assignment by puffing on a hookah (introduced into the scene with a predictably corny pun). The Sheik takes a few mild puffs, telling Lovelace that, "You don't have to take a lot into your mouth," and encouraging her with the very timely, "Try it, you'll like it." Lovelace, thanks to (all together now) her incredible sucking ability, creates a cloud of smoke that completely envelopes her (and her face) and sends the Sheik running from the tent, choking and gagging on the fumes. A similar reaction could probably be recalled by anyone unfortunate enough to sit through this film in a theater.

## THE LAST PORNO FLICK (1974)

**Directed by Ray Marsh**
**Starring Frank Cagnini, Michael Pataki, Robyn Hilton, Mike Kelin and Jo Anne Meredith**

Linda Lovelace is only here in spirit, but that spirit is unmistakable.

A sleazy director gives Noo Yawk cab driver Tony (Frank Cagnini) a film script as collateral while he runs off to get change of a hundred-dollar bill for a $10 fare. When the not-only-sleazy but also broke director skips out on the fare, the hack drives off with the script, which is for a movie called *Temptations of Cynthia.*

And get this: It's a fuggin' paw-no!

After Tony cons investment money from his taxi company boss Mr. Balinkoff and his mother-in-law and her friends, filming on *Temptations of Cynthia* begins. Enter big-titted, gum-chewing starlet Linda Loveman, played to dubble-bubbled, bimbotic perfection by the extremely sexy Robyn Hilton. One great scene finds her mind wandering a little too far during a conversation, a glassy-eyed stare overtaking her with a beautiful subtlety that is very, very funny. Later on after Loveman is brought on set, she finds herself under the wing of Mr. Balinkoff (more a caricature of the foppish David Winters than Chuck Traynor), and almost immediately pushes back against doing another porn film by whining, "I'm a serious actress. . . ."

Of course, Loveman winds up doing the flick, and the crew's reaction shots to her sex scenes show her to be a sexual dynamo. One clip re-creates the "I got Blue Cross!" scene from *Deep Throat* word for word.

Personally I love *The Last Porno Flick*, even though it plays like a so-so episode of *The Odd Couple* and owes more than a little to Terry Southern's hilarious book *Blue Movie*. It's not a bad movie for a bad movie, but it's a lot more fun to watch if you're in on the joke. Which is a lot funnier because the movie's executive producer is Joseph Peraino—yes, of the Brooklyn Perainos.

She does
for politics
what she did
for sex.

**LINDA
LOVELACE
FOR
PRESIDEN**

Starring:
Linda Lovelace
and a cast
of thousands.

A GENERAL FILM CORPORATION RELEASE

## LINDA LOVELACE FOR PRESIDENT (1975)

**Directed by Claudio Guzman**

**Also features Micky Dolenz, Joey Forman, Roberta Kent, Scatman Crothers, Marty Ingels, Vaughn Meader, Joe E. Ross, Chuck McCann and Louis Quinn**

*Linda Lovelace for President* was meant to cash in on bankable celebrities reportedly approached to appear in or create it. Maybe Milos Forman was in pre-pro with *Cuckoo's Nest*; maybe Johnny Carson couldn't book a guest host, but they were nowhere to be found when the cameras started rolling in the great state of Kansas to capture Linda Lovelace's final film performance.

One-part calculated shocker, one-part bedroom (make that boardroom) farce and one-part *All in the Family*-type social satire, the film isn't offensive, it's trite—and these days completely politically incorrect. The jokes are an unsettling combination of predictable and embarrassing (when you can understand them at all), and the characters are all drawn with incredibly narrow strokes, their stereotyping meant to add to the film's satirical stance. You got yer mincing fag, yer jackbooted Kraut, yer fedora-wearing Wop and yer afroed, dashiki-clad spook, all of whom manage to come together to help guide the world's greatest cocksucker into the Oval Office. Less than 25 years later, American life would parallel if not quite imitate Lovelace's art, and the small-worldism involved with this film becomes too depressing to think about unless you're really jaded. Or a Republican.

Truth be told, *Linda Lovelace for President* is probably Linda Lovelace's "best film," basically because one of them has to be. People going to their local drive-in to catch this weren't going to see her give head (despite the film's occasional although undeserved X rating), but they did get to see her perform her lines better than in *Deep Throat*. She deserves some credit for that, not only because it would be hard for her not to act better than she had in *Deep Throat*, but because some of her lines in *President* are even more ridiculous. Linda's dialogue reaches its nadir in a scene where she leads a conga line of political delegates out of a meeting room to a chant that makes "Schlemiel! Schlimazel! Hasenpfeffer Incorporated!" seem like Lennon and McCartney.

The contrived comedy and bad acting don't make this a good film, but they don't necessarily make this a bad film, either. In fact *Linda Lovelace for President* is better than some other B-comedies from the same time that now enjoy cult status. Some scenes are actually pretty funny, in a so-bad-they're-good, cheesy '70s B-comedy kind of way. It's just too bad that not too many of those scenes feature Linda Lovelace. The film's best-developed joke comes in a scene when tall, stout comic Chuck McCann (in his second of two roles, this one an assassin) prepares to sneak into the German stereotype's birthday party so he can poison the Presidential hopeful. McCann drags the first redcap to cross his path—who must be five feet tall—behind a door, only to emerge seconds later in a perfectly fitting bellhop uniform. Then it's off to the party, where the assassin joins Linda Lovelace and her friends in a rousing version of "For He's a Jolly Good Nazi."

**BONUS CONTENT**

Listen to a *Linda Lovelace for President* radio ad by scanning this QR code or logging onto **bit.ly/LLQR12**

# RIPPED FROM THE HEADLINES

## PERVERTED STORIES 35 (2002)

**Directed by Jim Powers**

*Perverted Stories* was a vignette-based porn series in which often outrageous and sometimes topical stories are turned into truly grim fairy tales, kind of like *Fractured Fairy Tales* with plenty of fucking and no moral at the end. The vignette "Coma," produced about six weeks after Linda Lovelace's death following her removal from life support after three weeks in a coma, is tacky, tasteless and tailor-made for JM Productions fans (a brotherhood in which I certainly count myself).

Hospital intern Johnny Thrust checks in on comatose patient Alaura Eden while doing his rounds and sees on her chart that she's soon scheduled to be taken off life support. Noticing what a pretty girl she is and what a shame it is she's going to die such an ignoble death, Thrust decides to ease her pain the best way he knows: by pulling up her hospital gown, giving her a four finger handjob, eating her pussy, fucking her face and asshole and blowing his load into her slackjawed mouth. Then pulling the plug.

Alaura remains absolutely silent and completely motionless during the entire scene; as a result, Thrust has a hard time flipping her soon-to-be-dead weight onto her tummy so he can buttfuck her. Thrust also gets in some truly demented dialogue: when she flatlines, Thrust replaces her oxygen mask and whispers, "Don't die on me… I'm not a pervert. I don't like fucking dead girls." Later he asks, "Who's my favorite vegetable? Who's my favorite little broccoli? That's right, you are. You know what goes good with broccoli? Cucumber!" right before he sticks his dick in her.

Director Jim Powers went on to greater glory for his work on this disk, being named Best-Director (Non-Feature) at the 2003 Adult Video News Awards, while Thrust and Eden unfortunately had to settle for the respect of their peers.

## MIDNIGHT BLUE COLLECTION: THE DEEP THROAT SPECIAL EDITION (2005)

**Various Directors**

This early entry in the DVD release of episodes from Al Goldstein's legendary public-access cable TV show *Midnight Blue* compiles interviews done by Goldstein, Associate Producer Alex Bennett, and *Screw* Art Director Bruce David of the major players in *Deep Throat*: stars Harry Reems and Carol Connors; director Gerard Damiano; and Linda's husband, manager and *Deep Throat* Production Manager Chuck Traynor, who is grilled in two separate interviews. Linda is the only key figure missing.

In keeping with the legal history of *Deep Throat* and the theme of many episodes of *Midnight Blue*, the *Deep Throat Edition* starts off mentioning issues of censorship and the First Amendment as they relate to both Harry Reems' 1976 obscenity conviction and the nuts and bolts of getting *Midnight Blue* on the air. Broadcast from 1975 to 2003 on city government supplied cable space, each episode had to be pre-approved by Manhattan Cable TV [MCTV], who previewed the show for any possible obscenity violations and acted accordingly. It was a love/hate relationship that would continue for the show's entire run.

The hate part of that relationship is best documented in the DVD's opening segment. Bennett sets up a 1975 interview with Carol Connors by explaining that the segment was heavily censored by MCTV, apparently for no good reason (elements of the interview to which MCTV objected are juxtaposed with interviews from previous episodes of *Midnight Blue* that met no such resistance). After Carol describes the way she likes having her pussy eaten—tame, frankly, by *Midnight Blue* standards—the show cuts to British sex writer and Sex Maniac's Ball founder Tuppy Owens, who describes how she likes to go down on a cock. To truly drive the point home, Carol's laughably low-tech but still sexy striptease from a nurse's uniform is intercut with footage of Owens driving her previous point home—by sucking Bennett off, shot with Owens just out of frame.

During the interview clips that did make it to broadcast, Carol cheerfully submits to The Goldstein Probing ™, answering questions about her sex life with a smile and playing along when Al suggests she address the camera as if the home viewer was giving her head. Goldstein, of course, asks Connors why she was the only member of the *Deep Throat* cast who didn't become a superstar while Linda became a household word, an observation that history would prove to be not entirely accurate; that distinction should probably go to their co-star Dolly Sharp. Connors would achieve bigger and better in blue movies as star of the *Candy* franchise of porn flicks, a place in the history books as one of porn's first female directors and, perhaps most impressive to this writer, national mainstream exposure of a different kind as one of the hostesses of *The Gong Show*.

Goldstein asks Connors about her deep throat ability (she gives great head despite the fact that she can't do it, although she claims to have been teaching women the art of fellatio) and learns that when people on the *Deep Throat* set saw Linda do her thing, "They thought [deep throat] was an unusual gimmick. They joked around a lot, asking if she was a sword swallower, but that was just her way of sucking cock."

Of her experiences with Linda, Carol says that she and Linda didn't necessarily have the adversarial relationship Linda implies five years later in *Ordeal*; far from being alienated from her on the set of *Deep Throat*, Connors claims that she, Linda and Chuck furthered their personal and professional relationships.

"We were very good friends for a period after *Deep Throat*," Carol says. "As a matter of fact Lin and I made a stag film together. Chuck was into filmmaking and we got together one night, we all got high, we were all feeling very good and we put together a movie. We did everything. What the movie was about was that Linda and I seduced a young girl. We used a little bit of bondage in the film. I think it turned out very well, from what I've heard."

Goldstein avoids the L word in his 1975 interview with Gerard Damiano, who appears on the show to promote the release of *The Story of Joanna*, but he gets back on track while speaking with Chuck Traynor and Harry Reems.

Friends from the *Deep Throat* days, Goldstein and Reems catch up on the occasion of Reems' return to adult film in the flick *Society Affairs*. Reems comes across as well-spoken, sensitive and sincere—and slightly coked up—and he's typically forthcoming when they discuss changes in the business, the problem with having relationships as a porn cock (one of Goldstein's favorite topics) and of course, Reems' history with Linda.

Reems calls bullshit on *Ordeal*, which he wouldn't let Goldstein identify by name:

"I knew Linda for eight days (during *Deep Throat*)" he says, "and two days the year before. My only frame of reference of knowledge for Linda Lovelace and her relationship with Chuck Traynor was those eight days, and there was no sign of any brutality. She was not forced to do anything at any point. She was not beaten, there was never any make-up to cover her bruises. There was no make-up man! We had an $18,000 budget. We were lucky to have costumes! One need only to look at the film to see that the girl is having a terrific time. When Linda did *Deep Throat*, there was an innocence, a naivete, a sexual exuberance, a warmth, and a genuine electricity to the girl." Further, he challenges Goldstein, "Answer the question, 'Why is Linda Lovelace not there as a representative of Women Against Pornography?' Because her stories and her arguments, they're not credible!"

Reems then recalls his relationship with Linda beginning with the second doctor scene in *Deep Throat*, claiming it was shot a year before *Deep Throat* and inserted later—a story both Damiano and Lovelace would dispute later.

A 1987 interview conducted in a Circus Circus hotel room broaches the subject of Linda's claims in *Ordeal* to Chuck Traynor, who in typical fashion offers a self-effacing, non-denial denial in response. During his sign-off Goldstein thanks Traynor for being Traynor and writes Linda off in his own typical fashion for being "a dumb cunt."

## INSIDE DEEP THROAT (2005)

**Directed by Fenton Bailey and Randy Barbato**

Since reaching his executive excitement stage in 1996, Hollywood producer Brian Grazer's hard-on for bringing The Linda Lovelace Story to the big screen was teased by bad scripts, fluffed by loads of mainstream media publicity but left frustrated and unsatisfied by corporate cockblockage when funding just didn't come. But his cinematic chubber was finally brought to wide-screen, Technicolor tumescence when he acquired the services of filmmakers Fenton Bailey and Randy Barbato, directors of the documentaries *The Eyes of Tammy Faye* and *Monica in Black and White*, to help him rub one out with the so-provocative-you-could-taste-it title *Inside Deep Throat.*

(In the spirit of full disclosure, I submitted to a 90-minute interview for the film but didn't appear in the final product, even as a DVD extra. I can only figure but cannot prove that Bailey and Barbato's decision to leave my footage on the cutting room floor had less to do with my screen presence than the fact that I didn't talk shit about Linda during the sit-down and, perhaps more on the money, wouldn't loan the production—budgeted at $2 million—my entire, extensive, bordering-on-endless archive of Linda-related magazines, books, video and ephemera for free. I had offered one of the film's staffers full, unfettered access to the collection for a $5,000 stipend, which was declined. That turn of events in no way skews my keen editorial insight to the final product. Honest.)

That said, *Inside Deep Throat* is a good, not great documentary; it is, however, an excellent example of what I call a "talkumentary."

As defined by the Academy of Motion Picture Arts and Sciences, the governing body that hands out the Academy Awards, a documentary is "a theatrically released nonfiction motion picture dealing creatively with cultural, artistic, historical, social, scientific, economic or other subjects. It may be photographed in actual occurrence, or may employ partial re-enactment, stock footage, stills, animation, stop-motion or other techniques, as long as the emphasis is on fact and not on fiction."

In that case, sure, *Inside Deep Throat* is a documentary and certainly met all the criteria for its 2006 Academy Awards nomination. Which it lost.

In addition to the above criteria, a quality documentary should rely on some degree of investigative journalism, practiced either during the course of production or as a reflection of the source material on which the film is based, over and above corroborating interviews, to advance some semblance of a thesis. A successful documentary adds something to the discussion at hand—some new fact, some new revelation, some new opinion, some new something.

As defined by me, a "talkumentary," on the other hand, just gathers together a group of interview subjects and has them talk, if you will, about the topic at hand. Examples of excellent documentaries include most anything by Ken Burns or a film like Michael Moore's *Sicko*. Examples of excellent talkumentaries: *Edgeplay: A Film About the Runaways; God Bless Ozzy Osbourne*; and, well, *Inside Deep Throat*.

*Inside Deep Throat* accomplishes little other than getting the same people to answer the same questions the same way they have for, in some cases, 40 years. As such, it's difficult to ascertain what *IDT* proves: That *Deep Throat* changed America's attitudes towards sex in general and oral sex in particular? That the government made a concerted effort to clamp down on the film after its initial popularity, after Congress' decision that the 1970 President's Commission on Pornography Report, which found no causal relationship between fucking on film and violent crime, was incorrect? That appearances in *Deep Throat* had sometimes serious consequences for its cast and crew? That *Deep Throat* was... funded by the Mob... who made 600 million billion dollars from it?

Some talking heads are there for good reason, others less so. Interviews with Gerard Damiano, Harry Reems and Larry Parrish provide good insight to the film's creation and legacy, thoughtfully examined and placed in its proper chronological, cultural and creative contexts. Some talking heads, however, seem included solely for their "hep appeal." John Waters' outlaw filmmaker credentials are beyond question, having rightly positioned himself as Grande Dame of Alternative Cinema at roughly the same time *Deep Throat* was released. Hef was there, to be sure, as were Norman Mailer, Erica Jong, Helen Gurley Brown, and Andrea True.

But what does comedian Bill Maher contribute aside from pointing out that many major American corporations, including not a few hotel chains, make a nice but largely under-the-radar living off porn—and cracking wise about how that's good for the hotels but bad for the chambermaids? (His own fiduciary connection with HBO might give a clue to his inclusion.) What does Dick Cavett contribute at all, considering he starts things off by mentioning that he's never even seen the film?

*Inside Deep Throat*'s strong points rest in the archival footage documenting the ensuing obscenity cases and its interviews with *Deep Throat* tech crew members like the charmingly irascible set designer Lenny Camp; film distributors; the FBI agents, prosecutors and defense attorneys who fought on both sides of the issue during those obscenity trials; and the opportunity to include the truly awesome clip of Linda Lovelace performing the stunt that made the whole project possible.

According to imdb.com, *Inside Deep Throat*—made on an estimated budget of $2 million, the standard price tag for an HBO documentary—grossed just over $650,000 in its first two months of release, opening on 12 screens on February 13, 2005, reaching a high of 27 screens the next week and falling to 9 screens the weekend of April 17 that same year. It presumably made its seed money back (and more) with DVD sales and rentals.

# Chapter 4:
# THAT'S ALL SHE WROTE
## A Deep Throat Speaks Volumes

**Dozens of writers have spilled gallons of ink in honor of Linda Lovelace, and they haven't all been pornographers, either. Scattered among the cheap porn novels and the cheesy porn biographies are serious think pieces about feminism and popular culture and entertainment and obscenity law. And then there are a few more cheesy porn biographies thrown in for good measure.**

# REQUIRED READING

## *Inside Linda Lovelace*

**Linda Lovelace**
**(Pinnacle Books, 1973)**

The first of Lovelace's four autobiographies, *Inside Linda Lovelace* is one of the most tawdry, exploitative and sensational celebrity bios ever to appear in bookstores—even more so than Lovelace's later chart-topper *Ordeal*. As Lovelace recounts in that book through coauthor Mike McGrady, *Inside Linda Lovelace* should have been titled *Inside Chuck Traynor*, since it was he and not she who actually wrote it, contributing a series of sexual experiences and sexual fantasies that, like some of the episodes recounted in *Ordeal*, become progressively more bizarre.

Thanks in no small part to America's changing erotic landscape and the underlying reason that the book was written—a dose of fantasy, titillation and innuendo in exchange for the consumer's dollar—*Inside Linda Lovelace* is an amazing example of literary pornography. "I come at least 50 times a day," Lovelace claims at one point, going on to describe a huge list of sexual and social episodes in which she's indulged, almost all of them breaking one sexual or social taboo or another. From her first kiss (with a girl) to a pedophilic grope session committed by a friend's father during a camping trip (which of course was fine with the hypersexual starlet), Linda has done it all, seen it all and will continue to do it all until she can't do any of it anymore.

The only sexual thrill Linda denies involvement with in *Inside Linda Lovelace* is bestiality. While claiming to have watched a pair of husband and wife friends fuck a poodle and Great Dane respectively, Linda writes that while she's never indulged in the act, the thought arouses her:

> "I have to be honest with you [that] the action was exciting in a voyeur's way. The very disgust of it turned me on. But I wasn't in on the act, nor do I think I ever could be, even when I'm 90 and a dog is all I can get. But my reaction was to go home and fuck my man, and later, in the bathtub, if the memory popped up, I might stick a Prell shampoo bottle in my pussy and masturbate with the thought of it."

Needless to say, *Inside Linda Lovelace* is almost wholly bullshit as far as Lovelace herself is concerned, sprinkled with the odd amount of truth and seemingly written almost as much for legal cover as anything else. Lovelace tells the "real" story behind the *Dog Fucker* still printed in *Screw*, while revealing the real story behind the real story: that *Screw* publisher Al Goldstein wanted Linda to star in his own film, *It Happened in Hollywood*, and became incensed when she refused. (Harry Reems took the lead role in the film and stayed in Goldstein's good graces.)

There's a healthy amount of nose-thumbing in the book, not only at Goldstein but also at the likes of photographer/director Bunny Yeager (the famous Bettie

HER EXCLUSIVE, INTIMATE STORY!

523-00240 ★ $1.75

FOR THE FIRST TIME IN PAPERBACK
CENTERFOLD PHOTO IN FULL COLOR

INSIDE
LINDA
LOVELACE

BY LINDA LOVELACE
STAR OF DEEP THROAT

..."Linda is the new sex goddess of the 70s!"
—Hugh Hefner, *Playboy*

523-240394-7★$1.75

# The Intimate Diary of Linda Lovelace

Page photographer who was a friend of Traynor's and had shot Linda a few times). But in the end, *Inside Linda Lovelace* is exactly what you'd imagine it to be: a commercial literary device meant to exploit the popularity of a notorious film star that will occupy space on the discerning pervert's book shelf somewhere between *Lolita* and *Teenage Farm Girl Sex Slaves*.

As part of her promotional tour, the author hyped *Inside Linda Lovelace* with a personal appearance at the American Booksellers Association convention in Los Angeles, where she hobnobbed with the likes of Rosey Grier and pitcher Bo Belinsky and was late for her own autograph session. One appointment Linda did honor was a panel discussion that included an exchange between herself and none other than Henry Miller—who called pornography "sly" and admitted he liked "obscenity" because it was more "forthright," adding that "pornography is killing sex."

Linda disagreed with Miller and told him, "Sex was already dead and films like *Deep Throat* are bringing it back to life." (Any ABA member or Miller collector with a tape of this meeting of the minds must contact the offices of Power Process Publishing immediately.)

## *The Intimate Diary of Linda Lovelace*

**Linda Lovelace**
**(Pinnacle Books, 1974)**

Despite being a similarly titillating exercise in fictional and fantastical fucking, *The Intimate Diary of Linda Lovelace* is decidedly more accusatory in tone. By this time Linda's ex had gone from being referred to in print as "Chuck Traynor, the Creator" to "Chuck the Shmuck" (he's never referred to by his whole name in the American edition, but the British version does identify him completely).

Still and all, *IDOLL* is like *ILL* in its description of the prowess and endowment of her boyfriends. Describing her deflowering by Traynor in *ILL*, Lovelace states:

> "I automatically pushed him back when his big cock started pushing into me, and I may have tried to sneak out and run away. The fat rocklike muscle tore into me, and I nearly fainted from the shock. It hurt. The explosive pain shot from my groin over every inch of my body. But it wasn't that bad. In fact, at the same time I yelped in pain, I was already pressing my pussy up instead of away. I came in seconds and the rockets were all on time."

In *IDOLL* she says the consummation of her affair with David Winters took place after begging him to fuck her in a hospital while being treated for facial pain:

> "With a tremendous thrust, he put that surging, gorgeous cock inside me. A pulsing jackhammer that kept driving, driving, driving, plowing into me, over and over. I could feel some pain where the doctor worked on me, but I didn't care. I was past it; I was flying in another world. At the top of a high, high mountain the two of us came together in a giant explosion, the supreme moment of my entire life. My cunt was awash with his come, and I loved it."

Like *Ordeal*, *IDOLL* drops its fair share of names, some explicitly and some cryptically. Ann-Margret and Elvis Presley and Harry Nilsson and John Lennon appear with others referred to as Mr. Dynamite (Sammy Davis Jr.) and the King of Sex (Hugh Hefner).

*IDOLL* ends on a not-too-surprisingly commercial note. The final chapter "Wrong Number" tells the story of a randy, piggish telephone repairman who expects sexual service in return for his mechanical ones with vague allusions to how Linda would change the world if she were President. To that end, the book includes a final page that readers could mail back to Pinnacle Books to show their support for Linda in the upcoming election. The reverse of the book's centerfold noted that "When you say 'Linda Lovelace for President,' you've said a mouthful."

## *Ordeal*

**Linda Lovelace**
**with Mike McGrady**
**(Citadel Press, 1980)**

Ordeal is without a doubt the best-known and most controversial of Linda Lovelace's four autobiographies. Unfortunately, if there's little new and insightful to say about *Deep Throat*, there's even less of note to say about *Ordeal*, except maybe that it's gone on to become one of the most discussed, debated and deconstructed pop-culture autobiographies ever published—and it earned that achievement in spades.

One of the most sensational aspects of *Ordeal* is "The Inquisition," the marathon lie-detector test demanded by publisher Lyle Stuart before he would release the book. We all know that (the former) Linda Lovelace took the test—and presumably passed it—but not everyone knows the questions:

**From:** Nat Laurendi
**To:** Curto, Meservey, Armstrong, Waller & Smyth
Attorneys at Law

**Subject:** Polygraph Examination of Linda Lovelace

During September 26, 1979, writer was contacted by Mr. Jeff Waller of the above firm, relative to giving a polygraph (Lie Detection) examination to Linda Lovelace in connection with her forthcoming book.

Writer was later contacted by Mr. Curto of the above firm about scheduling and to discuss the areas of inquiry on the polygraph with Mr. Mike McGrady, the author of the book *Ordeal*.

THE BESTSELLING TRUE STORY
EVERY WOMAN IN AMERICA
WILL WANT TO READ!

LINDA LOVELACE

WITH MIKE McGRADY

Ordeal

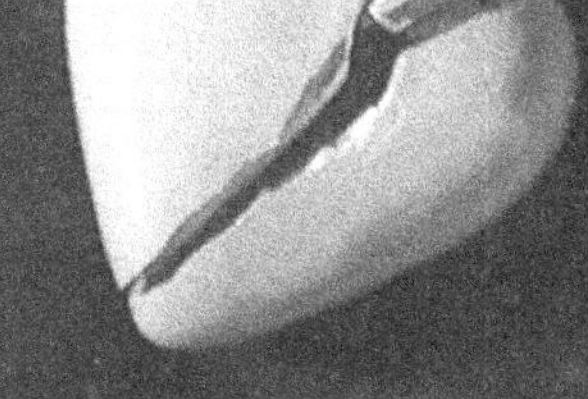

"It happened to me. It could
happen to any woman..."

Subsequently, Mr. Mike McGrady came to this office and supplied writer with galleys of a book entitled *Ordeal* published by Citadel Press.

In addition to the galleys, Mr. McGrady supplied writer with a list of 114 questions regarding the subject matter in the book. There were additional questions to be asked by the publisher.

Writer and Mr. McGrady discussed the general area and background of critical questions to be asked during the polygraph test. Writer read the galleys and reviewed the questions supplied.

On Friday, October 26, 1979, Linda Lovelace came to this office for a polygraph examination with Mr. Victor J. Yannacone Jr., Attorney of Yannacone & Yannacone P.C.

Before the examination Linda Lovelace signed two copies of a form stating she was taking the test voluntarily. The examination commenced at 3:07 P.M. and terminated at 4:44 P.M. Mr. McGrady and Mr. Yannacone were outside the polygraph examination room during the administration of the test.

A 4-pen stoelting 22695 desk model polygraph was used. The mixed control question type procedure was utilized including a numerical stimulation and a "silent answer test."

**PRE-POLYGRAPH TEST INTERVIEW**

During the pre-polygraph test interview Subject stated she was born January 10, 1949, in the Bronx.

Linda Lovelace gave background information about herself and her previous lifestyle. She is presently married and has one son.

**PHASE 1**

The following pertinent test questions were asked while Subject was attached to the polygraph during this phase.

**POLYGRAPH TEST**

**QUESTION/ ANSWER:**

4. Did the thing[s] you described in *Ordeal* really happen to you? YES.
6. Did you see Sammy Davis Jr. go down on Chuck Traynor? YES.
8. Were you forced by Chuck Traynor to have sex with five guys in Coral Gables in 1971? YES.
10. Did you go down on Lou Peraino in his office in New York? YES.
12. Did you ever have sex games with Phillip J. Mandina in Florida? YES.

**Analysis and Comments:**

There were no emotional reactions indicative of deception to the above pertinent test questions and it is my professional OPINION that Subject's answers to the above questions were truthful.

**PHASE II**

On Saturday, October 27, 1979, Linda Lovelace returned to this office for a continuation of the polygraph examination.

Before the examination Linda Lovelace signed two copies of a form again stating that she was taking the test voluntarily. The examination commenced at 1 P.M. and concluded at 3:50 P.M.

During this phase other areas of her life were discussed with Linda Lovelace and the following critical questions were asked while Subject was attached to the polygraph.

**POLYGRAPH TEST**

**QUESTION/ANSWER:**

4. To your knowledge, did Dr. Gross of Miami insert silicone into your breasts? YES.
6. Did Arthur Marks tell you at one time to get ready for the "fucking and sucking" scenes? YES.
8. Did Bob Phillips lie during the trial of Chuck and Bob Inglesby in Florida? YES.
10. Is it a fact that during your time with Chuck Traynor you feared for your life if you tried to get away? YES.

**Analysis and Comments:**

There were no emotional reactions indicative of deception to the above pertinent test questions and it is my professional OPINION that Subject's answers to the above questions were truthful.

**PHASE III**

During the pre-test interview and while in the process of formulating the questions to be asked on the polygraph for this phase, Subject broke down and cried.

After a rest period the interview continued and the activities of Linda were discussed. After regaining her composure the following pertinent test questions were asked while she was attached to the polygraph.

**POLYGRAPH TEST**

**Question:**

4. Did Bob Wolfe direct you in a movie where you had sex with a dog?
6. Did Hugh Hefner want to see you have sex with Chuck's dog named "Rufus"?
8. Did you tell the truth about the two dogs?

**Analysis and Comments:**

This was a Silent Answer Test where Subject was instructed to answer to herself. There were no emotional reactions indicative of deception to questions #6 and #8.

When Subject was asked during the first run of the Silent Answer Test #4 "Did Bob Wolfe direct you in a movie where you had sex with a dog?" there were highly emotional reactions following that question, specifically a blood pressure rise, sweat gland activity and in the breathing patterns.

During the asking of that question (#4) with verbal response by Lovelace a second time, there were strong reactions in both pneumographic reading tracings and a violent and dramatic blood pressure rise to that question. Subject was crying and holding back tears.

It is my professional OPINION that Subject was answering truthful to questions #6 and #8. Because of the violent and dramatic reaction to question #4 which was followed by Subject crying, no opinion could be given.

However, writer is convinced that Subject was not attempting deception. Since she broke down and cried writer did not deem it proper or wise to re-examine her further on the polygraph. This phase terminated at 2:30 P.M.

**INTERROGATION PHASE**

After a short rest period the interview continued without Lovelace being attached to the polygraph. This time the questions supplied by Mike McGrady and the publisher were reviewed. All the questions outlined in that question sheet were asked of Linda Lovelace.

The only area where Subject had any problem was with a question which dealt with whether or not Chuck Traynor ever had sex, oral or otherwise, with Altovise Davis. Subject stated she wasn't sure since she did not see them.

During this phase of the questioning Subject again broke down and cried and after a short rest period the interrogation recommenced.

**Analysis and Comments**

Based upon the information supplied, the galleys of *Ordeal* with Mike McGrady, Citadel Press, Secaucus, N.J., the pre-polygraph test interviews prior to each phase of the test, the analysis of the emotional reactions on the polygraph to the above critical questions and post-test conversation and interrogation of Subject, it is my professional OPINION that Subject's answers to the above critical questions were truthful.

The question "Did Bob Wolfe direct you in a movie where you had sex with a dog?" aroused violent and dramatic reactions. Therefore no opinion could be given and writer did not desire to put her through another ordeal.

Respectfully submitted,
Nat Laurendi
Polygraphist

Following is the complete list of questions Linda Lovelace was asked before the publication of *Ordeal.*

1. Did your mother beat you when you were a child?
2. Did your mother hit you with a broomstick?
3. Did you ask your mother what "fuck" meant and did you get hit for asking?
4. Were you known as a straight-arrow during your school days?
5. Did you always have great respect for the institution of marriage?
6. Did your father ever come home drunk?
7. Did your mother ever go after him with a butcher knife in her hand?
8. When you were in Florida after your accident, would your mother hit you if you came home late?
9. Did Chuck Traynor run a house of prostitution, a string of prostitutes?
10. The first night with Chuck Traynor, did he not have a full erection?
11. That same night, did he ask you to suck him?
12. Did Chuck Traynor hypnotize you?
13. Did the barmaids at Chuck's bar go topless?
14. Did you see the barmaids in an orgy?
15. Did Chuck Traynor urge you to help run a prostitution business?
16. When you refused to do this, did Chuck hit you?
17. Did beating you seem to excite Chuck sexually?
18. Did Chuck tell you to stop talking to your mother?
19. Did Chuck Traynor have a .45 caliber pistol?
20. Did Chuck have a semiautomatic machine gun?
21. When Chuck took you to the Holiday Inn, did he have five men waiting to have sex with you?
22. Did Chuck force you to have sex with them? Did you have sex with them of your own free will?
23. Did Chuck point a gun at you and threaten to kill you if you didn't have sex with them?
24. Was the Holiday Inn scene true as you described it?
25. Did Chuck then make you have sex with men for money?
26. Did he beat you from time to time?
27. Did Chuck keep the money that you made? Did you keep a percentage of the money you earned as a hooker?
28. Did Chuck give you the least-attractive customers?
29. Did Chuck bring you to a pornographic photographer named Leonard Campagno, or Lenny Camp?
30. Did this photographer take pictures of you with another naked model?
31. Did he take pictures of you with a dildo?

32. Did you enjoy working as a hooker? Did you experience orgasm while working as a hooker?
33. Did Chuck teach you how to relax your throat muscles?
34. Did Phil Mandina know who "Mister X" was? Did he speak with "Mister X" about the trial?
35. During one of your escape attempts, did another hooker turn you over to Chuck?
36. Did Chuck invent the story about the sky-diving club? Did Mandina know it was a lie?
37. Did Bob Phillips perjure himself at the trial?
38. Did you pay for Chuck's defense? Did Mandina get to handle your case in New York?
39. Did you want to marry Chuck Traynor? Did Chuck marry you so that you couldn't testify against him?
40. Did you say no, you wouldn't marry him?
41. Did he beat you the night before you were married?
42. Did you call your parents immediately after the wedding ceremony?
43. Did you have sex with Chuck's cousin's husband while Chuck was working with Sheetrock?
44. Did your sister Jean see the pictures of you and Cricket?
45. Did your mother permit Chuck to come over to the house when you were trying to escape?
46. Did Chuck threaten to shoot your sister's son if you wouldn't go back with him?
47. When you were out with others, would Chuck tell you not to speak?
48. Did you have to ask Chuck's permission to go to the bathroom?
49. Did Chuck and Mandina brag about their hypnotizing prowess?
50. Did Chuck give you a posthypnotic suggestion to undress and have sex with Mandina's girlfriend, Barbara?
51. Did Barbara say that Phil Mandina wanted her to deep-throat him?
52. Did Chuck and Mandina have a contest to see who could bring a woman to orgasm first?
53. Did you and Barbara have a similar contest with the two men?
54. Did you have oral sex with Phil Mandina?
55. Did Chuck ever ask you to put cinnamon candies in your vagina while you were driving?
56. Did Chuck ask you to proposition salesmen in stores?
57. Did Chuck threaten you by saying you were going to have sex with donkeys in Juarez?
58. Did you have a job interview with Xaviera Hollander?
59. Did Bob Wolfe direct you in a movie where the actors urinated on each other?
60. Did Bob Wolfe direct you in a movie where you had sex with a dog?

61. Did you say that you would not have sex with a dog?
62. Did Chuck threaten to kill you if you didn't make the movie?
63. Did you see a gun on the set of the dog movie?
64. Did you make 8mm pornographic movies with Gerard Damiano?
65. Did Harry Reems want to arrange pornographic film work for you?
66. Was your total pay for *Deep Throat* $1200? Did Chuck keep the money?
67. Did Chuck tell you to have sex with Lou Peraino?
68. Did you perform oral sex on Lou Peraino several times?
69. After the first day of filming *Deep Throat* did Chuck beat you viciously?
70. Did the movie crew members hear the beating? Did you cry out for help?
71. Did Gerard Damiano notice the bruises?
72. Would Chuck ask hitchhikers if they wanted to be hookers?
73. Did Chuck's mother say she had been friendly with mobsters? Did she call herself a "flower lady"? Did she say her store was a "front"?
74. When you escaped to Patsy's house, did Chuck threaten to kill you?
75. Did Chuck sometimes make you expose yourself in restaurants? In cars?
76. Did Chuck ever insert a garden hose in your rectum and turn on the water?
77. Did Chuck force you to greet your parents while you were naked?
78. Did Michelle poke you with a hot hair dryer?
79. Did Michelle insert a dildo into your rectum?
80. Did Michelle seem to lose control of herself?
81. Did the Florida proctologist treat you in exchange for sexual favors?
82. Did a Doctor Gross illegally insert silicone into your breasts?
83. Did Chuck bring home a dog named "Rufus"?
84. Before your interviews, did Chuck tell you what answers you should give?
85. Did Chuck offer Al Goldstein oral sex from you?
86. Did Hugh Hefner say he liked the movie you made with a dog?
87. Did Hefner tell Chuck that he had many animal movies?
88. Did Hefner have Rufus shipped in from Florida and did he then put the dog into his own kennels?
89. Did Shel Silverstein discuss making a country-and-western album with you?
90. In *Deep Throat Part II*, did you perform oral sex for the cameras?
91. Were you and Chuck and Andrea True involved in sexual acts together?
92. Did Andrea True introduce you to a top executive at Pinnacle Books? Did Andrea True say that this was one of her clients?

93. Did Hugh Hefner urge you to have sex with a girl named Lila at an orgy?
94. Did Hefner want to see you have sex with the dog named Rufus? Was he there when this was attempted?
95. Did Sammy Davis Jr. tell you that he considered sexual intercourse to be infidelity, but oral sex to be okay?
96. Did Chuck have sex with Altovise?
97. Did Sammy Davis Jr. talk about tying you down to a bed?
98. Did you and Altovise have sex while Chuck and Sammy watched?
99. Did Sammy ever express interest in marrying you?
100. Did you see Sammy Davis Jr. commit an act of oral sex on Chuck Traynor?
101. Did Buck Henry and Milos Forman ever discuss making a movie with you?
102. Did Chuck hit you when you were rehearsing for your stage act?
103. When you escaped from Chuck, did he come looking for you with a gun?
104. Did David Winters tell you he was millions of dollars in debt?
105. When you first wrote *The Intimate Diary of Linda Lovelace* with Mel Mandel, did the publisher complain about the lack of sex?
106. Did David Winters say you should tell a little bit of the truth now and the full story later on?

## *Out of Bondage*
### Linda Lovelace with Mike McGrady (Lyle Stuart Books, 1986)

If there's nothing new to say about *Ordeal* (and there's really not), then there's nothing even vaguely interesting to say about *Out of Bondage*. The book was essentially a contractual obligation, and that's exactly how it reads. Not that I'm not fascinated by every little thing Linda Lovelace does, but I'm not fascinated about what her and Larry's lives were like after *Ordeal* became a big hit—and if it sounds like I'm just about completely dismissing this book, I am. Pick up *Out of Bondage* only if you really need to read every last word about Linda Lovelace—otherwise stick with *Ordeal*.

**BONUS CONTENT**

Hear Lyle Stuart speak about Linda by scanning this QR code or logging onto **bit.ly./LLQR14**

"DON'T BELIEVE IT WHEN THEY TELL YOU PORNOGRAPHY IS A 'VICTIMLESS CRIME.' I WAS ONE OF ITS VICTIMS. I'M NOT ANY MORE..."

THE INCREDIBLE TRUE STORY CONTINUES... BY THE *NEW YORK TIMES* BESTSELLING AUTHORS OF *ORDEAL*

LINDA LOVELACE

WITH MIKE McGRADY

Out of Bondage

INTRODUCTION BY
GLORIA STEINEM

# MOVIE TIE-INS

## *Deep Throat*
## *Deep Throat Part II*
**D. M. Perkins**
**(Dell Books, 1973; 1974)**

The task of writing the novelizations for the two *Deep Throat* films fell to one man: D. M. Perkins, known to poetry fans as Michael Perkins, author of poetry books including *The Persistence of Desire* and *Praise in the Ears of Clouds*. He's also known to inky-fingered degenerates and spittle-chinned mouth-readers as the author of the "Fuckbooks" review column for *Screw* magazine, a position he held for more years than I'm sure he'd like to admit.

There's a reason why Perkins was tagged to do the job: He's a goddamn good writer. I can just see him writing these two books, hunched over a battered old Royal typewriter; his face, a combination of Errol Flynn and Clark Gable, bathed in the light of an old standing lamp; an ever-growing mountain of ribbon reels stacked in the corner as he considered how best to face the challenge of bringing the world's most notorious movie to those poor unfortunates who would never get a chance to see it. (I edited him for years at *Screw*, so believe me on this one. And he still does write on a manual typewriter.)

It was a challenge he definitely rose up to. As stated earlier, *Screw* takes great pride in its writers and doesn't hire hacks (I wrote for *Screw* for years, too, so believe me on that one as well), so the unenviable task of turning a 62-minute film into a 190-page novel was well assigned. His opening paragraph has echoes of Nabokov's *Lolita*:

> "Picture Linda Lovelace: just the sound of her name, Love-lace. Love. Lace. Panties. Close your eyes and hear her name; roll it around on your tongue, savoring it. Linda. In Spanish, beautiful. And love? A special kind of sweetness mixed with heat."

While he follows the film's plots he also embellishes, and in a way makes it something new with the creation of characters like "Case Number 666, Marco Polo, alias Nathan Vaseline, writer of erotic poetry," who I assume is based on writer Marco Vassi, a member of the '70s cliterati and Perkins' contemporary. Perkins puts serious thought into all his work and is more than capable of giving a little class to even the sleaziest project.

## *Linda Lovelace for President*

**John S. Margolis**
**(Playboy Press, 1975)**

If the movie was barely good, you can't expect the book to be any better. And this novelization lives up to those expectations.

Margolis, author of the wonderful book *A Child's Garden of Grass*, adapted this from his own screenplay, and in many ways it reads like a movie—not like a script, but like a movie. Some of the scenes from the film are recreated here, a few written in black-out style, but none come off as funny as anything that appears in the film. Which is kind of a shame. Really.

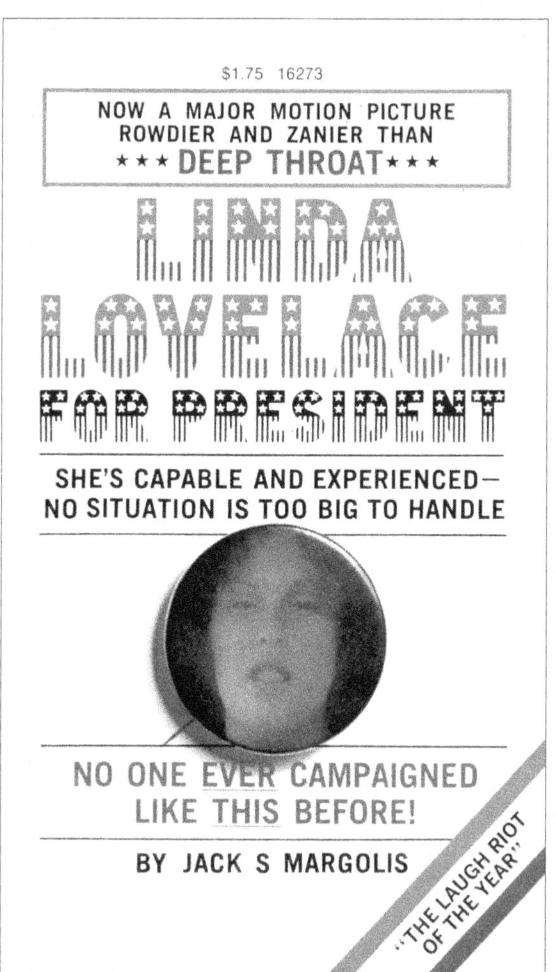

# REQUIRED READING

## *Contemporary Erotic Cinema*
**William Rotsler**
**(Penthouse/Ballantine, 1973)**

This otherwise excellent early look at X-rated film pays only minor attention to Linda and *Deep Throat*, although it's obvious from that attention that Rotsler truly enjoyed the film and Linda's presence in it. Far from going overboard about *Deep Throat*'s technical wizardry, which always has been debatable, he honestly states that the film is of average technical appeal ("The photography was shaky, the direction sloppy and there were technical errors galore"); the starlets are not beautiful but of "at least acceptably attractive" appearance; and while not always funny the film was often "amusing." In Rotsler's view, only the film's impact on American sexual mores, filmgoing habits and artistic boundaries is extraordinary. He does seem justifiably taken with its starlet. "One of the things I liked best about the film was Linda's obvious delight in what she was doing," he writes. "It was infectious and made the entire film more palatable." Pun intended, no doubt.

## *The Deep Throat Papers*
**Introduction by Pete Hamill**
**(Manor Books, 1973)**

Like *Getting Into Deep Throat* (see below), this is a collection of articles about the furor and phenomenon behind the film, its stars and especially the New York *Deep Throat* trial. Although much of the book originally appeared in *Bachelor* magazine, the publishers make the extra effort of securing rights to Hamill's introduction, "Hix Nix Skin Flix," reprinted from the September 4, 1972, issue of *New York* magazine. That piece offers the journalist's take on his experiences seeing the film as well as his perspective of the furor caused by its prosecution (the film had only just been busted when the article first appeared).

Two articles—Peter Wolff's "The Movie That Swallowed Manhattan" and "(French) Culture Shock" by Greg Jackson—put the film into the proper legal and artistic perspective (as if people trying to sell a book about the film would slam it), making niceties about Linda, her looks and her considerable oral talents. Linda speaks for herself as Diana Helfrecht's oft-reprinted interview is reprinted here again, along with a few photographs taken by Traynor and another picture of Linda taken early in her history by Bunny Yeager.

Other chapters include: "*Throat*'s Nibbling Nurse," a sit-down with Carol Connors (identified as Carol Kyzer) and her boyfriend Jack Birch, who appears in the *Deep Throat* orgy scene as Number 11; "About *Deep Throat*," the obligatory retelling of the plot complete with "photographs of explicit sex acts" straight from the film (some shot directly off a movie screen); and excerpts from the *Deep Throat* trial, along with Judge Tyler's unexpurgated trial decision.

## *Getting Into Deep Throat*

**Richard Smith**
**(Berkley Medallion Books, 1973)**

Despite the appearance of a seductive, finger-lickin' Linda on the cover (in a photo from her first *Playboy* sitting) and an opening chapter titled "Linda Lovelace: The Blue-ing of America," *Getting Into Deep Throat* doesn't delve as much into Linda or the film as the media circus surrounding them. An interesting compilation of news, opinion and speculation concerning Linda and *Deep Throat*, the chapter uses Linda more as a springboard to wax philosophic about the film than impart any new information about its star. A lengthy section from the *Screw* interview is reprinted, as are several quotes from Nora Ephron's *Esquire* article, which was later included in her book *Crazy Salad*. Included also are in-depth interviews with Goldstein, Damiano and Reems, leading one to assume that Linda was not made available to the author.

Intentionally or not, the chapter also shows just how sad the porn consumer could be before the Sexual Revolution really took hold and people were more able to get in touch with their carnal instincts. Smith talks with one porn consumer, a raincoater who, when asked about the educational value of smut, says, "It really is educational. I saw one film about 15 minutes long, where you actually could see a vagina covering the whole screen and throbbing, with fluid running. You know for sure that she is coming, the same way you know a man is coming when you see the sperm moving out. Where else could you see a vagina 20 feet high, and learn how it works and looks?"

## *Blue Money: Pornography and the Pornographers*
### Carolyn See
### (David McKay Company, Inc., 1974)

See's brutally frank account of her sentence as ghostwriter for Lovelace's ill-fated *Oui* magazine advice column spills as many beans about professional sex journalism as about its most famous subject. She recounts Traynor's Florida youth as crop-duster assistant and his fabled three-year stint in the Marines before the short leap to pilot, photographer and, of course, pornographer (when the newly legal crotch-shot market opened wide, Traynor jumped right in).

See kicks off with the story of Linda's ghostwriter and the utter hell-trip that is conceptualizing a general-interest magazine column, not to mention an adult one. It's not necessarily unpleasant, but just like any job, sometimes it's not necessarily fun. Sounds like things haven't changed too much in the past four decades.

See eventually explores every possible dynamic of the Lovelace/Traynor relationship, except the possibility that it might actually be against Linda's will. Using various first-person voices in the form of party guests, See depicts Linda and Chuck as either a couple of freaky, stoned-out hippies who have fun (and make profit) with their sexuality, or a pair of pathetic, stoned-out hippies engaged not so much in acts of sexual revolution as in acts of mutual exploitation. Putting herself back in the third person, See hopes against hope that the pair really are in love. No conclusion is given one way or the other.

Incisive, honest and informative, this is probably the best thing ever written about Linda Lovelace. Aside from what you're reading now.

## *Crazy Salad: Some Things About Women*
### Nora Ephron
### (Bantam Books, 1975)

This collection of Ephron's columns about women includes her musings on her own burgeoning womanhood (and blossoming breasts); the feminine-hygiene-spray industry; the divorce of Maryland governor Marvin Mandel and his wife Barbara; and her interview with porn star Linda Lovelace. Originally appearing in the February 1973 issue of *Esquire*, the article "Deep Throat" is one of the best-known (feminist) tracts about the film, detailing her trip to see it with a few male friends.

She didn't enjoy the experience. After a slightly disingenuous comment about her expertise in watching porn ("I've seen a lot of stag films in my life—well, that's not true; I've seen four or five . . .") she assails *Deep Throat* for not being of the "sweet and innocent and actually erotic" variety. In one of the best-remembered quotes from the piece, she writes, "*Deep Throat* is one of the most unpleasant, disturbing films I have ever seen—it is not just anti-female but anti-sexual as well. . . . Give me the goriest Peckinpah any day."

Ephron apparently didn't like Linda Lovelace any better after she spoke with her, taking several opportunities to make fun of her youthful expressions, such as her penchant for describing things as "sort of a goof." Which is all well and good, because Linda eventually bests her during the interview section, giving great quotes for Ephron to work with. (When asked the difference between *Deep Throat Part II* and mainstream commercial films, Linda says, "To me, [*DTPII*] is just a movie, like all other movies. Only it has some much better things in it." Like what, Ephron asks? "Like me," is Linda's reply.) It's a shame this is all Ephron could do with them.

## *Outrageous Acts and Everyday Rebellions*

**Gloria Steinem**

**(Plume Books, 1983)**

Steinem, a writer of exceptional force and conviction and no little ability to persuade her reader, tackles Linda's claims in *Ordeal* in this, perhaps the most famous feminist tract written about Linda Lovelace. But just as the Drs. Kronhausen took everything in *Inside Linda Lovelace* on blind faith, so does Steinem accept as gospel everything Lovelace has written in *Ordeal*, both examples illustrating the power of the written word.

Steinem can harness that power incredibly well. The conviction with which she writes about female servitude seemingly knows no bounds. To Steinem, everything relates to the male domination of women, even the interview technique of Phil Donahue. Linda recounts her horrific experiences from *Ordeal*, Steinem writes, "Yet Donahue, usually a sensitive interviewer, is asking her psychological questions about her background. How did she get along with her parents? What did they tell her about sex?"

Linda answers his questions, "and to many women [in the audience] the point finally comes through. But to some it never does. Donahue continues to ask questions about her childhood. If you accept the truth of Linda's story, the questions are enraging, like asking, 'What in your background led you to a concentration camp?'" Later, even Linda's willingness to answer questions put to her by an interviewer is the product of society's ability to dominate women: "Inside the patience with which she answers these questions—the result of childhood training to be a 'good girl' that may make victims of us all—there is some core of strength and stubbornness that is itself the answer."

But Steinem should know that Donahue's questions are not enraging, they're necessary in order to elicit the answers that will further the debate at the heart of Linda's appearance. Or else you just take what people write on blind faith, which sometimes can blow up in your face.

## *Kissing Dead Girls*

**Daphne Gottlieb**

**(Soft Skull Press; 2008)**

The award-winning San Francisco spoken-word artist crafts the conversational poem "Introducing Linda Lovelace as Herself," a narrative mash-up constructed of literary samples from three interviews with Linda Lovelace—conducted by Yvonne Postelle for *Venus* magazine in 1973, Diana Helfrecht for *Bachelor* that same year and me, for the first edition of this book—answered with lines of Linda's dialogue from *Deep Throat*.

Interestingly, the poem seems to deconstruct Linda not with its unique structure but with the dialogue from *Deep Throat*. She's alternately portrayed as sexually exploited ("How do you get along with all these celebrities I hear you're cavorting around with?" "Sex. Sex. I don't enjoy it. All right, that's not altogether right. It makes me feel sort of tingly all over and then . . . nothing.") and, somewhat paradoxically, sexually empowered in a Dworkinian way ("Does your openness about your sexuality threaten many of the men you meet?" "You don't know how good that makes me feel, to know that I've been of some help to you."). She also comes across as somewhat naive and occasionally less-than-bright ("What should the government do about pornography?" "I don't know anything about physiotherapy")—all valid insights to this most complex personality.

Does this reflect Gottlieb's perception of Lovelace? Obviously, to an extent. But if you believe that the purpose of poetry is to elicit some manner of emotional or visceral reaction from the reader or to create a dialogue about the work's theme or topic, her choice of subject and her approach to deconstruction is well done. Or as Linda might say, "I'm so glad! You don't know how good it makes me feel to know that I've been of some help to you."

# OF INTEREST

## *O'Grady: The Life and Times of Hollywood's No. 1 Private Eye*

**John O'Grady and Nolan Davis**

**(J. P. Tarcher, Inc., 1974)**

In clichéd but entertaining gumshoe lingo, O'Grady describes his work as bodyguard to the rich and famous. In one part of the chapter "You Heard the Lady, Buster!" he writes about the time when he crossed paths with a real doll after getting a call from a Linda's attorney:

> When I walked into his office, I recognized the star of *Deep Throat* right away. I didn't see the movie (I'm not a porno fan), but I recognized Miss Lovelace from her pictures in the papers and her appearances on TV. Immediately I saw that she was wearing a see-through blouse with no bra. It's hard, especially for a private eye, not to notice things like that. She was a corpus delicti, but not of the variety spoken of in cop flicks. Linda has short brown hair, a small, compact body, very delicate, attractive features and a petite but ample-looking neck. Details about the client are things every private eye should avail himself of, and I was hard at work. I decided to take the case. Actually I decided to do that the minute I walked in the door. She looked like a nice kid.

O'Grady goes on to describe that Linda was being threatened by members of the mob who wanted her to give them "a piece of her action"—the money she was receiving after having earned her $1,200 for *Throat*, which was coming from publicity, personal appearances, commercials and future film deals. O'Grady spent the next two weeks holed up in a hotel, a cheap flop-house, stuck with a blue-movie dame, the type of heartbreaker who can make the hairs on your neck stand up every time she—

Sorry, I got carried away.

O'Grady and a partner spend the next two weeks guarding Linda's body in a hotel while she sits and watches the Senate Watergate hearings in a see-through dress wondering, "Why does there have to be so much corruption?" The rest of the assignment turned out to be anticlimactic, as O'Grady reports it, with no violence and no real close calls. "But with Linda," he writes, "who needs violence?"

## *Here Comes Harry Reems!*

**Harry Reems**
**(Pinnacle Books, 1975)**

I've always really liked this book. I don't think for a second that Reems actually wrote it, but it's a great read if only because it comes across as more honest than books by his porn compatriots. "I made a one-day wonder just the other day," he writes at one point. "The plot was stupid. The whole thing was ridiculous. And I had a hell of a lot of fun." Which kind of sums up his own book.

By the time this book came out, Reems had already made 407 stag films and was well past his relationship with Linda Lovelace. But his memories of her are friendly ones, and he never dishes any dirt on her, even confirming that she's a good cook. He tells some interesting tales from the set of *Deep Throat* and perpetuates the story that his first session with Lovelace was in a loop that was inserted into *Deep Throat*.

## *The Sex People: The Erotic Performers and Their Bold New World*

**Drs. Phyllis and Eberhard Kronhausen**
**(Playboy Press, 1975)**

Most of the chapter on "The Girls: Linda Lovelace, Tina Russell, Marilyn Chambers, Georgina Spelvin and Others" is taken from their respective autobiographies, *Inside Linda Lovelace* being Linda's contribution. Surprisingly, the Kronhausens actually seem to believe that book's wild sexcapades, the tales of flashing her teacher in high school and using a vibrator to get herself off "some 50 times or more" daily.

Eventually, though, Linda's stories become a bit much to swallow. "[Linda] asks us to believe," the pair write in the first sign that they may finally be taking Linda's autobiography with a grain of salt, "that she likes to go shopping at the local supermarket with a vibrator humming away inside her, firmly held in place by her thoroughly trained 'pussy muscles.' " The Kronhausens, perhaps to prove their expertise (and Linda's truthfulness), substantiate her foot-fucking story by citing examples of woodcuts and prints from their own erotic-art collection showing just such an act. The rest of *The Sex People* is an interesting read, but in light of Linda's later claims about *Inside Linda Lovelace*, this is an embarrassing chapter, especially when put up against Carolyn See's book.

## *Sinema: American Pornographic Films and the People Who Make Them*

**Kenneth Turan and Stephen F. Zito**

**(Signet Books, 1975)**

Turan and Zito's book is one of the best-known early works on the booming sex-film trade, and their chapter on *Deep Throat* is informative and entertaining. All the pertinent info (and not too much else) about the film is there, as always in some slightly different form than when it appeared somewhere else (was it shot in six days or 12?; was the budget $24,000 or $40,000?). Towards the end of the chapter the pair turn their attentions to Linda, mentioning her 8mm loops, her acting stints, arrests, etc. To their credit, the pair know a bogus autobiography when they read one, calling *Inside Linda Lovelace* just one of several money-making schemes meant to cash in on Linda's newfound fame.

## *I, Goldstein*

**Al Goldstein and Josh Alan Friedman**

**(Thunder's Mouth Press, 2006)**

If there's one thing I know after working for Al Goldstein for seven years, it's that he once got a blowjob from Linda Lovelace after he interviewed her—the literal embodiment of the in-your-face style of porn journalism I always referred to as "The Goldstein Probing." This might have been one of the first things I ever knew about Goldstein, whom I and a clique of literary rebels worshipped as English majors at The Big Man's own (almost) alma mater, Pace University. I certainly knew about his close ties to *Deep Throat* even before reading *Ordeal* in college, where we nicknamed one of my good dorm floor friends, a proud and resourceful masturbator capable of MacGyveresqe ways of whacking it, Chuck, after Mr. Traynor. And as you'd imagine, the topic of the groundbreaking blowjob came up with a comforting regularity in the workplace.

Said throat job rates an entire chapter entitled "A Blowjob From Linda" in this, Al Goldstein's autobiography as realized through the mind and fingertips of Josh Alan Friedman, himself a former *Screw* staffer and author of the seminal and semen-drenched classic, *Tales From Times Square*.

Rumors circulated through the grapevine of former *Screw* staffers—a brotherhood given to bouts of alcohol-fortified support-group reminiscing, sometimes years after their work at The World's Greatest Newspaper had ended—that Josh only had about 10 hours of interview tapes to work with, although his personal history with his subject would certainly inform his collaboration in ways very few others could boast.

Although I—spoiler alert—was Al's ghostwriter for two years (and what a pleasure it was hearing people compliment me on how insightful, intelligent and well-informed Al was, knowing I'd actually put those words in his mouth) I don't doubt for a second that Goldstein said (or wrote) every word in because the chapter is taken from at least three previously published sources: several paragraphs are reworkings of Goldstein columns from *Screw*; one paragraph uses the "If I was a faggot she'd be my Judy Garland," line from Fatman's October 1974 *Playboy* interview; and reference is made to Linda's interview with me from *Leg Show* where she admits being "exploited" by feminists in the '80s.

Despite Friedman's undeniable chops both as a writer and a scholar of sleaze, his research occasionally results in the type of editorial malfeasance that would have gotten him shitcanned if it had been committed as a staff member at *Screw*, such as the assertion that *Dog Fucker* was shot in 1969, a direct cop from Jim Holliday's essential but occasionally flawed mega porn review collection *Only the Best: Jim Holliday's Adult Video Almanac and Trivia Treasury*; the fact that Linda's first interview was in *Screw*; even the date of Goldstein's landmark *Deep Throat* review is incorrect. Which is a shame really, because even though Al Goldstein is an incredibly, uh, difficult person in myriad ways, his legacy deserves better than this, although the Linda Lovelace story he tells is not far off the mark, as his personal history with his subject informs his contribution in ways few others could—or frankly, would—boast.

## *Supermouth: A Juicy Banquet of French Love*

**William Rotsler**

**(Melrose Square Publishing; 1975)**

Oh, those must have been heady days, no pun intended, when you could earn something of a living writing on the topic of oral sex, on and off the big screen. Rotsler's opening chapter "Supermouth" sings the praises of the star of the otherwise unspectacular *Deep Throat* ("a goddamn pornie," as he describes it at one point), paying a requisite amount of lip service, no pun intended, to Linda's star turn along the way.

In not only telling the reader who Linda Lovelace is, why people know and love her and why you should too, Rotsler appropriates some of the chapter from Linda's first two autobiographies; provides some anecdotal evidence of Linda's influence on America's sexual psyche and experiences ("A girl in Los Angeles boasted proudly to me that she had mastered the 'Linda Lovelace technique' "...A businessman in New York informed me that certain of the street hookers there whisper that they are masters of the 'Lovelace method' . . . A black hooker in Miami approached a friend of mine saying, 'I taught Linda Lovelace everything she knows' "); offers his advice on how she can maintain and improve upon her star status in the mainstream world; and ends, as more authors of books on oral sex should, by comparing Linda's acting talents to those of Audie Murphy.

## *The Big Book of Porn*

**By Seth Grahame-Smith**

**(Quirk Books; 2005)**

*The Big Book of Porn* undertakes its big task in a light, breezy, easy-to-read style, unlike similar books that try to answer The Big Questions About the History of Smut with varying degrees of feminazi didactics or constitutional grandstanding. In making the "personal is political" philosophy of early feminist theory into something more, well, manly, Grahame-Smith reclaims the male pervert's inherent right to watch people fuck on film, at the same time empowering all his brothers-in-struggle who make their living toiling in the porno vineyards, regardless of what our parents or in-laws have to say about it.

He begins a list of "The 20 Essential Classics" by explaining the highly personal nature of his choices and explains his approach honestly, considering the shit-storm of criticism to which he opens himself up. "[O]f the hundreds of classic pornos I've seen, these are my favorites. That's it. . . . If I left yours off or picked one that you can't stand—let me apologize in advance. You have only my terrible taste to blame."

Apology accepted, mate. Happens to the best of us.

His choices are logical ones: He leads off with *The Opening of Misty Beethoven*, followed closely by *Behind the Green Door* and *Sex World*; *Deep Throat* gets stuck halfway down at number 10. Grahame-Smith addresses its technical merits (or lack thereof), acknowledges its commercial and cultural impact, and points out that it made a boatload of money, blah blah blah, comparing it, interestingly enough, to *Star Wars*, *Titanic* and the *Harry Potter* franchise. Whether Linda is Wan Sandage, Kate Winslet or Petunia Dursley remains undisclosed, and there's little mention of Linda's impact on *Deep Throat*'s impact, although he does politely describe her as "attractive."

Linda's also there for two of the book's "Great Moments in Porn": her ascension to smut queen-ness in 1972 (righteously paralleled with that of Marilyn Chambers) and her repudiation of same in *Ordeal*, although she doesn't even place on his list of 10 notable porn ladies later in the book.

## *The X List: The National Society of Film Critics' Guide to the Movies That Turn Us On*

**Edited by Jami Bernard**
**(Da Capo Press; 2005)**

A decidedly stiff approach to analyzing *Deep Throat* and, by default, Linda Lovelace is taken by film critic Emanuel Levy, a member of the National Society of Film Critics, an organization not unlike the adult industry's X-Rated Critics Organization (XRCO). But as members of Levy's brotherhood would balk at an XRCO member being assigned to analyze, say, The Symbolism of Nightmares in German Expressionist Film from 1920 to 1925, I will go on record (again) saying that mainstream film critics should never be allowed to review porn.

Most of his essay recounts the too-oft-recounted story behind the film's creation (it was made by the mob, made 600 gazillion dollars, blah blah blah), offering no opinion as to what it was that made *Deep Throat* the political and cultural flash-point of the sexual revolution and porno chic. He ends his piece with the widely accepted, hardly ground-breaking observation that "Going beyond artistic or personal values, *Deep Throat* represents a unique moment in American cultural history when buying a ticket to see a dirty movie was a political statement: movie-going as revolutionary act."

When you review fuck flicks professionally, it's not enough to know when the lighting sucks or what camera angle could have best captured a flash of genuine erotic emotion. And while *Deep Throat* is one of the few films whose mere attendance in the '70s was a huge part of the experience, the literary money shot in reviewing a porno is the tacit or explicit admission that you jerked off to it. Levy seems unwilling to let any of the right side of his brain spurt out onto the page, which is disappointing in a book written by mainstream cinematic literati promising to wax authoritative on "the movies that turn us on." Levy reveals nothing as to why this dark horse of a film "turns him on." In the end, all he winds up waxing, ironically enough, is the bishop.

# WORTH A LOOK

## *Playboy's Sex in Cinema 4*
**(Playboy Press, 1974)**

Richard Fegley's photograph of a pear-eating Linda graces the cover of this book, which reprints Arthur Knight's two "Sex in Cinema" articles—"Films" and "Sex Stars"— from *Playboy*'s November and December 1973 issues, respectively. Inside there are a few color stills from *Deep Throat* and three more color pictures from the Fegley photo session: two from the "Say 'Ah!' " layout of April 1973 and one previously unpublished.

## *Screen World 1972-1973 Season*
**John Willis**
**(Crown Publishers, 1974)**

Volume 24 of entertainment archivist John Willis' comprehensive motion-picture directory gives capsule information about practically every domestic and foreign movie screened in the United States in 1972—from *The Godfather* to *Godzilla vs. the Smog Monster*, from *Slaughterhouse-Five* to *The Thing With Two Heads*; from *Deliverance* to, yes, *Deep Throat*. Considering its lead time, it's understandable but unfortunate that *Deep Throat* didn't get more than the scant mention it did (Willis doesn't even note the film's rating, although a few other X-rated flicks like *Sexual Customs in Scandinavia* and *The Rise and Fall of the World From a Sexual Position* were mentioned), and no pictures are included among more than 1,000 in the book. Linda even missed out on being included in the book's list of the Top 25 Grossing Hollywood Stars or its list of Promising Personalities of 1972.

## *Sex Stars' Favorite Positions*
**(Merchandise for Mailers, 1980)**

This one's not as "educational" as you might think, despite its cover claim that "the world's top porn stars illustrate how they do it!", but it does have some pretty good stuff for collectors. The Linda Lovelace section runs four pages with exceedingly minimal text that mainly says, "Linda used to say she loved porn, now she says she hates it." Most of the pictures have run in other magazines dealing with Linda's pre-*Throat* career, but *Sex Stars' Favorite Positions* reproduces two rare photos of Lovelace with a clean-shaven Chuck Traynor.

## *Theatre World: 1973-1974 Season*

**John Willis**

**(Crown Publishers, 1975)**

Although Linda's box-office success was glossed over in *Screen World*, her star power is evident in Volume 30 of Willis' annual encyclopedia of stage performance. Unfortunately her on-screen success wouldn't be duplicated treading the boards. *Deep Throat* was shown in theaters across the country for years, but *Pajama Tops*, a bedroom farce based on playwright Jean de Letraz' *Moumou*, ran at Philadelphia's New Locust Theatre from December 26, 1973, until January 5, 1974. As shown in *Theatre World*, Linda's billing as Babette Latouche, originated by *Playboy* pinup June Wilkinson, was second-to-last, but she's pictured in both of the comedy's production stills: one showing her in a typically dramatic stage pose with Dick Patterson, the other showing a smiling Linda pulling the trousers off William Browder with the help of Simon McQueen.

## *Sex, American Style: An Illustrated Romp Through the Golden Age of Heterosexuality*

**Jack Boulware**

**(Feral House, 1997)**

*Sex, American Style* is a good-natured, porn-friendly look at all things smutty and salacious, from rock and roll groupies to Swedish stewardesses to X-rated magazines (the final chapter chronicles Boulware's trip up to the *Screw* inner sanctum and his impressions of my own nicotine-stained, smut-filled office). His section on *Deep Throat* in the chapter "Hooray for Hardcore" contains all the great *Deep Throat* stories (theater owners being busted around the country while suffering through bomb threats and protesting patrons paying their admission in pennies) told in a light-hearted, breezy way.

About halfway through it turns into a history of Lovelace, recounting all the appropriate and interesting stories (learning how to deep throat with Chuck Traynor, dipping her hands in cement at the Pussycat Theater and teaching Sammy Davis Jr. how to deep throat with Chuck Traynor). Boulware makes a few gaffes (he's not quite sure about Linda's well-documented real name and it wasn't me who asked Kaitlyn Ashley that stupid question, dude!), but they're really pretty minor considering what a huge topic he tackled. *Sex, American Style* is a great, fun read.

# PULP FICTION

## *Show Business Laid Bare*

**Earl Wilson**

**(Putnam, 1974)**

When he was still writing the musical comedy *Let My People Come*, Earl Wilson Jr., in need of some capital, went to an interesting potential investor: his mother. "I told her I was writing a dirty show," he says, "and she laughed and said, 'That's okay, your father is writing a dirty book!' " That father, of course, was legendary entertainment columnist Earl Wilson Sr., and the book he was writing was *Show Business Laid Bare*, in which he describes the time he had "two in one day": interviews, that is, with Linda Lovelace and Marilyn Chambers.

"Pornography must and should go," Wilson says in his introduction, before stating his intention that the book "prove to the most liberal-minded that some control is needed" by the government over Hollywood's wildly unchecked liberalism and permissiveness (said permissiveness described as the current level liberalism has reached) since, "because of their inability to police themselves, the media and Hollywood have brought censorship down upon their own heads."

Linda first appears in "Exhibitionists 'for Kicks'" when Wilson calls her "the face that sank a thousand ships," before describing his afternoon euphemistically probing Marilyn Chambers about infidelity, orgies and come shots. Dubbing this new, wondrous and enigmatic breed of blue-movie star the "Genitalia Generation," Wilson goes on to describe his attendance of the notorious *Inside Linda Lovelace* press conference at the Gaslight Club. So packed is the affair that the only question Wilson gets in is whether an unidentified reporter will let Wilson listen to him interview Linda. To Wilson's credit, he didn't eavesdrop and claim Linda's quote for his own. After describing the plot of *Deep Throat* to its "happy ending," he says the ending might not be too happy for the porn biz, which now has the Supreme Court breathing down its neck.

It's painfully obvious that Wilson is uncomfortable with his interview subjects and the new, prominent place of the Jizz Biz in Show Biz. Considering that Wilson is fairly intolerant of the new commercialization (and therefore cheapening) of the human sex act, it's amazing he even got the book done, going back to the sex-well time and again—all in the interest of journalism, of course.

## *Scandal!*
### Janet Street-Porter
### (Dell, 1983)

"Lovelace Goes Down Fighting" screams the title of this, another recounting of Linda's experiences in porn courtesy of *Ordeal*. It's a pretty bare-bones retelling of Linda's rise and fall, from her experiences with Chuck Traynor to her second marriage and life on welfare, with a brief side trip into the story of Marilyn Chambers and her dealings with Traynor. There's not much new here, except the idea that people didn't believe it when the woman who claimed she loved being a porn star came out against it.

Let's flash back to one of the things that pissed off Lenny Bruce for a second and state that *Scandal!* is an exploitative book that, like most such exploitative books dealing with such sordid topics (especially where the rich and famous are concerned), takes a morally indignant tone while at the same time using its stories to titillate the reader. The biggest surprise about *Scandal!* is that they didn't put Linda on the cover.

## *Deals: The World's Shrewdest and Most Lucrative Deals From Business, Entertainment, Politics and Sports*

**Cheryl Moch and Vincent Virga**
**(Crown Publishers, Inc., 1984)**

*Deals* rewrites information already available to anyone who's read *Ordeal*, with the original spin of contextualizing it in a lightweight reading of economics/business theory. The chapter "Below the Belt: Legal and Extralegal," contains the essay "Porn's Pawn: Linda Lovelace Stars in *Deep Throat*," which shows Linda's "deal" for appearing in the film was neither shrewd nor lucrative—at least not for her.

Moch and Virga reiterate what everyone's known for years about Linda's involvement with *Deep Throat*: she was paid $100 a day for 12 days' work; Chuck Traynor pocketed the money; the film went on to make 600 bajiggity zillion dollars; and Linda went on welfare.

Aside from a few well-placed, moderately funny oral-sex puns (about how Linda's talents "aroused" Damiano's creativity and how the fact that *Deep Throat* made millions and all its star got was notoriety would be hard even for Linda to swallow), the high point is a "business deal" quote in the margin that illustrates the main text: "Don't drink the Devil's broth if you won't eat the Devil's meat," credited to "Anonymous."

## *The Myth of Women's Masochism*

**Paula J. Caplan, Ph.D.**
**(Signet Books, 1987)**

Chapter Seven, "Women as Victims of Violence," gives major props to Gloria Steinem's "The Real Linda Lovelace" (Caplan's book even takes its title from one of Steinem's lines in that piece) and props Linda up as a poster child for the issue of domestic violence. Fair enough, as it's the domestic violence angle that makes Linda's story common; the pornography aspect merely makes it unique. But no new interviews are conducted and no new information is given on Lovelace, although lots of sources and statistics from other books are mentioned.

Among the other points Caplan makes in this chapter, which blithely names pornography as a weapon in man's oppression of women, is one often made: The difference between pornography and erotica is that erotica "gives the same importance to the woman's pleasure as to the man's and [it gives] dignity to both sexes." There are a couple of other definitions of the difference between porn and erotica, including: "In erotica you use a feather, in porn you use the whole bird," and the always-popular "What I like is erotica, what you like is porn."

By Caplan's own definition, then, *Deep Throat* is erotica, because that's exactly what expert witnesses said it was during the New York *Deep Throat* obscenity trial. But feminists weren't buying it back in 1972, so why should they buy it 15 years later?

## *Shaking a Leg: Collected Writings*
**Angela Carter**
**(Penguin Books, 1997)**

"Lovely Linda," Carter's critical essay of *Inside Linda Lovelace*, starts off the chapter "Fleshly Matters," which deals with matters of body politics, sometimes ass-backwards.

Carter is singularly unimpressed with Linda's fleshly talents or the insistence that she loves what she does. She even denies Linda (the '70s character, remember) the sexual freedom that she claims as her own, arguing that to be allowed sexual freedom by the societal or governmental entities that repressed you in the first place is to still owe them that freedom, and therefore not be free. Extrapolating this ridiculous logic to Linda's escape from Traynor, she must still be his captive, as she became free of him only after he ceased making demands that she return to him.

Elsewhere, Carter likens Linda's talents to a suppressed castration urge, writing, "If my sexuality had been as systematically exploited by men as Ms. Lovelace's has, no doubt I, too, would want to swallow men's cocks whole; it is a happy irony that she should have found fame and fortune by doing so." This makes Carter guilty of reducing Lovelace to the trace elements of her sexuality, not thinking for a second that there might actually be a living, breathing person locked up in that ability to swallow a cock or ingest a foot who is worthy of even the slightest amount of empathy.

After noting Lovelace's quote from *Inside Linda Lovelace* that, "My God is now sex. Without it, I'd die. Sex is everything," Carter imbues Lovelace's shaved mons with a less-than-practical *razor d'etre*: "Like a postulant, Ms. Lovelace shaves herself before she engages in these primal yet abstract confrontations. She has removed all traces of the animal from her body, so that it has the cool sheen, not of flesh, but of a mineral substance." (Actually she removed all traces of the animal from her body so no unsightly pubic hair would get her and Chuck Traynor busted in his bottomless lounge in Florida.) But as so many people before (and after) had done, Carter took the Lovelace mythos at face value, at one point declaring Lovelace "a shaven prisoner in a cage whose bars are composed of cocks. And she has been so thoroughly duped she seems quite happy there."

One can only wonder what Carter thought after she read *Ordeal*.

## *Ultra Flesh: A Connoisseur's Guide to the Halcyon Days of Pornography*
**Tony Clarke, editor**
**(Babzotica, 1998)**

Connoisseur's guide? Hardly. The only thing this book has in common with the halcyon days of pornography is the feeling that it was created in a single day on a shoestring budget. Full of inaccuracies, shitty art direction and even more typos than the first edition of this book, *Ultra Flesh* is a failed attempt to document some of the best (and worst) moments in porn. It is, however, an incredibly successful attempt to con people out of their money for same. The book has no direction, no context and no point of view, jumping from profiles of personalities like Russ Meyer and Gerry Damiano to reprints of porn-video ads to reviews of unrelated movies and videotapes.

The sections about Linda reprint loads of pre-*Throat* pics, all censored and looking like they were cropped with a butter knife and rehash all the same stories in a stumbling, ham-fisted way. "The People vs. Linda Lovelace," Clarke's history of *Deep Throat*'s legal woes, is full of clipped phrases, unfinished sentences and bad punctuation:

> Suddenly if you hadn't already seen it. You just had to, if only to see what all the fuss was about, needed or not, everybody had an excuse to take their date/partner to an adult flick, and it turned them on even better, it was the talk of the Country *Deep Throat* was on everybody's lips.

Throughout the book, photos are put in the wrong place, people are identified incorrectly and names are misspelled. *Ultra Flesh* is the type of shit that gives porn writers a bad name.

# Chapter 5:

# WRAP HER UP

## Getting into Linda's groove

**After the nation's media outlets began singing the praises of Linda Lovelace, it wasn't long before others followed suit. And follow suit they did: Musicians have been invoking the name of porno's premiere sex goddess in practically ever genre you could think of for over 40 years—and some you wouldn't imagine in a million.**

# The *Deep Throat* Soundtrack

Porn films are usually given short shrift for their soundtracks, to the point where their wah-wah-guitar, soft-suck high-hat and roller-rink organ riffs have become clichés. Said shortness of shrift is generally well-deserved. Any (good) film soundtrack ideally reflects a scene's action and in its own strange way, that's what (good) porn film music does, with a slightly different approach. But the reason that most porn soundtracks (usually) suck isn't because the musicians are untalented, but because the people bank-rolling them are cheap.

Not so Gerard Damiano, who by some reports spent as much as $10,000, or roughly a third of *Deep Throat*'s budget, on its music. The money wasn't wasted; novelty value aside, the music was generally well-received when the film opened. No less an authority than *Ace!* magazine called the film's music "excellent," and Vincent Canby wrote in his *New York Times* review "What Are We To Think of Deep Throat?" that its title song was "rather funny." Even Judge Joel Tyler, in his decision condemning the film as a "feast of carrion and squalor," noted that *Deep Throat*'s music gave it an air of legitimacy, however putrid that air was. Once the film became a legitimate phenomenon, it also became obvious that anything bearing the *Deep Throat* name would become a lucrative commodity. Hence, a soundtrack album for a porno film.

If things had gone as planned, the *Deep Throat* soundtrack might not be the collector's item it is today but rather a garage-sale perennial. It was once actually scheduled for mainstream, mass-market commercial release by a mainstream, mass-market record company before being pulled. According to photographer Earl Miller, best known for his work in *Penthouse*, the reason the project was shelved had nothing to do with interference from the government, the Mafia or even Chuck Traynor. It was shelved because of a much more innocent party.

"Warner Bros. Records had scheduled the *Deep Throat* soundtrack for release and they had done the album art," Miller says. "I was doing a lot of shooting for them back then, so the art director gave me a set of prints of the proposed album art. They had finished slicks, they were ready to go. I get to the final meeting and [Warner Bros. executives] looked at each other and said, 'Look, we really can't do this,' because at the same time they were also getting ready to release the soundtrack for the show *Sesame Street*."

The *Deep Throat* soundtrack album was finally issued by DT Music Productions in a run of about 1,000 copies. By some accounts it was given away as a promotional item at theaters showing the film (as if it needed any more publicity); by some accounts it was sold for $5. These days an original copy of the *Deep Throat* soundtrack album is a collector's item that will run you considerably more than $5: vinyl (and/or soundtrack) junkies can expect to pay at least $100 for a copy, if they can score one at all.

Like most collector's-item records, the outrageous prices commanded for an original *Deep Throat* soundtrack are in inverse proportion to what it actually delivers. Not that the music is so terrible. Considering the budget, the times and the vehicle it was recorded for, it's not that bad. After 40 years, though, it just hasn't aged well. The parodies of the Mickey and Sylvia song "Love Is Strange" and the jingles for Coca-Cola and Old Spice are as cheesy as they are notorious. The record's biggest legacy is probably that it set the bar for future porno soundtracks—and set it painfully low.

**BONUS CONTENT**

See the author's list of great cover versions of the *Deep Throat* theme song by scanning this QR code

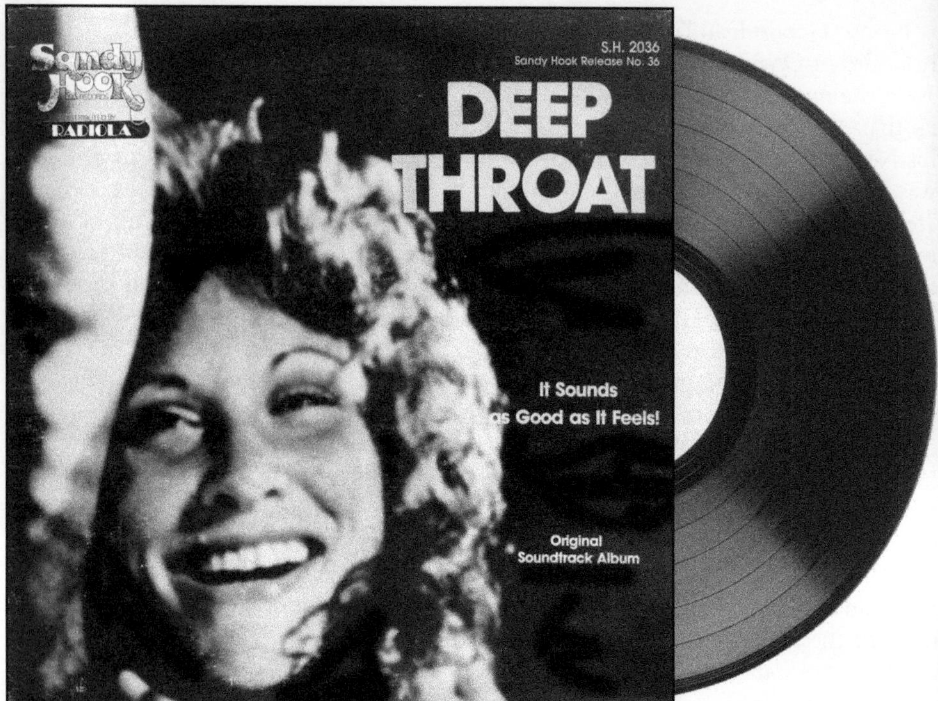


In 1980, the nostalgia label Sandy Hook Records re-released the album in an edition also highly prized by soundtrack collectors, despite its mercenary nature. Unlike the 1973 version, which features only the music and clocks in at just over 30 minutes, the Sandy Hook release contains the entire 62-minute audio track: music, dialogue, sound effects and all. Even so, the Sandy Hook version works because the music doesn't overlap the dialogue. Maybe the only thing better than the album is the foot-square album cover featuring Linda Lovelace's smiling face—right next to William Love's big, come-soaked cock.

The *Deep Throat* soundtrack was also issued by England's Bonk Records, who mimicked the Sandy Hook release by including both the music and dialogue and a picture from *Throat*'s final scene. Bonk also put out the first-ever CD version, which includes little information aside from a 17-track index so you can find your favorite part. The far-superior music-only version has yet to appear on CD.

When all is said and done, though, anyone who wants to save themselves the $100 to $200 a copy that the original or even the Sandy Hook version will set them back (or even the $15 to $20 for the CD) would do just as well popping in the DVD and not watching it.

Having been composed before the movie became popular, though, the songs in *Deep Throat* aren't really about Linda Lovelace, either as character or flesh-and-blood human being, but since the film's release Linda has served as muse for artists in a wide range of musical forms: country & western, cabaret, pop, jazz and rock. What follows is sort of a horny hit parade of songs dedicated to, inspired by and otherwise using the image of America's original porn queen.

# "'Polk Street Rag'"

## Barclay James Harvest
**(from the album *Octoberon*, MCA Records)**

"Polk Street Rag" recalls a special day when this British prog-rock band was in San Francisco to work on an album with producer Elliot Mazer. Unfortunately, Mazer wasn't in town, which left the band with a little bit of time on their hands. Guitarist John Lees' plan to keep his hands busy involved wandering down to Polk Street and taking in a screening of *Deep Throat*. The experience proved so profound that he was moved to write:

I was down on the East Side
On a block with no name
When I walked in a movie
You were blue, I was game

Didn't know when I entered
Second seat, second row
It was then I first saw you
But your mouth stole the show

Tell me, did you love it, baby?
Did you think your smile looked right?
Tell me, when you came together
Was it in your mind
'Cause it sure was out of sight

Combine the experience that inspired the song with the tune's flanged guitars, power chords and echoed vocals, and you can almost hear a "Stonehenge"-era Spinal Tap playing it. Loud.

Funny as that thought is, the tune provides even more comic relief when you realize that, when its members weren't out seeing Linda Lovelace suck cock, the band also killed time on their trip to the States by doing background vocals for an album being recorded by David (*Starsky & Hutch*) Soul.

**BONUS CONTENT**

See a rockin' quote about Linda Lovelace by scanning this QR code

# "Theme From Deep Throat"

## Linda and the Lollipops
**(Kama Sutra Records, 7-inch single)**

Several magazine and newspaper interviews made mention of a Linda Lovelace project that would have used her throat in a considerably more conventional way: as singer on an album with poet/songwriter Shel Silverstein. For better or worse that project never materialized (chances are it turned into the 1974 Barbi Benton album *Barbi Doll*); Linda told this writer that the idea was nothing more than idle conversation while they were in a hot tub. For better or worse, though, we do have this 1973 45, and my vote is "worse," for a couple of reasons: The singer on this record is not Linda Lovelace. The song being sung is not the theme to *Deep Throat*, it's the music from the film's title sequence, which had no lyrics. And the music isn't even from the original soundtrack, it's re-recorded.

The record begins with the pop of a cork and the sound of bubbly—recalling *Deep Throat*'s "Bubble Song"—being poured into a glass. The song's trademark organ riff begins and after about a minute and a half, and some semi-orgasmic moaning and groaning, a woman sings:

I would like to really turn you on
Won't you please let me turn you on?
If you love me let me turn you on
I will really, really turn you on

Those four vocal lines (the only lines in the song) degenerate into a series of sighs and whimpers whose sex appeal ideally should ring true but sound more like cash registers, which must have been music to the Perainos' ears at least. Novelty value aside, this song is second in inanity and minimalist lyrics only to "La La La" from the soundtrack of *Deep Throat Part II.*

Although a call to the recently revamped Buddha Records, who issued Kama Sutra in the early '70s, showed they had no idea who recorded it, played on it or, most importantly, Why It Was Made, according to Neil Kempfer-Stocker, the record was the creation of none other than Walter Carlos, the man who gave us *Switched-On Bach*, the soundtrack to *A Clockwork Orange* and, following his sexual reassignment surgery, Wendy Carlos.

"I was head of A&R at Overseas Music Services," Kempfer-Stocker recalls. "The firm 'placed' Tempi masters [Trans-Electronic Music Productions, Inc, Carlos' production company] with record labels for a licensing arrangement. Bob Reno, who signed David Bowie to Philips Music when Bowie signed to Mercury USA, took on the Lollipops master for Buddha/Kama Sutra." To the best of Kempfer-Stocker's knowledge, the project stopped there, although the record, with a picture sleeve depicting a topless Linda Lovelace from the opening scene of *Deep Throat Part II*, was released by Derby Records in Italy. "I know of no stock copies ever being pressed," he says. "I was given 25 copies as well as a commission for my work." His reaction to the disc? "It's a total gas, with Walter singing 'Wendy-style' femme vocals. The mind does boggle!"

# "Linda Won't You Take Me In"

## Murray McLauchlan

**(from the album *Day to Day* Dust, True North Records)**

In an August 27, 1973, *New York Times* article entitled "Salvos of 'Erotic' Songs Traded in Friendly Exchange of Ribs," John S. Wilson describes an early performance of this song at the Philadelphia Folk Festival. After performances of other erotic songs, some of them part of a workshop on women's folk, some of them "English dominance and submission ballads" and some of them just good old randy songs dating back to the 1920's, Wilson writes, "Murray McLauchlan, a young Canadian songwriter, brought the subject up to date with a bright, catchy song about an unlikely subject: Linda Lovelace, who starred in the pornographic film *Deep Throat*."

And bring it up he did, in more ways than one:

I've been around with other girls
But they just made me tired
I'm so unemployed but I want to be so hired
Put my dinner in your oven
Put my steak there in your fire
I know I ain't good-looking but I'm hungry with desire

Linda won't you take me in?
Linda won't you take me in?

"Linda Won't You Take Me In" was issued as a single in 1974, but it didn't last too long on public airwaves, although it had a promising start. According to McLauchlan's manager Bruce Davidson, "The song was picked up by radio and was starting to be played across the country. One day one of the music directors for one of the major stations figured out that the song was not just about any girl named Linda, but about exactly one girl named Linda! He put the word out, and the next day the song just disappeared from the charts."

# "Stove Bolt Six"

## Big Block 454
**(from the album *Three Lucky Boys*, Raspberry Records)**

Colin Robinson and Pete Scullion are the core members of Big Block 454, who describe themselves as a "semi-amorphous post-modern/situationist neo-dada musical compositional construct" hailing from Manchester, England. (This means that the boys know their way around a computer through which they filter electronic and acoustic instruments as well as "found" sounds.)

The chorus to "Stove Bolt Six," a track from their second album, consists of the lyrics "We are the Stove Bolt Six/ We are the angels of Mons/ We are household Gods/ Where did we go wrong?" followed by a list of seemingly random, seemingly unrelated transitional word-groups sung by Melissa Sinden and set against electronic tones and synthesized rhythms.

In great semi-amorphous post-modern/situationist neo-dada style, the phrases give way one to the other in concentrated bursts of wordplay. When a wondering writer questioned Robinson why he'd want to weave winsome webs with otherwise weird and whimsical words like "Lee Van Cleef, Garcia Lorca, Linda Lovelace, Linda Chalker, Lingua franca, linguaformal, lilienthal, linguaphone," he replied, "Probably because of the alliterative nature of her name."

# "The W*nker's Song (Misprint)"

## Ivor Biggun and the Red-Nose Burglars
**(from the album *The W*nker's Album (Misprint)*, Beggar's Banquet Records)**

Biggun is something of a cult star in England, sort of a mixture of Neil Innes and Tiny Tim (possessing the former's sense of humor but lacking the latter's sense of fashion), who has made his way to American airwaves courtesy of *The Dr. Demento Show* on the strength of the singles "Bras on 45" and "The Majorca Song" and the albums *More Filth! Dirt Cheap* and *Partners in Grime*. But this is his greatest shit (misprint).

Biggun describes dipping his hand in the masturbatory arts and lets us know how far that hand goes:

I've wanked over Italy, I've wanked over Spain,
I've wanked in an omnibus,
I've even had a wank in a train,
I've used a badger and a melon and a cat,
An inflatable Linda Lovelace and a Davy Crocket hat.

Although she's only mentioned briefly, "The W*nker's Song (Misprint)" marks one of the few instances in which Linda Lovelace actually received some sort of sustained radio play, however quickly the song came and went. Despite being banned by the BBC for sexually explicit lyrics after its September 1978 release, the song inched up the British charts for 12 weeks, shooting to number 22 before eventually dropping off the charts with a resounding splat into the dirty old sock of pop history.

# "I Can't Get Started"

## Maynard Ferguson
**(from the album *Chameleon*, Columbia Records)**

Jazz legend Ferguson recorded this song, originally introduced by Bob Hope in the Zeigfield Follies of 1936, as one of his rare vocal tracks. He even updated some of the original lyrics. After inserting the line "Stan Kenton made me a star," a reference to the man who helped establish his name, Ferguson replaces an original line with a reference to everyone's favorite porn star: "Linda Lovelace thinks I'm obscene."

Asked what led Ferguson to include the line, he recalls his first viewing of *Deep Throat*. "We were on the road a couple of years before we recorded that," he says, "and our band checked into a motel in a very small town in Pennsylvania. There was nothing happening, the motel we were in was in the middle of nowhere, but there was a small town right nearby. The TV wasn't very good at the motel, so we asked if there was a theater. We went to this small town with only one theater and a diner next door, a really small town.

"None of us had ever heard of *Deep Throat* or Linda Lovelace, so me and the band just said, 'Okay, let's go in and see this.' Whatever it was, we didn't care. We just thought if it was good, we'd stay. It was uproarious because we thought we were going to see some normal movie, like a John Wayne western or something. Needless to say, with all those young men in my band, we stayed. I thought the whole experience was hilarious, so that's why the line was inserted.

"After the record came out, I was in La Guardia Airport, and a guy came up to me and said he was with the publishers of the song. All the guys from the publishing house were waiting for their plane, too, because they were on their way to a convention. He told me that they just heard my version, and he said, 'But the Linda Lovelace line . . .'

"I thought he was gonna give me a problem because that wasn't how the lyrics were originally published. But he said to me, 'It's great! You gotta come upstairs and meet the guys!' "

While out on the road in the late '90s with his band Big Bop Nouveau, Ferguson replaced Linda's name with that of another woman with newsworthy oral talents: Monica Lewinsky. "I just sing about whoever's controversial at the time," he says. And when it comes time to find out who the latest girl of the moment is, "I know which guys in the band to go to and seek accurate information."

# "Wrap Her Up"

## Elton John
**(from the album *Ice on Fire*, MCA Records)**

"Wrap Her Up" was written by EJ with Bernie Taupin, Charlie Morgan, Paul Westwood, Davey Johnstone and Fred Mandel, but got its Linda Lovelace connnection from George Michael, with whom John formed an alliance that gave them several hits. Legend has it the pair were riffing at the end of the song, mentioning names of "ladies, illegal X's, Mona Lisas, well connected." Michael sings "Little Linda Lovelace," between Tallulah Bankhead and Little Eva.

The legend was more or less confirmed 15 years later when Michael pulled the same trick, so to speak, ad-libbing the name of Latin heartthrob Ricky Martin into his cover "My Baby Just Cares for Me" from his album *Songs of the Last Century*.

Any similarity between Martin and Lovelace is strictly coincidental. In Michael's mind, at least.

# "Sleep Wonderfully Warm With Linda Lovelace"

## The Fauves
**(from teh album *Surf City Limits*, Polydor Records Australia)**

One listen to this 1998 song and you'll see that this group of Australian pop-punksters is pretty serious about their love of the pornographic arts. This spunky two-and-a-half-minute rocker outdoes most other songs in the sheer number of porn stars in its lyrics, paying tribute not just to Linda Lovelace but to the late '90s porn industry in general:

> He's got a good thing going
> Northie's the biggest wad in the game
> Joey Silvera, a little gut but kicks ass just the same
> C'mon get into it, watch just a little bit
> Pause button on the money shot
> Sleep wonderfully warm with Linda Lovelace

Interestingly, considering that the only performers most porn fans care about are the women, the only performers mentioned here are men, and all of them are partners in Evil Angel Productions, also known as the Evil Empire. The other porno mainstays lauded in the tune are John Leslie and big-dicked Italian überstud Rocco Siffredi. "Northie" is Peter North, known for his copious come shots.

# "Linda, Georgina, Marilyn and Me"

## performed by Christine Rubens
**(from the *Let My People Come* cast album, Libra Records)**

During a decade-plus off-Broadway run, fans of musical theater were treated to this cabaret song about the up-and-(hopefully)-coming starlet Sally Streichermeyer, whose great ambition is to follow in the pecker tracks of her titular idols.

With an almost "Hey kids, let's put on a dirty show" innocence, Sally sings:

> I go to the movies almost every day
> There's not a porno film I haven't seen

Linda, Georgina and Marilyn
Are my favorite stars up on the silver screen

I'm leaving my old neighborhood
No longer a non-entity
I wonder how I'll like Hollywood
When it's Linda, Georgina, Marilyn and me!

After sending off her head shot, Sally elaborates on her other qualifications for blue-movie stardom:

I've seen every picture, I know every line
Linda Lovelace is an idol of mine!
She should have got the Oscar, she was the best
It would have been a little sticky, I guess!

Writer Earl Wilson Jr. says that far from being a vehicle to promote porn, the play was written to solve a more down-to-Earth problem. "Producer Phil Osterman and I had been working on another project which was going nowhere because we had no money and no reputation," he recalls. "He said, 'Why don't we do something outrageous and get known? Let's do a show about sex. Something very positive and very uplifting and very funny, the way young people think about sex.'

"Keeping in mind that the whole thing was to make this as light-hearted and as fun as possible, it seemed logical that there should be a song about porn movies, because porn movies were just becoming quite the thing. We had to figure out who the big female porno stars were: Linda, Georgina and Marilyn were chosen. I had never met any of those women before, but I had seen their films. I wasn't naive, and they were really all over the place."

If there's one thing Wilson remembers about Lovelace's film debut, it's that it was less than memorable. "I didn't think anything about *Deep Throat* as a film. It was just a piece of hyped porno. I most remember being shocked that I was watching it with other men and women. Before, you had to sneak into some 42nd Street theater and hope that nobody saw you. But this was quite different. People weren't ashamed. It was regarded as a fun, in, hip thing to do. It was the first time I remember that sex was acceptable on a fun level."

*Let My People Come* was an almost immediate hit, and with his newfound status as a songwriter came the chance to meet the women who inspired him. He met Spelvin and Chambers at the show, but had to wait to meet Lovelace. "I met Linda after some press agent set something up," he says. "She was wearing a see-through black dress. She was beautiful. You wouldn't know that she was a porn star. She looked like a movie star. I liked her. She impressed me by being very quiet, being very staid and being not at all what you would think. She was very classy, but it seemed to me that her relationship with her husband was a very Svengali kind of thing. She might have been restrained from saying anything, I don't know."

What does Wilson remember most about Lovelace? "She was very beautiful and she was beautifully dressed."

# "The Ballad of Linda Lovelace (L.A. Porno Queen)"

## Geronimo Whitewing
**(White Wing Records, 7-inch single)**

Geronimo Whitewing isn't an American Indian band with a taste for Linda Lovelace, but the name of a country band led by Lynn Groom, who still plays on the Texas nightclub circuit.

Groom wrote the song, full of pedal steel, twangy guitar and honky tonk piano, in 1975 about a girl "at the eye of a hurricane of controversy that catapulted her to the status of a rock star, and the irony that it was the controversy that elevated her to that level more than it was the piece of film."

Groom sounds almost apologetic when he discusses the song now. "It had a very simplistic view of her," he says, "seeing it all as a big joke, living in the lap of luxury and that it had no cost to her whatsoever." He recalls the line, "And all it cost her was her modesty," admitting, "Time proved that to be wrong. It was a tremendous personal cost to her. But you're 20 years old, like I was at the time, you only see what you want to see. The rest of the song was just my fantasy of what I hoped her life was like. But who knew? It's just great that Linda survived it!"

Despite knowing so little about her, some of Groom's lyrics are pretty perceptive considering Linda's later claims:

> She was such a good girl in her younger years
> She always did just what her mama said
> She always went to church but never did quite understand
> Just exactly what that preacher said
>
> So it was screen test after screen test
> On that long road to the light
> Showing off her most peculiar self-esteem
> And now her name's a common word
> And she's a star in her own right
> But success was not at all the way she dreamed
>
> 'Cuz she's an L.A. porno queen
> The courts call her obscene
> She's living her life under camera lights
> She's America's sex machine

Groom laughs that there are only about 600 copies of this record, the B-side to his song "Fade Away." The first pressing of 500, made for promo and airplay, had the misspelling "Prono Queen." The band couldn't wait to get 500 correct copies, so they used what they had. They let go of about a hundred and destroyed the rest when the good ones were delivered.

# "Linda Lovelace"

## David Allan Coe

### (From the album *Nothing Sacred*, DAC Records)

The most notorious ode to Linda comes courtesy of David Allan Coe, author of such hits as "Take This Job and Shove It" and "Would You Lay With Me (in a Field of Stone)?". It originally appeared on the incredibly rare *Nothing Sacred*, a self-released album that includes the songs "Cum Stains on the Pillow," "Pussy-whipped Again" and "Masturbation Blues." He also released a similar album called *Adults Only*, and they're both fucking great.

Coe sets the scene when he has his fantastical session with his favorite fuck-film starlet thusly:

Old Harry Reems fell apart at the seams
When he saw me fuck that whore
She sucked my dick and swallowed my nuts
And I still hollered for more
She sucked my asshole, she sucked my toes
She's the suckingest bitch alive
I made her call up two more cunts
And friend that ain't no jive
So don't give me no shit
About being no big-time lover
Or some movie star with a Jag
'Cuz you ain't shit if you can't git
Linda Lovelace to gag

Coe's lyrical flip side to this was the equally charming "Little Susie Shallow Throat," about a gal whose problem is the polar opposite of Linda Lovelace's.

# Linda Lovelace (Come Sit on My Face)

**Paul Craft**
**(from the album *Warnings!*, Peabody Records)**

More downright outré than straight-up outlaw, country songwriter Paul Craft has an impressive package of tunes under his presumably turquoise-buckled belt, written while busting his chartmaking chops in Nashville, blending compact lyrical and musical rhythms with a hook you could hang a hat on. Music Row cred came as author of, among others, The Eagles' "Midnight Flyer" and "Keep Me From Blowing Away" by Linda Ronstadt; he also proved able to lighten and liven things up with "Dropkick Me, Jesus (Through the Goalposts of Life)," "Too Bad You're No Good" and, as a member of bluegrassers The Seldom Scene, the toe-tapping elbow-bender "Through the Bottom of the Glass." That decidedly homespun sense of humor gets exposed on his 1986 debut solo album *Warnings!*, softcore cornpone not so much David Allan Coe as Ray

Stevens—who, coincidentally, scored a minor hit with Craft's "It's Me Again, Margaret" the previous year.

Bouncy accordion riffs lend the lead-off tune a Tejano feel as Craft solicits his subject (and her services) in the tune's opening lines:

> Linda Lovelace, come sit on my face
> Just we two
> Do like you done in *Deep Throat* number one
> And *Deep Throat* number two

After a PG paean to Linda's body of work and a verse-long take on the "Nixon watching *Deep Throat*" joke, Craft again extends Linda his invite to the seat of honor with the promise "I'll do the same to you." Which, if nothing else, makes him the only musician offering to return the favor. The 2008 CD reissue of *Warnings!* features a good-natured, well-received live version of the song among its three bonus tracks.

# "Religion: Lovelace-a-Go-Go Mix"

## Front 242
### mix by J.G. Thirlwell (Epic Records promo EP)

Belgian industrial band Front 242 are among the granddaddies of the electronica scene, gaining cult status in Europe before making a name for themselves in the States. Australian J.G. Thirlwell, who has released albums under the names Foetus, Clint Ruin and Wiseblood, among many others, is sort of a granddaddy of industrial music. Their two distinctly trendsetting worlds converged in 1993 with this promo-only single, released on 12-inch vinyl and CD. It's a shame this never got wider release.

Thirlwell, whose perhaps greatest strength lies in his sonic manipulation of other people's music, provides some of the most exciting and challenging mixes committed to vinyl, using sound clips from a variety of sources. "I had done a few remixes where these random elements came in," Thirlwell says. "For EMF, I did a Jonestown kind of thing. For Nine Inch Nails I did one with Timothy Leary." Here he places the dialogue from *Deep Throat*'s examination scene and Damiano's fey reading of "What's a nice joint like you doing in a girl like this?" with the band's scratchy guitars, heavy drums and some assorted electronic noise.

**BONUS CONTENT**

For a fun fact about Linda Lovelace, scan this QR code

Of his decision to use Linda's dialogue in general and the examination scene in particular, Thirlwell says, "That came about through a series of happy accidents. I like that bit where she says 'I try, but I choke,' and I thought the way that part leads into the song's break was perfect. There was this sort of insidiousness juxtaposed with the beat which worked really well and heralded that next bit. There was just something a bit more sinister about that section."

# "Dogs Are Not People, Linda!"

## Ultra

**(from the album *Youthful Pleasures*, DOM Records)**

A cacophonous mix of clattering sticks, dissonant chords and howling dogs over lyrics that are spoken instead of sung, this tells of reports from "a reliable source close to Sammy Davis Jr." that Linda still loves animals and is trying to find Rufus and Norman, "those brilliant beasts who provided Linda—and us—with so many hours of hard-core entertainment." The speaker says Linda is willing to pay to find some canine companionship (and provide video) then gives out a phone number so the listener can get in touch with her. The phone number is bogus.

To say this song is in bad taste is an understatement, but it's also an interesting bit of tape collage. The vocals are buried deep in the mix at points, so you really have to listen to catch everything, which isn't really too pleasant because the music is pretty unnerving.

# "She's Got To Have It"
# "La La La"
# "Deep Throat"
# "Deeper and Deeper"

**(from the *Deep Throat Part II* soundtrack, Bryan Records)**

The soundtrack to *Deep Throat Part II* contains four vocal tunes and four instrumentals, some surprising players and an interesting history. The man who made the record is composer/arranger Tony Bruno, a music-industry veteran whose career began with the Deltones in 1959. He also helped to found Kama Sutra Records after producing a few hit singles like "All in My Head" for Maxine Brown. Yes, that's the same Kama Sutra records of Linda and the Lollipops fame, although Bruno denies any responsibil-

ity for that single. "At Kama Sutra," he explains, "we were a bunch of guys who did a lot of things, but we didn't ask each other about them. We just did it, and if we made money we shared it. If not, we forgot about it." The Lollipops single, he suggests, was probably something Lou Peraino did with someone else in the record company.

Bruno's involvement in scoring dirty movies came about through his involvement with the Perainos (Lou Peraino shares in most of the songwriting credits on the album). "I knew some people from my days as a kid in Brooklyn, and they approached me to do some music for their movies," he says. "They were doing X-rated pictures. I couldn't say no, so I would do music for them under another name, like Johnny Seven." Bruno appears on the soundtrack album as T.J. Stone, vocalist of "She's Got To Have It," "Deep Throat" and "Deeper and Deeper," and as songwriter M. Colicchio.

He says of the sessions he helmed, "I used to see who wanted to come in and get paid in cash. Anybody who dropped by was welcome." That list of guest stars includes Marty Kupersmith and Kenny Vance of Jay and the Americans (Kupersmith has also worked with Steely Dan and Kiss guitarist Ace Frehley); Steve Nathanson; Pete Anders and Vinnie Poncia, Brill Building songwriters who worked with Phil Spector and were members of the Tradewinds; and Bobby Bloom, who had a hit with the song "Montego Bay."

The music was recorded in an abandoned church on 57th Street and 9th Avenue in New York, without charts or preparation. "The guys would ad lib, I'd record them, then I'd take a single instrument and put a melody line over it and put it to the picture." There wasn't a lot of money to be made, so the recordings were done for the love of making music. Bruno says, "I was offering a good time. Come and play your instruments. There was more fun in the making of the music than in the movie itself."

And he should know. Scoring pornos gave Bruno a good excuse to check out the films, which is how he saw *Deep Throat Part II*. "It was funny. It wasn't excellent acting or anything, but for a porno flick, it had a good storyline: the Russians wanted to kidnap Linda so they could take her to Russia to teach the girls how to do things. I saw it once and then that was it." Of the film's disappearing act, Bruno says, "The Perainos were having trouble with lawsuits for *Deep Throat*, and there was so much turmoil. They were getting busted all over the place and the trial was going on in Florida. They had to keep going back and forth. I think that's how [the film's hardcore footage] got lost."

Bruno and crew's songs show the elements that make up good soundtrack music: The lyrics reflect the story in a subtle and sometimes poetic way, considering the story line they're reflecting. In "Deeper and Deeper," relating Linda's need to take a cock down her throat to reach orgasm, he sings:

Deeper and deeper
Inside you my love grows
Deep, so deep
You keep the love that flows from me
But does it touch the part
That makes the heart within you sing
Until you reach that note?

But *Deep Throat Part II* is a porn soundtrack, hence the song "La La La," in which Laurie Greene sings, "La la lala la la lala/ Linda Lovelace . . ." and little else.

Today we know that a song like "Deep Throat," with its James Bondian theme, evokes suspense in response to the film's Soviet intrigue. But sometimes Bruno's music evoked feelings even he couldn't explain. "There was a guy in the Midwest who kept ordering the single from the soundtrack," he remembers "He used to order 10, 15 at a time. We were wondering, 'Who's ordering all these records?' We were wondering if we had a record that was getting some action. We found that the guy owned a funeral parlor, and he was playing the instrumental of 'Deeper and Deeper' in the viewing room and giving away copies of the records."

# Chapter 6:

# SO HELP ME GOD

## Preaching to the Choir

**Of all the public appearances Linda Lovelace made, none had as big an effect on her public image as when she testified against pornography. Everyone knows she spoke in several high-profile legal arenas, but not everyone knows exactly what she said. Did America's original porn queen really advocate censorship? Here, Linda Lovelace goes on the record, once and for all.**

**On Monday, December 12, 1983, the former Linda Lovelace appeared in public using her married name of Linda Marchiano and testified before the Minneapolis City Council in support of a proposed ordinance that would provide civil as opposed to criminal remedies for pornography, holding the distributors, producers, retailers and consumers of sexually explicit adult material liable for prosecution in regard to any crime committed by someone under its "influence."**

**The legislation was drafted by radical feminists Andrea Dworkin, author of *Pornography: Men Possessing Women,* and Catharine A. MacKinnon, an Associate Professor at the University of Michigan Law School. They had been asked by a group of citizens to testify at hearings meant to get adult bookstores out of their neighborhoods by changing zoning statutes. The pair did wind up testifying—against the proposal—and drafted their own, which they submitted to the Council.**

**Linda Lovelace's testimony was among the most anticipated at hearings for the Dworkin/MacKinnon Anti-Pornography Civil Rights Ordinance, resulting in a packed house and considerable media coverage. This is the complete transcript of her testimony.**

**Chairman White:** Prior to Ms. Marchiano's speaking, I would ask there be no discussions during this because once again, to reiterate, the stenographer is taking down testimony. You now have the floor if you wish to begin.
**Ms. MacKinnon:** We are trying to arrange so that you can see the witness. Go ahead.
**Chairman White:** Give your name and spelling for the stenographer.
**Ms. Marchiano:** I feel I should introduce myself and tell you why I am qualified to speak out against pornography. My name today is Linda Marchiano. Linda Lovelace is the name I bore during a two-and-a-half-year period of imprisonment. For those of you who don't know the name, Linda Lovelace was the victim of this so-called victimless crime.

Used and abused by Mr. Traynor, her captor, she was forced through physical, mental and sexual abuse, and often at gunpoint and threats to her life, to be involved in pornography. Linda Lovelace was not a willing participant but became the sex freak of the '70s.

It all began in 1971. I was recuperating from a near-fatal auto accident at my parents' home in Florida. A girlfriend of mine came to visit me with a person by the name of Mr. Charles Traynor. He came off as a considerate gentleman, asking us what we would like to do and how we would like to spend the afternoon and opening doors and all so-called manners of society.

Needless to say I was impressed, and started to date him. I was not getting along with my own parents. I was 21 and resented being told to be home at 11:00 and to call and say where I was, and to call and give the phone number and address where I would be.

Here comes the biggest mistake of my life. Seeing how upset I was with my home life, Mr. Traynor offered me his assistance. He said I could come and live at his home in Miami. The relationship was platonic, which was fine with me. My plan was to recuperate and then go back to New York and live. I thought then he was being kind and a nice friend. Today I know why the relationship was platonic. He was incapable of a sexual act without inflicting some type of pain or degradation on a human being.

When I decided to head back north and informed Mr. Traynor of my intention, that was when I met the real Mr. Traynor and my two-and-a-half years of imprisonment began. He began a complete turnaround and beat me up physically and began the mental abuse. From that day forward my hell began.

I literally became a prisoner. I was not allowed out of his sight, not even to use the bathroom. Why, you may ask. Because there was a window in the bathroom. When speaking to either my friends or my parents, he was on the extension with a .45 automatic eight-shot pointed at me. I was beaten physically and suffered mental abuse each and every day thereafter.

In my book *Ordeal: An Autobiography*, I go into greater detail of the monstrosity I was put through. From prostitution to porno films to celebrity satisfier. The things that he used to get me involved in pornography went from a .45 automatic eight-shot and M16 semiautomatic machine gun to threats on the lives of my family. I have seen the kind of people involved in pornography and how they will use anyone to get what they want.

So many people ask me, "Why didn't you escape?" Well, I did. I'm here today. I did try during the two-and-a-half years to escape on three separate occasions. The first and second times I was caught and suffered a brutal beating and an awful sexual abuse as punishment. The third time I was at my parents' home and Mr. Traynor threatened to kill my parents. I said, "No you won't, my father is here in the other room," and he said, "I will kill him and each and every member of your family." Just then my nephew came in through the kitchen door to the living room. He pulled out the .45 and said he would shoot him if I didn't leave immediately. I did.

Some of you might say I was foolish, but I'm not the kind of person who could live the rest of my life knowing that another human being had died because of me.

The name Linda Lovelace gave me a great deal of courage and notoriety. Had Linda Boreman been shot dead in a hotel room, no questions would have been asked. If Linda Lovelace was shot dead in Los Angeles, questions would have been asked. After three unsuccessful attempts at escaping, I realized I had to take my time and plan it well. It took six months of preparation to convince Mr. Traynor to allow me out of his sight for 15 minutes. I had to tell him he was right: a woman's body was to be used to make money, that porno was great, that beating people was the right thing to do. Fortunately for me, after I acquired my 15 minutes out of his presence I also had someone that wanted to help me.

I tried to tell my story several times. Once to a reporter, Vernon Scott, who works for the UPI. He said he couldn't print it. Again on *The Regis Philbin Show*, and when I started to explain what happened to me, that I was beaten and forced into it, he laughed. Also at a grand jury hearing in California, after they watched a porno film they asked me why I did it. I said, "Because a gun was being pointed at me," and they just said, "Oh, but no charges were ever filed."

I also called the Beverly Hills Police Department on my final escape attempt and told them that Mr. Traynor was walking around looking for me with an M16. When they first told me that they couldn't become involved in domestic affairs, I accepted that and told them that he was illegally possessing these weapons, and they simply told me to call back when he was in the room.

During the filming of *Deep Throat*, actually after the first day, I suffered a brutal beating in my room for smiling on the set. It was a hotel room and the whole crew was in one room, there was at least 20 people partying, music going, laughing and having a good time. Mr. Traynor started to bounce me off the walls. I figured, out of 20 people there might be one human being that would do something to help me and I was screaming for help, I was being beaten, I was being kicked around and again bounced off of walls. And all of a sudden the room next door became very quiet. Nobody, not one person came to help me.

The greatest complaint the next day is the fact that there was bruises on my body. So many people say that in *Deep Throat* I have a smile on my face and I look as though I am really enjoying myself. No one ever asked how those bruises got on my body.

Mr. Traynor stopped searching for me because he acquired Marilyn Chambers, who I believe is also being held against her will.

A reporter from the Philadelphia newspaper did an interview, his name is Larry Fields. During the course of the interview Ms. Chambers asked for permission to go to the bathroom and he refused it. Mr. Fields objected and said, "Why don't you let the poor girl go to the bathroom? She's about to go on-stage . . ." and he came back with, "I don't tell you how to write your newspaper, don't tell me how to treat my broads."

I have also been in touch with a girl who was with Mr. Traynor two months prior to getting me, who was put through a similar situation, but not as strong. And as it stands today she still fears for her life and the life of her family. Personally, I think it is time that the legal system in this country realize that one, you can't be held prisoner for two-and-a-half years and the next day trust the society which has caused your pain and resume the life you once called yours. It takes time to overcome the total dehumanization which you have been through.

It is time for something to be done about the civil rights of the victims and not criminals, the victims being women. But realize it's not just women who are victims but also children, men and society.

**Chairman White:** Thank you for your testimony, Ms. Marchiano. I would like to say, because of time again, there are those who are a little irate that they are here thinking that they would have the opportunity to participate in this public hearing by getting in a comment. So I think we are going to have to be expeditious in terms of questions and answers. We should move this right along so we give people who are here this morning who will not have the opportunity to speak this evening, to have their day to speak. So would you begin?

**Ms. Dworkin:** Thank you. I will try to do that. Ms. Marchiano, I have to ask you some questions that are difficult for me to ask and I apologize to you for asking them. It is important that we get the answers. Could you describe for us the first time that Mr. Traynor prostituted you?

**Ms. Marchiano:** It happened in Florida. I thought we were going to visit a friend of his and we pulled up to a Holiday Inn. So my second reaction was a buffet, I thought we were going to lunch. And he took me up to a room and there was five men in the room and told me that I was there to satisfy each and every one of them. And I said that I wouldn't do it, so what he did is he took me into this little dressing area and he told me that if I didn't do it he would shoot me. And I said, "You won't shoot me, there's five men in this room. You just won't do it. Somebody will say something and do something." And he just laughed hysterically. He said that my body would be found and I would just be another dead prostitute who was shot in her hotel room or something like that and that none of the men would do anything. They would just laugh.

During this event I started to cry and while these five men were doing whatever they wanted to, and it was really a pitiful scene because here I was, they knew I wasn't into it. One of the men complained and asked for his money back because I was crying and I wasn't the super freak that Mr. Traynor usually brought around. And he was given back his money. And the other four men proceeded to do what they wanted to do through my tears and all.

**Ms. Dworkin:** Thank you, Ms. Marchiano. One of the major themes in pornography is that women are portrayed having intercourse . . . Of doing the various . . .

**Mr. Daughtery:** Could you speak into the mike, ma'am?

**Ms. Dworkin:** One of the situations that is commonly portrayed in pornography is women being . . . women having sexual intercourse and doing various sex acts with animals. You were forced to make such a film. Could you describe for us the situation in which you were forced to make this film?

**Mr. Daughtery:** Would you like to respond?

**Ms. Marchiano:** Yes. I think it is important that everyone understands. Prior to that film being made, about a week, Mr. Traynor suggested the thought that I do films with a D-O-G and I told him I wouldn't do it. I suffered a brutal beating. He claims he suffered embarrassment because I wouldn't do it.

We then went to another porno studio, one of the sleaziest ones I have ever seen, and then this guy walked in with this animal and I again started crying. I started crying. I said, "I am not going to do this," and they were all very persistent, the two men involved in making the pornographic film and Mr. Traynor himself. And I started to leave and go outside of the room where they make these films, and when I turned around there was all of a sudden a gun displayed on the desk, and having seen the coarseness and the callousness of these people involved in pornography, I knew that I would have been shot and killed. Needless to say, the film was shot and still is one of the hardest ones for me to deal with today.

**Ms. Dworkin:** Thank you. I am sorry, but this is something that I had to ask. There was one other incident you described in your book *Ordeal* that involved Mr. Hefner,

Hugh Hefner at the Playboy Mansion, that was about the same theme. Would you tell us briefly about that?
**Ms. Marchiano:** Yes. Well, we first met Mr. Hefner. Mr. Traynor and him sat around discussing what they could do with me, all kinds of different atrocities. And it seemed that Mr. Hefner and Mr. Traynor both enjoyed seeing a woman being used by an animal. And so Mr. Hefner had Mr. Traynor's dog flown in from Florida to the L.A. Mansion. And one evening they decided that it was time and they had one of the security guards bring the animal down to Mr. Hefner's bathhouse and fortunately, during my two-and-a-half years in imprisonment, there was a girl who tried to help me in her own sort of way. She told me the tricks to avoid that kind of situation, and I did what I could to avoid it but Mr. Traynor and Mr. Hefner were both very disappointed.
**Ms. Dworkin:** Thank you. Would you explain to us how it was that Mr. Traynor taught you to do what is now known popularly in this culture because of the movie *Deep Throat* as the sex act of deep-throating?
**Ms. Marchiano:** Well, he used hypnotism. He told me that it would overcome the natural reflexes in your throat that would prevent you from gagging and it was through hypnotism that I was able, I guess, to accomplish the feat, I guess you could say.
**Ms. Dworkin:** So that hypnotism was added to the prostitution?
**Ms. Marchiano:** Yes, it was.
**Ms. Dworkin:** My final question is this: Some people may think that you could have gotten away, for instance, when Mr. Traynor was sleeping. Could you explain to us why that was impossible?
**Ms. Marchiano:** Well, at night what he would do is put his body over my body so that if I did try to get up he would wake up. And he was a very light sleeper. If I did attempt to move or roll over in my sleep he would awaken.
**Ms. Dworkin:** Thank you very much.
**Ms. MacKinnon:** How do you feel about the film *Deep Throat* and its continually being shown?
**Ms. Marchiano:** I feel very hurt and very disappointed in my society and my country for allowing the fact that I was raped, I was beaten, I was put through two-and-a-half years of what I was put through. And it's taken me almost 10 years to overcome the damage that he caused. And the fact that this film is still being shown and that my three children will one day walk down the street and see their mother being abused, it makes me angry, makes me sad. Virtually every time someone watches that film they are watching me being raped.
**Mr. Daughtery:** All right. Catharine, do you have another witness?
**Ms. MacKinnon:** We were going to allow the space for a member of the public who was given the wrong information. She is not part of what we were going to proceed with. We thought it was best to be more brief with Ms. Marchiano so this woman could speak. We have a couple of documents to submit.
**Ms. Dworkin:** May we do that first?
**Mr. Daughtery:** Thank you, Ms. Marchiano, for showing up.
**Ms. Marchiano:** Thank you. I would like to say thank you for everybody who made it possible for me to be here tonight. I want to speak out for what happened to me and for the other members of society. I feel that it is important that victims have a chance today in our society. I also want to say that my children thank you.

**Ms. Dworkin:** I would like to just put into evidence . . . In support of Linda's testimony, we will be providing you with a copy of her book *Ordeal*, which tells the facts. We are also providing you with a copy of her lie-detector test that bears out the truth of everything that she has said to you today. In addition, I would like to read a letter by Dr. Kathleen Barry, who is a Professor of Sociology and who is an author of the book *Female Sexual Slavery*. We will also put this into evidence:

"In this memo I intend to identify the practices related to pornography which constitute a violation of women's civil rights, and in accordance with the International Declaration of Human Rights, they constitute a violation of women's human rights. As I have already conducted, reported and published the research in this book," she goes on to say that she is not going to reiterate all of the conclusions.

"Number one, pornography is used by pimps as part of the illegal action of procuring and attempting to induce young girls and women into prostitution by presenting young women and girls with pornography which fraudulently represents actually painful sexual practices and acts as pleasing and gratifying to the female represented in the pornography. The pimp attempts to convince young and vulnerable, usually homeless, young women to prostitute themselves for him. Pornography plays a large role in the deception that is necessary to put naive young women into prostitution.

"When a young girl or woman is procured, pornography is often used as part of the seasoning and blackmail strategies which will force her into prostitution. Prior to being 'turned out' to prostitution, many pimps 'season' or break down their victims through sessions of rape and other forms of sexual abuse. Sometimes these sessions are photographed or filmed and used in a variety of ways which include personal pleasure of the pimp and his friends, blackmailing the victim by threatening to send them to her family and selling them to pornographers for mass production. This constitutes the use of pornography as a form of torture and the marketing of actual torture sessions in the form of film and pictures as a pleasure commodity.

"Pornography is a form of prostitution and consequently pornographers are pimps. There have been several court cases upholding the convictions of pornographers as pimps for having been supported off the earnings of prostitutes."

That is a small portion of Kathleen Barry's letter, which I will submit with her book. I would also like to read just two paragraphs to you from the U.N. report on the suppression of the traffic in persons and the exploitation of the prostitution of others. I will also put this into evidence. . . .

**Chairman White:** Ms. Dworkin, I would like to . . . I hate to continually talk all the time, [but] if you could just submit them for the record . . . The media, if they wish them, they can get them from the committee clerks and so we can just move right along.

**Ms. Dworkin:** Thank you. There is one other point that I want to make. I won't read the whole letter. I will tell you that we have a letter here from a New York crisis worker about the increased existence of rape of the throat since the distribution of the movie *Deep Throat*. And in addition the increased use of cameras in actual rape situations.

**Chairman White:** We are going to move quite quickly now. Ms. Marchiano, I want to thank you for coming to testify.

**Ms. Marchiano:** Thank you very much.

1

EXHIBIT 9

I feel I should introduce myself and tell you why I feel I am qualified to speak out against ponagraphy. My name is Linda Marchiano, but Linda Lovelace was the name I bore during a 2½ year period of imprisonment. For those of you who don't know, the name, Linda Lovelace was the victim of this so called victimless crime.

Used and abused by Mr. Traynor, her captor she was forced through physical mental and sexual abuse and often at gunpoint and traits of her life to be involved in ponagraphy. Linda Lovelace was not a willing participant but became the sex freak of the 70's.

PAUSE

It all began in 1971, I was recuperating, from a near fatal car accident, at my parents home in Fla. A girlfriend of mine came over to visit me with a person by the name of Mr. Charles Traynor. Mr. Traynor came off as a very considerate gentleman. Asking us what we would like to do

Entered into evidence with Linda Marchiano's testimony, a copy of her book *Ordeal* and the chapter "The Real Linda Lovelace" from Gloria Steinem's book *Outrageous Acts and Everyday Rebellions* were these handwritten notes Linda made in preparation for the hearing.

and how we would like to spend the afternoon. Opening doors, lighting cigarettes and all the so called good manners of society.

Needless to say I was impressed and started to date him. I was not at the time getting along with my parents. I was 21 and resented being told to be home at 11:00 and to call and say where I was and give the phone # and address.

Here comes the biggest mistake of my life. Seeing how upset I was with my homelife. Mr. Traynor offered his assistance. He said I could come and live at his home in North Miami. The relationship at that point was platonic, which was just fine with me. My plan was to recuperate and then go back to N.Y. and the life I was living before my accident. I thought then he was being kind and a nice friend.

Today I know why. the relationship was platontic He was incapable

The Dworkin/MacKinnon Anti-Pornography Civil Rights Ordinance proposed a legal definition of pornography: "The sexually explicit subordination of women, graphically depicted, whether in pictures or in words," in which women are dehumanized and enjoy sexual humiliation and rape.

of a sexual act without inflicting some kind of degracation or pain upon another.

When I decided to head back North and informed Mr. Traynor of my intention that was when I met the real Mr. Traynor and my 2½ years of imprisonment began. He made a complete ~~tur~~ turnaround and beat me up physically and began the mental abuse, from that day forward my hell began.

I literally became a prisoner I was not allowed out of his sight, not even to use the bathroom. Why? because there was a window in the bathroom. When speaking to either my friends or my parents he was on the extention with a 45 revolver pointed at me. I was beaten physically and suffered mental abuse each and every day.

In ~~so~~ my book "Ordeal" an autobiography I go into greater ~~deta~~ detail of the attrosides I was put through.

In addition to Linda Lovelace, several victims of sexual abuse testified about the effect that pornography had on their lives, speaking of beatings and violence at the hands of husbands and boyfriends who had become desensitized by reading and viewing smut.

From prostitution, porno films to celebrity satisfier. ~~Th~~ The things that he used to get me involved in pornagraphy from a 45 automatic 8 shot + M-16 semi-automatic machine gun to threats on the lives of my family. I have seen the kind of people involved in pornagraphy and how they will use anyone to get what they want.

~~So~~ many people ask me ~~I~~ why didn't you escape? Well I did I'm here today. I did ~~[illegible]~~ try during 2½ years, to escape on 3 separate occasions. The 1st +2nd time ~~[illegible]~~ I was caught and suffered a brutal beating and an awful sexual abuse as punishment. The 3rd time I was at my parents home and Mr. Traynor treatened to kill my parents. I said "no" you won't my father ~~was~~ is here he said "I kill ~~him~~ and each and every member of your family as they come ~~thru~~ the door. Just then my ~~ne~~ newphew came thru the kitchen door to the living room. He pulled out

Opponents of the bill charged that it was a blatant violation of the First Amendment guarantee of Free Speech and the 14th Amendment guarantee of due process of law. All involved in the hearings agreed that if passed, the Ordinance would eventually end up before the Supreme Court.

his 45 and said he'd shot him if I didn't leave immediately. I did. ~~S~~
Some of you might say I was foolish but I'm not the kind of person who could live the rest of my life knowing others had died to make it possible.

~~On my final~~.

~~NOTARY~~ NOTARITY GAVE ME COURAGE

After 3 unsuccessful attempts at escaping I realized I had to ~~pl~~ take my time and plan it well. It took 6 months of preparation to convince Mr. Traynor ~~I~~ to ~~was~~ allow me out of his sight for 15 min. I had to tell him he was right a women's body was to be use to make money, that porno was great that beating people was the right thing TO DO Fortunately for me ~~a~~ after I acquired my 15 min. I also had someone who wanted to help me.

I tried to tell my story several times. Once to Vernon Scott a U.P.I reporter who said he couldn't print it once on Rejis Philibin show. but he just laughed. And also at a grand Jury ~~[illegible]~~

Although Mayor Donald Fraser tried to delay further movement on the bill, on Friday, December 30, 1983, the Minneapolis City Council voted on and passed the Dworkin/MacKinnon Anti-Pornography Civil Rights Ordinance by a vote of 7 to 6. Fraser soon after announced that he might not sign it.

Jury trial in Calif. after they watched a
porno film they asked why I did it
and I said because a gun was being
pointed at me. They said Oh! "No
Charges WERE FILED." Police Dept.
During the filming of D.T. actually
after the 1st day I suffered a brutal
beating in my room for smiling on the
set. EXPLAIN — — — —

COVERING BRUISES BIGGEST ~~[illegible]~~ COMPLAINT(S)E.

Mr. Traynor stopped searching for me
because he acquired M.C. Whom I
believe is also being held against her
will. ~~[illegible]~~ Larry Field.
A reporter from the Phila. Paper
did interview. — . . —

Stop-
~~Gloria Steinem sent NOTE~~ . . . .

~~Marty Yen~~

But . ~~and~~ some of you out ~~those who are~~

~~members of society~~ came ~~here~~ to

A few days later on January 6, 1984, Mayor Fraser vetoed the bill, albeit reluctantly, he said, in fear that it was too unconstitutional to be enforced. He then sent the ordinance back to the City Council so they could work on rewriting the objectionable parts.

~~What helped me ...~~

I have recently been in touch with a girl or VICE VERSA who escaped from M. Traynor 2 months prior to his acquireing me. Escaped herself from MR. Traynor. Will helped me but still fears the safty of herself + family.

~~So all some of you today have come to snicker some have come to learn. And I hope that those of you who came to snicker have learned.~~

~~All I can ... ask~~ a

~~SIGN OUT~~.

~~My children thank you.~~

The COURTS HAVE to REALIZE / HELD PRISONER 2½ YRS. / FREE

IT'S TIME SOMETHING should BE DONE FOR THE VICTIMS AND NOT THE CRIMINALS.

Mayor Fraser had called the bill "a travesty on the First Amendment and unacceptable not only to the [Minneapolis] Civil Liberties Union but to the right of Minneapolis citizens to make their own judgements about the content of books and movies."

It is Time The Legal System In This Country Realizes You Cannot Be Held Prisoner For 2½ yrs. And The Next Day; Thrust The Society which Has Caused Your Pain And Resume The Life You Once Called Yours. It Takes Time To Overcome The Total Dehumanization Which You Have Been Thru.

It is time For Something to Be Done About The Civil Rights of the Victims And Not The Criminals. The Victims Being Women. ~~I Grew Up At A Time When A Women Was Sacred~~ But Realize Please It Is Not Just Women Who Are Victims But Also Children, MEN ~~Males~~, AND ~~and~~ our society.

After Mayor Fraser vetoed the bill, the City Council reintroduced it and formed a task force to look into possible changes. Their report did nothing to help the measure get passed, and the bill was eventually dropped from the City Council's agenda.

**Linda Lovelace's most notable public testimony—certainly her most notorious—was given in Washington, D.C., on September 12, 1984, when she appeared before the Attorney General's Commission on Pornography, more commonly known as the Meese Commission hearings. Linda's testimony would go on to fuel both sides of the pornography debate, providing anti-porn activists with justification for their calls to ban adult entertainment (again based on its effects on women and children) and providing pro-porn advocates the fodder with which to accuse Linda of promoting censorship. A reading of Linda's testimony shows it to be somewhere between the two extremes. Questioned by Senator Arlen Specter, Linda only discussed pornography's effects on herself, and she never called for the outright ban of all smut, just showings of the film *Deep Throat*.**

**Senator [Arlen] Specter:** We appreciate your coming. As it is with the other women who have testified, we understand that this is not easy, but the subject matters are of importance, and they do provide a factual background for the Congress to make an evaluation as to what action should be taken, it is a matter of public policy, and what action may be appropriately taken, given the First Amendment rights which we have discussed earlier.

You may proceed.

**Ms. Marchiano:** Okay. First of all, I want to say thank you to all who are responsible for my being here to speak. I only hope that your doing so means that my government, and therefore my society, is ready to address the dark side of pornography.

My story is a common one. I was young and naive. My ordeal began when I had the misfortune to meet a Mr. Charles Traynor, whom, when I first met him, was a gentleman, so much so that he was the kind of guy that your mom would want you to know.

When I first met Mr. Traynor, my parents and I were not getting along, and Mr. Traynor offered a way around the problem. I look back now, and I know he was definitely taking advantage of the situation.

We had a platonic relationship until the day I told him that I wanted to leave, and at that point I was beaten physically and mentally, and my imprisonment began. From that day forward, I was not my own human being.

Mr. Traynor would be the first to say that he took a naive girl, who was embarrassed to take her clothes off in front of a man, and turned her into what he thought was a super sex freak.

I was then forced into a marriage with Mr. Traynor, on advice from his attorney. I literally became a prisoner of his, and was not allowed out of his sight, not even to go to the bathroom, for he feared that with a window in the bathroom I could make an escape.

Mr. Traynor, through threats on my life and the lives of my family and friends, by means of an automatic .45 eight-shot PPK, through a semiautomatic M16 machine gun, forced me into prostitution, pornography films and ultimately celebrity satisfier.

Due to my involvement in pornography, I have seen the type of people involved in it, the callousness and the inhuman way that they are only looking to make a dollar. It does not matter to them whose little girl they use.

So many people ask why I did not get away. Well, I did, but it was not easy. I made three unsuccessful attempts at escaping, and suffered a brutal beating for trying, and some sick sexual perversion as punishment. After three unsuccessful attempts at escaping, I realized that I would have to create a master plan, and so for the next six months I did what I could to convince Mr. Traynor that I was into what he was into, and thank God, when my time came, I had someone who wanted to help me, and when I first escaped from Mr. Traynor, I was hiding out in hotels, and I had someone who was bringing me different colored wigs, and clothes, and going from one hotel to another, and I hired two bodyguards, 24 hours a day, to protect me, until I ran out of finances.

Then someone said, "Why do you simply not call the police?" So I did. I called the Beverly Hills Police Department, and I told them that my husband was running around with a .45 and an M16, to kill me, and they just told me they could not get involved in domestic affairs. So I said, fine, I can accept that, but he is illegally possessing these weapons, can you do something about that? They said, "Lady, call us back when he's in the room."

If Linda Boreman, which was my name when I grew up, had been shot in that hotel room, when I was thrown into a hotel room that day, had I been shot that day, no questions would have been asked. I would just simply have been another prostitute, or someone who was beaten and abused by her clientele. But had Linda Lovelace been shot in California, there would have been questions asked. Fortunately, for me, in one respect, and unfortunately, the name Linda Lovelace gave notoriety, and therefore gave me some sort of protection. It took me six months of convincing Mr. Traynor that I was into beatings, that sexual perversion was all right, and the fact that a woman was to be used by a man, to be abused, and make money.

And after six months, I acquired 15 minutes out of his presence. I am free from Mr. Traynor today, but my ordeal still goes on. The film, *Deep Throat*, still shows, and virtually every time someone watches that movie, they are watching me being raped, and it is very difficult, because I have two beautiful children, and I do not think it is fair. I tried to raise my children to go by the rules of our country, and the rules of the schools, and the laws, and the regulations we all should abide by, but the other day my eight-year-old son said to me, "Mommy, if this country is so great, how come people are still hurting you?" And I had a hard time with that one, trying to answer him, and give him an honest answer.

I am also still being financially raped by Traynor's lawyer, who has already used me and abused me physically. So many people have said that I have such a smile on my face in that film, and that I was having such a good time, but you know what, no one ever says, "Where did the bruises come from?"

After the first day of shooting I suffered a brutal beating in my room. The whole crew of the film *Deep Throat* was in an adjoining room, and Mr. Traynor and I were in another, and he started yelling and screaming at me for smiling on the set that day.

And in my mind, I thought, "Well here is a chance, there is a whole room of people, somebody is bound to help me." And as he was beating me up, and bouncing me off walls, and punching me, and everything, the room became very quiet, but nobody came to help me.

And the next day, the greatest complaint was the fact that there was bruises on my body, because Mr. Damiano felt that destroyed the little-girl-next-door, innocent look that he was looking for.

**Senator Specter:** How many people were present when he was punching you, as you describe it?

**Ms. Marchiano:** Well, I was not in the other room, but I would say there would have to be 10 to 12 people in the other room.

**Senator Specter:** But they were in the adjacent room, and not in the precise room that you were in?

**Ms. Marchiano:** No, not in the precise room. In the hotel they run one room after another. Well, there was a door adjoining the two rooms. We were in this room, and they were in the next room.

**Senator Specter:** But you believe that they could hear what was going on, from the noise?

**Ms. Marchiano:** Oh sure, because they were all partying and laughing, and music was going, and when I started getting beat up, they became quiet, and the music was shut off. Nobody came to help, and the next day, the greatest complaint was the bruises, and how to cover them up, and what kind of makeup to use, and that was the thing they were really interested in.

**Senator Specter:** Ms. Marchiano, you referred to bruises; as a point of corroboration of what you have testified to here today, and have said in the past, what physical bruises, and what marks are left on your body as corroboration for what you have said here about Mr. Traynor?

**Ms. Marchiano:** My physical health, right now?

**Senator Specter:** Yes.

**Ms. Marchiano:** Well, I had to have surgery on my right leg. I used to use my right leg to protect my body, when he was kicking me. So all the surface veins in my right leg are broken, and need to be removed.

I was also forced to have illegal silicone injections, and I have to have—they have to remove my breasts, and see how much tissue damage there is from the silicone, and then, depending on how much damage they find, is whether they will be able to, you know, do plastic surgery, and rebuild them.

I guess the greatest scar of all was about two years ago. Because of all the beatings I suffered from Mr. Traynor, and everything else, I had to have an abortion. My doctor told me that because of what I went through, there was a good chance that I could be crippled for life, and so that was the only time, that is part of what Mr. Traynor did to me and I think that is the first time that I ever really felt hatred upon him.

**Senator Specter:** Ms. Marchiano, one of the questions we have been exploring here, in a variety of contexts, involve the possible remedies that women have when they are wronged by somebody. Have you or your attorneys considered suing Mr. Traynor for damages or to stop future showings of *Deep Throat*?

**Ms. Marchiano:** Well, first of all, in our country the statute of limitations on your own personal self is only two years, whereas on property it goes up to 20 or more. I think it is fairly important that the society realize that when you are held prisoner for two and a half years, and you have gone through so much degradation and humiliation, when you are finally free, you do not bounce back to where you were before. It takes time. It's been 12 years for me, and there are still times, when I am with my children, that I just cry when I think of something that I went through.

**Senator Specter:** How about the aspect of suing to stop the further showing of *Deep Throat*?

**Ms. Marchiano:** I was told that an injunction could be placed on the showing of the film, but I was also told that it would take at least $500,000 to get everything started. I do not have that kind of money.

**Senator Specter:** So you have not started that kind of an action, because of the expense involved?

**Ms. Marchiano:** I cannot afford it, no.

**Senator Specter:** Please proceed with your testimony.

**Ms. Marchiano:** Okay. I think that I was mentioning about the bruises on my legs and all. And I think it is really important that when people do not care enough about people, it should become an issue.

This accepted film caused me pain, and my society and government have accepted pornography, knowing its smiles. Now I am telling you about its bruises. *Deep Throat* made $600 million, and I received physical pain and the brand Linda Lovelace. The wounds may heal someday, but Linda Lovelace remains, because that is the law, so far.

Pornography destroys the family unit, and the family unit is a foundation of our country. If you have any doubt, remember that the youngest victim of child pornography was 13 months old. Remember also the women and young boys who are raped and murdered and look down to us to care about them and others, and then to do something in our lifetime to make it change. My contribution here today is one of informing you of what I went through. The so-called classic film that had created a myth and had helped give pornography acceptability was made under physical duress. I can only tell you of my ordeal, but I must add that I believe there are many others out there in a similar situation.

I have been on a program in Boston, with a psychiatrist, and he said that the only difference between my story and what goes on in society today is that I am alive to tell about it. He said most of the women are abused by pimps and pornographers, and they are injected with heroin or some sort of drug, and tossed in an alleyway, and he said when the police find them they assume it is a prostitute, or a junkie who has OD'd, and it stops their investigation.

We have gone from the acceptability of *Deep Throat* in 1972 to child pornography to snuff movies and the mutilation of women in 1983 in Arizona, to the sexual abuse of young children in our day-care centers, by city employees in the city of New York. My question is, what is next?

I hope that I have helped you. If you have any more questions, I would be happy to answer them.

**Senator Specter:** So your basic point is that *Deep Throat* got $600 million and you got a lot of bruises?

**Ms. Marchiano:** That is not the main point. The main point is that they took a human being, and through pain and degradation and beatings and constant threats, forced me to do something that I would never have become involved in, had it not been for a .45 put to my head.

**Senator Specter:** And you believe, Ms. Marchiano, that the pattern of women's responses, who are actresses or models, who are subjects of photographs, that to a significant extent replay your situation of being coerced, forced to do so?

**Ms. Marchiano:** I think some of them are. I am sure there are those out there who want to do it, that are doing it voluntarily, but there are those, you know, who do not, who would never get involved with it at all.

**Senator Specter:** And what is your response to those who say that a movie like *Deep Throat* ought to be permitted to be shown, under the Constitutional protection of the First Amendment?

**Ms. Marchiano:** What about my First Amendment rights? What about my rights as a human being? You know, it is not fair. Like I said before, every time someone sees that film, they are watching me being raped, and I am trying to teach my children good, and then they turn around and see that, I was raped, I was beaten, and this film is still being allowed to be shown, and people are still making money off it, and my family and my children and I are suffering because of it. It is not fair. It is unhumane.

# Chapter 7: SPEAK OF THE DEVIL

## Linda Opens Up, Again

**It may not be definitive, but it sure is defining. For the first time in 25 years, the original porn icon sits down to talk with a member of the adult press. In the following interview, the former Linda Lovelace talks about censorship, pornography and . . . *Christian Slater*?**

T

**The following interview—Linda's first with a member of the adult press since 1975—was conducted in a hotel room near Linda's home in Englewood, Colorado, in April 2000. Once she accepted my offer speak her piece in this book, she soon agreed to the one basic ground rule: Everything was on the record once the tape started rolling. In return, she had my guarantee it would only be edited for grammar and length, not for content. I offered to let her see the interview before it was printed; she declined.**

**Danville:** Why was Linda Lovelace the world's first porn queen?
**Boreman:** Hmmm. That's a good question. Why was Linda Lovelace the first porn star? How did I get so lucky? I don't know. The luck of the Irish, I guess. [laughs] From what I've heard, it was the fact that *Deep Throat* was a comedy, quote unquote, and because it was on the big screen. The humor in *Deep Throat* made it easier for other people to go into a theater and view it. At least that's what I've always heard.
**Danville:** Your billing in *Deep Throat* says, "Introducing Linda Lovelace as Herself." Did people believe you were literally that character?
**Boreman:** Yeah, people thought that's the way I was. No doubt. I do think people believed that.
**Danville:** What aside from the way you gave head made people notice you?
**Boreman:** Gerry Damiano thought it was the fact that I had that sweet, innocent look. I didn't have bleached blonde hair, I wasn't chewing bubble gum and counting the cracks in the ceiling. Again, that's just what I've heard. As far as what I was doing, I just thought everybody else did that. I didn't know any better. For me, it was cool, because after being with Mr. Traynor and being forced into prostitution, if I did that I felt like I wasn't being abused sexually. As much.
**Danville:** Did you used to read the articles that people wrote about you?
**Boreman:** No. I read a couple of articles and just got frustrated because they would take things out of context, so I never bothered reading anything after that. Every once in a while I would read something, but it would just get me annoyed.
**Danville:** You've always said that being famous helped you get away from Traynor. Have you ever thought that was because Al Goldstein made it popular?
**Boreman:** I've never thought that, no. Al Goldstein's an obnoxious person. He's fat

and ugly. No, I've never thought that. Not at all. Goldstein "made" that movie? I don't think I can really totally agree with that. When I went out, even after *Ordeal* was published, it was me that the people got to know. I think it was more me than him, and not being the bleached blonde chewing bubble gum and that kind of thing. That attitude and stuff like that. And the answers that Traynor gave me. I think Chuck Traynor was the success of *Deep Throat*, if you want to get right down to it. He gave me all the answers. He knew what he wanted me to say. He was perverted enough that he knew what would stimulate other people. He gave me answers for every question he could think of.

**Danville:** Goldstein wrote that *Deep Throat* was the best porn movie ever made.

**Boreman:** It probably was at that time. Before that, you know, I'd only seen maybe three seconds of a porn movie. One time my girlfriend and I were at her uncle's house and he had a movie and we put it on to see what it was then shut it right off. That was the only time I'd ever seen a porn movie. But like I started to say, it probably was the best porn film because it wasn't the seedy kind of films that I hear were made. Again, back to the bleached blonde looking around like she's supposed to be having an orgasm. I thought, and I still do think, that pornography is sleazy, but *Deep Throat* was not as sleazy as what had been shown or shot.

**Danville:** How did the fame you achieved affect your life? Was it ever good to be "Linda Lovelace"?

**Boreman:** Definitely. I felt protected because of the media. I felt safer with the notoriety, because with that notoriety I didn't think Traynor would kill me or really, really abuse me. He would keep it limited as far as beatings went because he didn't want people to see bruises all over my body. So it gave me a sense of protection. Like I've said many times before, if plain old Linda had been shot in a hotel room, no questions would have been asked, but had "Linda Lovelace" been shot in a hotel room, there would have been investigations. People would have tried to figure out what really happened. So I felt more protected.

And there were times when I had fun. Not so much with Traynor, more after I got away from Traynor and was with David Winters, because he was in a whole other league. Yeah, there were times it was fun. I met a lot of people. When I was with Traynor, the only thing that I really enjoyed was the fact that the fame protected me. I felt safer. I didn't feel like he was gonna pull that .45 out and shoot me. When I was with Traynor, it was still, "You can be with her if you do this . . ." I met Sammy Davis Jr. when I was with Traynor, and I had a lot of fun with Sammy. He protected me a lot of times, an awful lot of times. So there were good times during it. After I got away from Traynor it was a lot more fun, because I wasn't being sexually abused. I was walking around with transparent clothes on, but that wasn't too bad. I didn't think looking sexy was a terrible thing. And I wasn't being forced into having sex with quote unquote celebrities. I had many, many good times when I was with David. [smiles] When I was with David I had an awesome time. I went to see my first play. I saw Richard Chamberlain in *Cyrano DeBergerac*, I saw *Grease* in Manhattan. [laughs] I became cultured, I guess. I'd never been cultured. I saw the Alvin Ailey dancers. I met a lot of people and had a lot of fun at that point.

**Danville:** It's interesting that you say there's nothing wrong with looking sexy. A lot of people think you don't enjoy sex.

**Boreman:** That's not true! That's not true at all. I enjoy sex a lot more now that I'm divorced from my husband. [laughs] That was a kind of prostitute situation, too. I think that I started enjoying sex most after I got away from him, divorced him and met some other people. My husband was drunk all the time. Who wants to have a drunk person laying on top of you every night?

**Danville:** Did being forced into prostitution and pornography turn you off to sex?

**Boreman:** No, because right after it all happened, I ended up with Larry. There were times like he would touch me in a certain way and I would have a flashback [to something bad] and I would get totally turned off, but I wasn't that turned on by him to begin with. I just wanted kids. That's what I wanted. When I got pregnant with my son, I didn't care if my husband stayed or went. I just wanted my son. I fought to keep my son. My husband wanted me to have an abortion. He never wanted [the baby]. Then I deliberately got pregnant with my daughter. That's what I wanted. I wanted kids.

Maybe the first six months that I was with him, I enjoyed sex. The next 24 years I didn't. I've had two boyfriends since my divorce, and I've had an awesome time! I've come more in the past four years than I have in my whole life! I think sex is great. When two people click and everything happens just right, there's nothing better. The only thing I'm disappointed about is getting older. There are a lot of sexy clothes that I'd like to wear, but I'm not gonna gross anybody out by wearing them! [laughs]

**Danville:** You love sex, you're just not into the commercial aspect of it?

**Boreman:** I think it's sad. I really do. I think that if two people can't communicate and enjoy sex together, they shouldn't be together. To have to watch somebody else having sex to be stimulated, I think shows you've got a problem.

**Danville:** Let's say there's a guy in a wheelchair . . .

**Boreman:** Oh no! I hear this all the time! "What about the guy in the wheelchair?"

**Danville:** Or a guy so socially inept that his only sexual outlet is watching porn?

**Boreman:** Like I'm saying, they've got a problem.

**Danville:** Can't that guy's problem be dealt with by watching porn in the privacy of his own home?

**Boreman:** I don't think so. Because most of the porn that's out there, I'd say, 70 percent of it is kiddie porn, child porn. How can that stimulate anybody?

**Danville:** Actually, it's not that high a percentage.*

**Boreman:** It's the biggest seller. Kiddie porn is the biggest seller in magazines, photographs . . .

**Danville:** That's not the kind of pornography I'm talking about, though.

**Boreman:** I don't watch pornographic movies, so I really don't know what's out there. From what I read and the research I see when we do lectures, most of it's very degrading to women. Somebody's always being degraded. It's not real passion. If they had a movie where there was real passion, I could see the guy who's in a wheelchair watching it. Seeing it for what it really is. To show a woman wanting to get beat up

* As it turns out, we were both wrong. A U.S.Customs agent I asked for an official stat on the ratio of "mainstream" porn to "child" porn said there is no official stat, explaining that you can't measure child porn against legit porn because of the unknown quantity of porn they don't seize, likening the situation to measuring illegal drugs against prescription drugs. Customs measures their success, he said, on the number of arrests per year, which he claimed were up.

and smacked around and pissed on and shit on, no, I don't think that's healthy for anybody, even the person in a wheelchair. So it really depends on the content.

**Danville:** Anti-porn activists always bring up piss videos and shit videos. We're not allowed to do them here.

**Boreman:** You still do them here, don't give me that.

**Danville:** Not in a big mainstream commercial sense.

**Boreman:** It's all the stuff that's under the table.

**Danville:** Most of that stuff comes from Europe.

**Boreman:** Then how come they get away with making kiddie porn? Do you know the youngest victim is 13 months old?

**Danville:** "They" don't get away with making kiddie porn. The police and the FBI are always busting people for kiddie porn. But we're not talking abut kiddie porn.

**Boreman:** You can go to any pornographic theater or store anywhere in the country, and if you wanted kiddie porn, you could get it.

**Danville:** No, you can't.

**Boreman:** I don't agree with that.

**Danville:** When's the last time you were in a porn store? [laughs]

**Boreman:** I haven't been! [laughs]

**Danville:** Kiddie porn is an underground industry. Everyone's against kiddie porn.

**Boreman:** That to me is what's happened because of *Deep Throat*. I feel that *Deep Throat* gave pornography credibility and people were able to accept it. Husbands and wives went to see it together. Maybe I'm wrong, maybe back then they did have kiddie porn. It just seems that if people are stimulated to a certain point they eventually want something different. Maybe something more aggressive, maybe something more abusive, maybe something more bizarre. Then they make movies where women are getting beaten up. And they make child pornography.

**Danville:** That's where these porno debates always get fucked up. Pro-porno people talk about mainstream porn made by consenting adults, and anti-porno people always bring kiddie porn into it.

**Boreman:** Yeah, it always does come up, because it's there. Most of the world doesn't realize it or think about it, and they should. That's why I bring it up all the time. To make people aware that it's out there. Childhood is such a small part of your life, and it's so beautiful. I look at my grandson, and he's so innocent and so wonderful, and to think that somebody would sexually abuse him just blows me away. People have to be aware. I think if somebody wants to make a porno movie and they enjoy it, then go for it. But it's like, why did it happen to me? There were plenty of women out there who would have done that. Andrea True would've been in seventh heaven if she had been Linda Lovelace. Why was it me? Why did I have to be beaten up and forced into it? If that happened to me, then I'm sure it's happened to a lot of women out there, besides children. That's the part of it that I don't like.

**Danville:** What do you say to people who say you're the type of person who needs to be dominated?

**Boreman:** I've heard people say that before. I'm a submissive person and I like someone controlling me, and that kind of thing. . . .

**Danville:** You wrote in *Ordeal* that your parents hit you.

**Boreman:** My father hit me once in my whole life. My mother was the one who hit me with a broom, hit me with a rope, smacked me across the face, stuff like that. She was old-school, but it wasn't a daily thing, you know? It was worse when she was going through menopause. That was the time she hit me with the broom because I brought home the wrong thing from the store. She said if I didn't have my mind on boys so much that I would've brought the right thing home. She was going through menopause, she was going through a lot of changes back then. She hit me a few times, but like I said it wasn't on a daily basis or anything like that.

I would never say the things to my mother that my daughter says to me, and I've never hit my daughter. I think I turned out to be a decent person. I care about other people. I don't try to deliberately hurt other people. Whereas I look at my daughter, and right now she's hurting, so she's hurting everybody around her.

**Danville:** Are people wrong to think that you became involved with Chuck Traynor because of a cycle of sexual or physical abuse?

**Boreman:** I was an obedient child, alright.

**Danville:** You had a very strict Catholic upbringing.

**Boreman:** Yup. I was obedient. I skipped school once in my whole life, and I was so scared to death that my mother was gonna see me that I never did it again. It wasn't worth it. She didn't hit me. It was just, "If my mother sees me, she's gonna kill me!" Not beat the crap out of me or anything. She would yell. My mother would raise her voice and I'd be on my knees praying, Ohmigod, ohmigod. It was that kind of thing. It was just something that you knew. She was strict, but she was very loving. My boyfriends over the years were never abusive. I went out with one guy who hit me and I never saw him again. So, no, I wasn't always in abusive relationships. It wasn't something I was searching out. And my dad never, never raised his voice at me. Not once in my entire life. One time he hit me because he caught me lying to my mother. I'd told my mother I was going to the hospital to visit a friend and my girlfriend and I went and met these two guys and rode around in their car all night, you know? I mean, I got home on time. And my mother asked where I was, and I told her, "Oh, I was at the hospital." And she said, "No you weren't, I called there." My father got mad at me for lying to her and he smacked me on my butt, once in my whole life. It wasn't like I grew up in an "abusive house." But I grew up in a house where I was disciplined, no doubt.

**Danville:** Some people assume that you just have a submissive personality and that you actually loved what was going on.

**Boreman:** Oh, I was definitely submissive. My mother didn't raise no fool. Traynor had beaten me enough times that I knew what I had to do in order to not get a beating—and that's what I did. I wouldn't deliberately screw up so I'd get beat up. I did everything I could the right way so that I wouldn't get beat up. He definitely had control of me. I was scared shit of him, no doubt.

I'd never been around somebody like that. I mean, yeah, my mother hit me a

couple times in my life, but I was never around somebody that was constantly being verbally abusive. The mental abuse was definitely the worst. That was worse than getting beaten. I got beat up, I got threatened with knives—you know, knives to my face—a machine gun, the whole nine yards. Whoa, I wasn't ready for that [mental abuse].

I wasn't strong enough. I don't know if I wasn't strong enough to stand up for myself because there were a couple of times that I tried to, but I ended up getting some kind of sexual perversion as punishment and then getting beat anyway. I always knew someday, somewhere, somehow I would get away. That it was just a nightmare and I would wake up someday.

I was disappointed that my friends didn't do something more for me. There was one guy who called one time while Traynor was on the other line, and he was saying, "This isn't you." I had dated him for like six months, almost a year. He knew that wasn't me. We'd had sex together and he knew I wasn't the crazy person they were portraying.

He was asking if there was anything that he could do to help me, but I knew Traynor was on the extension, so I couldn't say anything. I was just disappointed he didn't realize [I was thinking], "You were right when you said that this isn't me. Don't give up, don't leave me now. Come get me."

**Danville:** Why did you join up with feminists trying to ban porn instead of feminists trying to fight domestic abuse?

**Boreman:** The people fighting domestic abuse never approached me. Catharine [MacKinnon] was the first person to really approach me. Women Against Pornography asked me to come to a press conference in Manhattan. I was married, I was pregnant with my daughter, I was in my home raising my family. And here comes someone who says, "Come down here and do this." I didn't say, "Well, what are your credentials? What are you fighting for?"

I used to have a girlfriend who lived across the street whose husband would give her so much money to buy groceries, and whatever she could save on groceries was her money for the week. To me, that's domestic abuse. You know what I'm saying? My daughter went through that when she was with her boyfriend. He never let her have 10 cents. He controlled the money. He didn't say, "Oh, I just got paid, here's 100 bucks, or even here's 20 bucks." Nothing. She would have to ask for money. That, to me, is domestic abuse.

**Danville:** What's the difference between pornography and erotica?

**Boreman:** I get asked that question all the time. I have no clue. You know, I really don't. Erotica? I actually don't watch this kinda stuff. When I think of erotica, I think of sensual, I think of stimulating. I think of nice things. When I think of pornography, I think of somebody smacking you across the face or kicking you in the gut. I mean, I've seen movies that have sexy scenes in them, and they're stimulating if they're done right. But I don't think I could watch a pornographic movie and find it stimulating at all. Especially because of what happened to me.

**Danville:** You don't ever go for the cheap thrill?

**Boreman:** I like love stories. Prince Charming comes in and sweeps you off your feet and takes you away and life is perfect, you know? Yeah, there are times when I'll look for something that has some kind of passion in it, that's stimulating.

**Danville:** Who's an actor you think is cute?

**Boreman:** Christian Slater. Tommy Lee Jones. Not cute, but there's something about them. And Powers Boothe. Oooh! [laughs]
**Danville:** If you see that a Powers Boothe movie is gonna be on, you might put the time aside to watch it for a cheap thrill, right?
**Boreman:** Oh yeah!
**Danville:** How's that different from someone watching porno for a cheap thrill?
**Boreman:** Because porn isn't real.
**Danville:** No one says it is.
**Boreman:** To me it's not really what having sex is all about.
**Danville:** Of course it's not. It's fantasy.
**Boreman:** It's cold to me. Pornography's cold to me. Like I said, it's not real. I just don't like it. And I'm looking at it from my perspective, what happened to me. If there's somebody that wants to do it, fine. I can't imagine doing porn all day long and then going home to the person that you love and enjoying having sex with them. I can't imagine that. It's like, God, leave me alone, you know?
**Danville:** What's your relationship with the feminist movement now?
**Boreman:** I think they got a good start on what they were trying to do because of me. They haven't really helped me. They've all made a lot of money off me. They used to say, "All these people make a lot of money off of you, but you don't want to go after that money. It's dirty money." And I'm like, "Okay, are you gonna take care of me for the rest of my life?" I guess I'm more disappointed in the women's movement than anything else.

There's a rape crisis group around here who go out and raise funds for women who have been raped. One time I told them, "I've been raped, and if there's anything I can do to help out, please let me know. I'd like to be a volunteer." But I didn't say who I was. And they never called me. That really blows me away, because I think I could be helpful to someone who's been raped.
**Danville:** Have you ever thought of becoming a rape counselor?
**Boreman:** No, because you'd have to go to school to be a rape counselor, and I can't afford it. I can't afford to go to school. That's the bottom line. I'd love to be a kindergarten teacher. That's what I'd really love to do. I love little kids. I used to be a teacher's aide, and that was one of the most joyful times I can remember. They look at you and they're like, "Miss Linda, what are you gonna tell me now?" They look at you with these big eyes, just wanting to learn so much. I'd like to go to libraries on Saturday mornings and read to little kids.
**Danville:** Why don't you?
**Boreman:** I'm afraid that someone's gonna find out about the Linda Lovelace thing and think all these horrible things about me. I mean, if I knew that that person that lived across the street was Linda Lovelace, after all the things that I'd heard, I wouldn't want my kids around her. I can understand that. And that hurts me, because people don't understand that's not me, you know? I'm me. I'm a sensitive person. I love kids and I would never do anything to hurt a child. And that would really be too hard for me to deal with, if that happened.
**Danville:** What should the government do about pornography?
**Boreman:** I think society should do their job about pornography.
**Danville:** Which is . . .?

**Boreman:** Just be aware of it. Make yourself aware of what's out there. If there's not a demand for it and a market for it, it's gonna go away. Most people go, "Oh, well it's just two people making love," and throw up their hands. But that's not all it is.
**Danville:** You don't think commercially available pornography made by consenting adults should be legislated out of existence?
**Boreman:** You can't do that. That's censorship.
**Danville:** And you're not in favor of censorship?
**Boreman:** No, I'm in favor of awareness. My son is desperately working three jobs, because he's got this baby coming. I said to him, "Why don't you go down and do some dancing? You're a nice-looking guy, all you have to is crack a nice little smile and you'll make a couple thousand bucks a week."
**Danville:** Being a male dancer?
**Boreman:** Yeah. I tried desperately to talk him into that. He's like, "I can't do that, Ma. Oh, I can't do that, I can't do that." One of my daughter's friends is a dancer, a topless dancer, and she wanted my daughter to come down. She asked me about it. I said, "Hey, if it helps you get on your feet and nobody touches you, it's okay with me. Just don't make it your whole life's profession, because it's gonna make you cold and callous and you don't want to do that because love is a beautiful thing." To me, doing that constantly makes you cold and callous towards sex. So yeah, here I am telling my kids, "Go ahead, be dancers. Get on your feet and then walk away."
**Danville:** When's the last time you were in a male strip club? [laughs]
**Boreman:** I've never been in one. [laughs] I've never been in one! My niece goes to one every year for her birthday, though.
**Danville:** You've never gone with her?
**Boreman:** No. She lives in New York. But she goes every year. It just blew my head. I said, "You? I mean, of all people!" And she goes, "Oh, yeah! I pull them things out and I stick that money down there!" I couldn't believe it! [laughs] I asked my other nieces about it and they're like, "Yeah!"
**Danville:** Do you want to go to one? We could leave right now! [laughs]
**Boreman:** I've never really thought about it. I figure that most of the guys are probably gay anyway. If they weren't gay, then I might go. [laughs]
**Danville:** A law similar to the Dworkin/MacKinnon Anti-Pornography Civil Rights Ordinance you testified for was passed in Canada. Written descriptions of sex can't be degrading, there can't be blood or feces or urine, no bestiality, no humiliation, no pain. One person wrote to *Penthouse Forum* that he wanted to fuck someone so bad it hurt. I had to take that out, because it equated sex with pain.
**Boreman:** Isn't that ridiculous? That's just because there are too many extremists in this society. To say no bestiality, no kiddie porn, no pissing and shitting on people, that's good. Society should realize that it's a good thing to eliminate that. People that watch kiddie porn or someone being beaten up or pissed on, they should think about that happening to their child, and then see how you feel. Society should have made the decision. It's just not healthy. They've done studies in colleges where they've taken young male students and showed them some mild pornography, just two people having sex, then they increase it to violence and then they throw in something else, and these guys become geared into that. They start to become more abusive with their girlfriends. It definitely does have an effect on some people in our society.

**Danville:** I'm sure there are some people who are negatively affected by pornography, but I definitely think they were fucked up before they watched porn. I also think that just because some people can't handle whatever their vice is, it shouldn't be taken away from those of us who can.
**Boreman:** But it could cause another human being to be hurt. That's my point. Even if it's just a few people. It's still another human being that's gonna be hurt, and I'm totally against that.
**Danville:** I saw you have a copy of *Natural Born Killers* you said you wanted to watch.
**Boreman:** It's my daughter's.
**Danville:** Is sex in movies more harmful than violence in movies?
**Boreman:** Yes. [pause] Well, I think it's equal. Look what we've done. Look at what's going on in our society. A kid in third grade killed a little girl. Look what happened at Columbine High School and where that stemmed from. Those kids were being abused every single day at school. Teachers were told about it and didn't do anything. The jocks in most schools could be totally screwed up, but they're jocks, so people say, "He's my star football player. We'll let that slide." That's wrong. That creates the violence. And yeah, there's just as much harm by violent movies as there is with pornography. And it's the few people. Some people can watch *Natural Born Killers* and say, "Wow, that was a really violent movie. I don't really want to see that again," but then somebody else will go, "Wow, that was really cool. I wanna go do that myself." It's the same with pornography. Society is doing all this. And does the government get involved? No, it's not the government's business. They screw people left and right as it is. They don't need to do anything more. It should be up to the people in our society.
**Danville:** So you're more likely to watch *Natural Born Killers* than *Deep Throat*?
**Boreman:** Mm-hmm. I have no desire to see pornography—at all. I know what I like sexually. I know what I can do sexually. I know how to do it! [laughs] I enjoy it. I don't need to watch it. To me, pornography is a total turn-off. If someone says to me, "Why don't we go get this porn tape?" I'm like, "Go away. You're a loser."
**Danville:** Ever had a date suggest watching porn?
**Boreman:** Yeah. I had someone suggest that to me. I was right there, ready to go, you know? [laughs] He said that shit? Nope! My whistle's not wet anymore. [laughs]
**Danville:** You never watched a porn movie just to see what it was you were coming out against?
**Boreman:** I was basing it all on *Deep Throat* and what happened to me. It's about what happened to me. If it happened to me, it's happened to another human being. And no human being should be treated and abused like I was.

**Danville:** What's it like when you do a speaking engagement?
**Boreman:** I took my daughter and my son's ex-girlfriend to see Gloria Steinem when she spoke. She did her lecture, which lasted about 45 minutes, and she did about 10 minutes of questions and answers. People still had questions but her

time was up. You got her for one hour, and that was it. I'm not like that. What they usually do is say, "Okay, everybody, we have to be out of the room by such and such a time," but I'll stay till the very last question is answered. And when they say there's no more questions, I'll say, "Come on, you gotta have one more question!"

When everybody leaves, there are usually some women who come up to me and give me a hug and say that they see me with my self-esteem back, going forward with my life, and because of that they were able to get out of a similar situation or feel better about themselves. And that's really great. But most people who do lectures won't stay and answer the questions, because they lie, and if they stay there too long they're gonna get caught in their lie. You can ask anybody. That's especially true with politicians. They get paid like $30,000 or $50,000 to do a lecture. They do some Q&A at the end and then they leave. Honesty is just like my ultimate thing.

**Danville:** Who makes up the audiences when you give a lecture?

**Boreman:** Students, some parents, a lot of professors and teachers. But it's mostly students. It's funny, there's always somebody to introduce me, and I get the biggest kick out of it. I always do this if they're nervous: I'll go, "You wanna trade places? I'll introduce you and you can give the lecture!" And they're like, "No, no! This is hard enough for me to do." But while they're introducing me, I'll watch and I'll look at all the faces in the audience. I put my glasses on and I check everybody out. I see the guys who are like, "Huh-huh, this is cool!" Making all these stupid smirks and stuff like that. But when I'm done, I look at everybody and it's totally different. And it's kinda cool. I found that most from the first lecture I ever did. I was really, really nervous, because I was thinking, "Oh God, these are college-educated kids. I never went to college." I never finished college, anyway. I got really nervous about that. But when they started asking me questions, I was like, "Man, these are college kids? What are we doing in this country?" It's incredible!

**Danville:** What do they ask?

**Boreman:** All kinds of things. What's Chuck Traynor doing now? Isn't there anything that you can do to him? Aren't there any laws written? Things like that. Most of those kids were in diapers when this happened to me, if they were even born when *Deep Throat* was out. At the last couple of colleges I've done, there have been a couple of guys that kinda lingered in the back and waited till everybody was gone to talk to me and ask me if there were any books that they could read because they were abused. They were too embarrassed to admit that in front of their peers, but I'm finding a lot more of that.

**Danville:** Do guys ever show up just to give you a hard time?

**Boreman:** One time, there was a group of about 10 of them that had that attitude. When I was done, this one kid from the fraternity house stood up and said, "You know what? We have pictures of naked women all over our frat house and I'm goin' back and I'm rippin' 'em all down." That's a good thing, that awareness. Just because you want to have sex and your girlfriend doesn't, you don't smack her in the face and do it anyway. That's not how it works, you know? How can you have pleasure in that?

**Danville:** People always wanted to know how you were planning to explain Linda Lovelace to your kids.

**Boreman:** When *Ordeal* first came out, I told my son, who was about four or five, that some people had hurt Mommy very badly and that Mommy goes out and talks about it and tries to help other people. My daughter has read *Ordeal*. She looks very much like me. She had one situation where she was at a friend's house and some guy pulled out an old copy of *Playboy* that I was in and asked her, "Is this you?" She's like, "Look at the fuckin' date, stupid!" She said, "No, that's my mother. You wanna know what really happened to her?" She'll get right into it. My son, on the other hand, he's never read it. He doesn't want to read it. He says, "Ma, I love you too much. If I read about what they did to you, I don't think I could handle it." He had one friend who made a comment to him about Linda Lovelace and he's never seen that friend again.

**Danville:** Have your kids ever seen *Deep Throat*?

**Boreman:** Not that I'm aware of. But my son does watch pornography. He did when he was 16, 17, 18, right around there. Boy, he made me mad. I told him, "I don't want this shit in my house. You wanna watch this stuff, you go somewhere else."

**Danville:** But you didn't say, "You cannot watch this."

**Boreman:** No. I just said to him, "Do you realize that sometimes people are being abused? That it's really not real? That's not what sex and love are all about. I'd rather you go out and get a girlfriend and experience hand on hand. You're watching that, you're stimulating yourself in a negative way." As far as I know, he doesn't watch it anymore.

**Danville:** Was it the typical teenage interest in porn?

**Boreman:** I think so. He's very shy. Not the kind of guy who'd go out with a lot of girls. He's told me like three or four stories about girls he went out with for one night who wanted to have sex. He told me, "Ma, I can't do that. I have to have some feeling. I can't just. . . . " He's like that. He's very sensitive. He has to care about somebody. He can't just say, "I'm goin' out with the guys tonight and I'm gonna get laid." Plus he's scared shit about getting a disease. I think that helps, too.

**Danville:** Why has it been so hard to make the movie of *Ordeal*?

**Boreman:** Personally, I think they get offered a deal they can't refuse.

**Danville:** Why wouldn't the Mob want them to make it?

**Boreman:** [facetiously] What's the Mob?

**Danville:** The Mafia. [not quite getting it] Who would make them an offer that they can't refuse?

**Boreman:** People. [still being facetious]

**Danville:** Are you afraid of the Mob? [finally getting it]

**Boreman:** No.

**Danville:** Are you afraid of "people," whoever those people might be, who might not want someone to make a movie out of *Ordeal*?

**Boreman:** No.

**Danville:** What are you afraid of?

**Boreman:** I'm afraid of being raped again. I'm afraid that someone's gonna think my daughter is Linda Lovelace and rape her. Things like that. But that's something that will always be there. That's why I can't sleep in hotel rooms. I always have a dream that someone's coming in and raping me.

**Danville:** You never went to therapy for that, though.

**Boreman:** I found that people were getting stimulated when I'd talk. I didn't like that. I'd been raped by lawyers, doctors. Why would I trust a doctor or a psychiatrist now? How can I look up to somebody after that happened? Michael McGrady was good therapy for me. When I do my lectures, that's great therapy for me. It really is. I feel so good when I'm done. Every time I think, "What am I doing?" My stomach goes into such knots and it's like, "Why am I doing this? What am I doing here? Why don't I just go home?" I get so nervous and my voice quivers when I start. But when it's over I feel so good.

**Danville:** Why did you agree to be interviewed for this book?

**Boreman:** I want people to be aware of what's going on. To let them know what I'm really like. The pros and cons, I guess. And the dollar. There's no doubt about it, I'm tired of being broke and poor. I am. I'm tired of being broke and poor.

**Danville:** There's a script based on *Ordeal* being passed around that deals a bit with the making of the book, like you taking the lie-detector test. I thought that took away from what your story is.

**Boreman:** I don't think that should even be in. That should only be a little clip in the movie. It shouldn't be the whole movie. It should be a two-second flash or something.

**Danville:** Where should the movie version of *Ordeal* begin?

**Boreman:** I think it should start with my childhood. Police officer father, PTA mom, Tupperware dealer. My childhood. My friends and I growing up and having a party in my basement every month. We were so corny, we used to lip-sync songs. We'd practice for three weeks. We'd have a party once a month and for all the time in between we'd be practicing the motions and everything. That was kids growing up then. The movie should show that I had a good upbringing. That I had fun with my friends. That my friends loved to be around my mom. And then Chuck Traynor coming in. To me, that's how it should be told: right from the beginning.

When *Ordeal* first came out, everybody was like, "What in your childhood led you to this?" That's what Gloria Steinem said was like asking Holocaust victims, "What in your childhood led you to a concentration camp?" I just think the whole story should be told from the beginning right into the bitterness and the awful things that happened. Maybe a little bit about how it was when *Ordeal* was first written, people trying to blame my mother or my father. "Well, your father must have abused you, sexually abused you." My God! I can't even imagine that! That's so far from the truth. That's how I think it should be told; right from January 10, 1949. Right from the beginning. I think that's the way it should be done. So you take people and show them what the person was really like. What happened in her life. Don't let them think, "Wow, what was her childhood like? Wow, what happened in her childhood that made this happen to her?" Answer the question right from the beginning. I was just a normal human being. And then, I don't know, big turn in the road. [laughs]

**Danville:** As you lived her, what's the character of Linda Lovelace like?

**Boreman:** She was a robot. People think she's a super sex freak who couldn't get enough. She probably has an orgy every night at her house. She walks around naked in the streets and picks up anybody. I'm sure that's what people think. That's not me. That's another reason I wanted to talk to you. I want people to know me for who I really am, not just for what happened to me.

**Danville:** Do you get recognized in public anymore?

**Boreman:** Not where I live now. I don't think I've ever been recognized here. Rarely, when I go somewhere else, but not very much.

**Danville:** What do people do when they realize it's you?

**Boreman:** Just smile. The last time I was recognized I was at the dog track with my dad and my sister and my nephew. A television interview had just aired a few nights earlier. I think it was *The Fox Files*. This girl looked at me, and she grinned. She looked at her boyfriend and he just smiled. That's all they did. There's a definite look in people's eyes. It was more the eye contact and the smile.
**Danville:** When people do recognize you, do they ever ask you for autographs?
**Boreman:** Not anymore. I think that's so silly.
**Danville:** What do you think about the fact that people care about both you and that character after 30 years?
**Boreman:** I think it's kinda corny, that's all. I really do. Everybody says to me, "Oh, why don't you just leave it alone and forget about it? Why don't you just forget about this Linda Lovelace thing?" I can't do that. It won't leave me alone. So I'm not gonna just turn my back. As far as talking to you for your book? It's been 30 years? Okay everybody, here it is again! Here's the real truth. Here's what really happened. I'm all for that, because of my children, my grandchildren, my great-grandchildren. I want them to know that even though this happened to me, I survived and people respected me enough to write the truth.
**Danville:** Do you still picket *Deep Throat*?
**Boreman:** Yes. I don't like the fact that *Deep Throat*'s still being shown. Like this one college in Ohio, they couldn't come up with enough money to have me speak there, but after the spring exams they decided to show *Deep Throat* to take away the stress. That makes me mad. That makes me really mad. Don't I have rights as a human being? If I had done that willingly and was all gung-ho for it, then it wouldn't bother me. But I was forced into that. I was abused. Why are you still showing it? I understand that you can't go on knocking on everybody's door and get every copy of *Deep Throat* out of everybody's house. I understand that. But I don't think it should be shown at a college after exams. I don't think it should be shown in a theater. How come I don't have any rights? That was three weeks of my life. I'm 51 years old and that was three weeks of my life. Twenty-one days that changed my life forever.
**Danville:** Deep Throat changed other people's lives in positive ways, like changing how they were able to think about sex.
**Boreman:** I remember I got one fan letter from a girl who said she hated me because, when *Deep Throat* came out, her husband made her watch it and then invited some of his friends over to have sex with her. She always blamed it on me. After she read *Ordeal*, she said she was so sorry that she felt that way. So there were a lot of women who got hurt because of [*Deep Throat*]. And yeah, there are some people that were able to be more open sexually because of seeing it, so ... [trails off]
**Danville:** You have the right to protest it.
**Boreman:** Yeah, but why isn't my government saying, "What happened to her isn't right. No, this can't be shown in theaters anymore."
**Danville:** Isn't that the same censorship that you were saying before you oppose?
**Boreman:** No, it's not. I was abused. I was used and abused in that movie. To me, that's not censorship. That's humanity.

Lightning Source UK Ltd.
Milton Keynes UK
UKHW042047211019
352023UK00001B/104/P

9 780985 973308